Your Affectionate Daughter, Isabella

Ann Williams

For Judy

Ann Williams

Historical Images
Asheville, North Carolina

Historical Images is an imprint of Bright Mountain Books, Inc.

Maps and genealogical charts created by James M. Daniel

The silhouette used on the cover is of an unknown woman, not Isabella Torrance. Pictures of only a few family members are known to exist at the present time. Please contact Ann Williams at the above address if you know of additional materials about or pictures of Isabella and her family.

Printed in the United States of America

ISBN: 0-914875-34-5

Library of Congress Cataloging-in-Publication Data

Williams, Ann, 1940–
  Your affectionate daughter, Isabella / Ann Williams
      p. cm.
Includes bibliographical references (p.   ).
  ISBN 0-914875-34-5 (pbk. : alk. paper)
  1. Torrance family—Correspondence. 2. Latta family—Correspondence. 3. Reid, Isabella Torrance Smith, 1818-1893—Correspondence. 4. Torrance, James, 1784-1847—Correspondence. 5. North Carolina—Biography. 6. Southern States—Social life and customs. I. Title.
  CT274.T67 W55 2001
  975.6'03'0922-dc21
                                        2001001890

Contents

Dedication

For Jim

Acknowledgments

I became acquainted with the Torrance family during the early 1990s as a volunteer interpreter at the Hugh Torance House and Store, the log house of Isabella's story. This small historic site is operated by a group of highly dedicated citizens and is well worth a visit. The interpretative focus of the site was its original settler, Hugh, and his merchant son, James. As I absorbed the details of their interesting lives, my curiosity was piqued by the next generation, whose biographies, all thirteen of them, had been squeezed into three scant pages of our training manual. The manual had been compiled from the original documents housed at the University of North Carolina at Charlotte library, so I went to the source and was immediately hooked. There were over 15,000 documents, some long and detailed, many just torn scraps of paper, that could be fit together to fashion the pattern of the family's life. I am deeply indebted to the Torrances who saved papers and to the university that preserved them. Many afternoons at the log house and a number of visits to the adjacent Cedar Grove (a private residence) helped me to feel that I had nearly walked in Isabella's footprints.

Isabella's story would have remained untold without the assistance of two gentlemen who are no longer with us, Richard Torrance Banks and Chalmers Davidson. Dick Banks, great-grandson of James Torrance, was the conservator and interpreter of the Torrance-Banks Family Papers. His handwritten notes attached to many of the documents and his accumulation of supplementary materials were invaluable in my research. Dick was a journalist, an able investigator, and a clear and competent writer. I knew him casually some years ago, but he was seriously ill when I began this project and passed away shortly before its completion. I deeply regret that I did not have the opportunity to thank him for his beautiful work.

While preparing the endnotes, I was surprised that Chalmers Davidson, a constant posthumous companion, appeared in only one citing, and a minor one at that. His contributions, noted in the bibliography, are the scaffolding that supports the story. His exhaustive research provided me with numerous birth, death, and marriage dates and brought to order the chaos of the many interconnected families. He documented where people lived, when they lived there, and told the histories of the churches. Much of the information in the maps, family trees, and the epilogue can be attributed to him. Chalmers was a professor of history and library director at Davidson College for many years and was a descendant of Wilson and Betsy Latta Davidson. I had the opportunity to meet this delightful Southern gentleman many years ago, long before I knew the role he would play in my work.

Among the living, I would like to thank Jane Estep and Karen

McConnell who proofread the letters, and, who along with a number of my "history friends," gave me tidbits of information gathered from hither and yon, often before they knew what I was up to. Martha Matthews and Elizabeth Myers read the manuscript, offered literary and historical suggestions and much enthusiastic encouragement. Robin Brabham and his staff at the University of North Carolina at Charlotte Adkins Library were always helpful, having the appropriate boxes of documents at my fingertips, at my pleasure. The staff at Latta Plantation, now a midsized historic site, were more than generous with their support and their archives. I especially appreciate the countless hours spent there in peaceful immersion in the time and place, honing my perspective. Pat Veasey of Historic Brattonsville, another beautifully preserved plantation, provided me with information on the Bratton family. Susan Taylor of the Salem College Library was always prompt with names and dates from the boarding school files. And again, time spent at Historic Brattonsville and Old Salem helped me feel a kinship to "my girls." Kay Moss helped with a number of things, including the mystery of hive syrup. Jim Daniel is perhaps the most accomplished amateur historian of my acquaintance. His exquisite skills in cartography and calligraphy transformed my crude maps and family trees into works of art.

Dorothy Riddick, of Coffeeville, Mississippi, shared census records and other details to point me in the right direction. On a delightful visit to Mississippi, I was assisted by Joyce Snider at the Coffeeville Public Library. Sarah Pullen of the Chancery Clerk's Office cheerfully led me through large dusty volumes of land records and photocopied at my slightest whim. The rest of my Mississippi sojourn was spent on back roads and dusty trails acquainting myself with the Torrance landscape. I found both the people and the place charming beyond expectations.

Cynthia Bright and her staff at Bright Mountain Books bravely took on an untried, unpublished neophyte as an author. Thank you so very, very much.

Most of all I am indebted to the person who listened to me ramble endlessly about Isabella and her family, who shared my excitement when a snippet of paper revealed the ambiguous evidence of another document, who understood my glee when a gravestone turned up in an unexpected cemetery, who weaned me from the typewriter to the computer (then graciously rescued me from the self-inflicted computer mayhem), and who gave me the grandest compliment of all upon reading the manuscript: "I tried to look for errors but kept getting caught up in the story," my dear beloved husband, Jim.

Your Affectionate Daughter,
Isabella

Introduction

The story of Isabella, her father James Torrance, and their large, convoluted family is largely wrought through letters and other records they left behind. This incredible cache of documents, accumulated over generations and tucked carefully away in an attic, illuminates the Torrance family and life in the nineteenth century. Providing flesh to liven the bare bones of history, it begins with the story of their ancestral home.

Cedar Grove, a glorious example of the Greek Revival fashion, suffered the infirmities of old age after cotton was last planted at her doorstep. Her structure was sound, but her patina had faded from handsome to shabby, and the appurtenances of modern life were nonexistent or in bad repair. After the cotton days, the family stayed with her as long as they could, but employment dragged them one by one to the cities and towns. She was rented for a time and empty briefly until the 1940s when James Torrance's great-grandson Richard Torrance Banks reclaimed the old homeplace and embraced her once again with familial love.

Over the next several decades his restoration efforts were combined with the necessities of earning a living and raising a family. He had noticed the boxes of papers in the attic but kept them at bay until he was no longer threatened by leaning chimneys and frazzled wires. When he began to study the papers, he realized that they contained his family's history in incredible detail. His ancestors were savers of all sorts of papers including wills, land records, ledger books, school records, business papers, financial records, doctor bills, slave records, inventories, sales receipts, and many beautiful, compelling letters. He spent some years sorting, cataloging, and organizing these thousands of documents. He augmented them with public records and family correspondence and wrote several brief family histories. When he was finished, he generously donated the collection of papers and the fruits of his labor to the Rare Books and Manuscript Collection of the Adkins Library at the University of North Carolina at Charlotte. There they are kept in tidy boxes safe from the elements and accessible for research.

The earliest document is a note that James Torrance's father brought with him from Ireland dated 1763. It describes the bearer as an unmarried man of honest and reputable parents who "alwaise behaved himself orderly and supported a very fair character." This extraordinary collection progresses from that date to the twentieth century, shedding light on the everyday life of the family in great detail.

Other original documents, public information (mostly census data and land transactions), and secondary histories of the time and region have also been used to tell of Isabella's life. The story is factual. Some liberties have

1

been taken to flesh out the characters and fill a few gaps. Obviously we are not privy to their conversations, but many of their thoughts and the nuances of their personalities emerge neatly from the letters. Endnotes have been included to document the facts and their sources and to make note of the few liberties. The story is written from the points of view of those who lived it and told in the language they spoke.

The backdrop is the northwestern corner of Mecklenburg County, which lies along the southern border of North Carolina slightly west of center. It was largely rural then, comprised of rolling hills and red clay soil, an ideal spot for men to prosper from cotton. Nearby Charlotte was a small town; Salisbury, some thirty miles to the northeast, was the primary seat of commerce. The story takes place in the first half of the nineteenth century—a time of great change in America. The new nation sought to create her own cultural identity separate from England, and the unprecedented melding of state and federal authority created problems with money and commerce. The Industrial Revolution brought advances in technology from the cotton gin to railroads, western lands were opened, and cotton became king.

The years embraced by this story were the pinnacle of the cotton economy in the piedmont of North Carolina. By the 1850s, the coastal lands of South Carolina and Georgia had converted from rice to cotton, and the Gulf Coast and Mississippi River environs were thriving. The Piedmont's lack of railroads and navigable rivers doomed all but its largest planters. The Civil War tolled the death knell. Southern agriculture was forever changed.

North and South Carolina with inset of Mecklenburg County

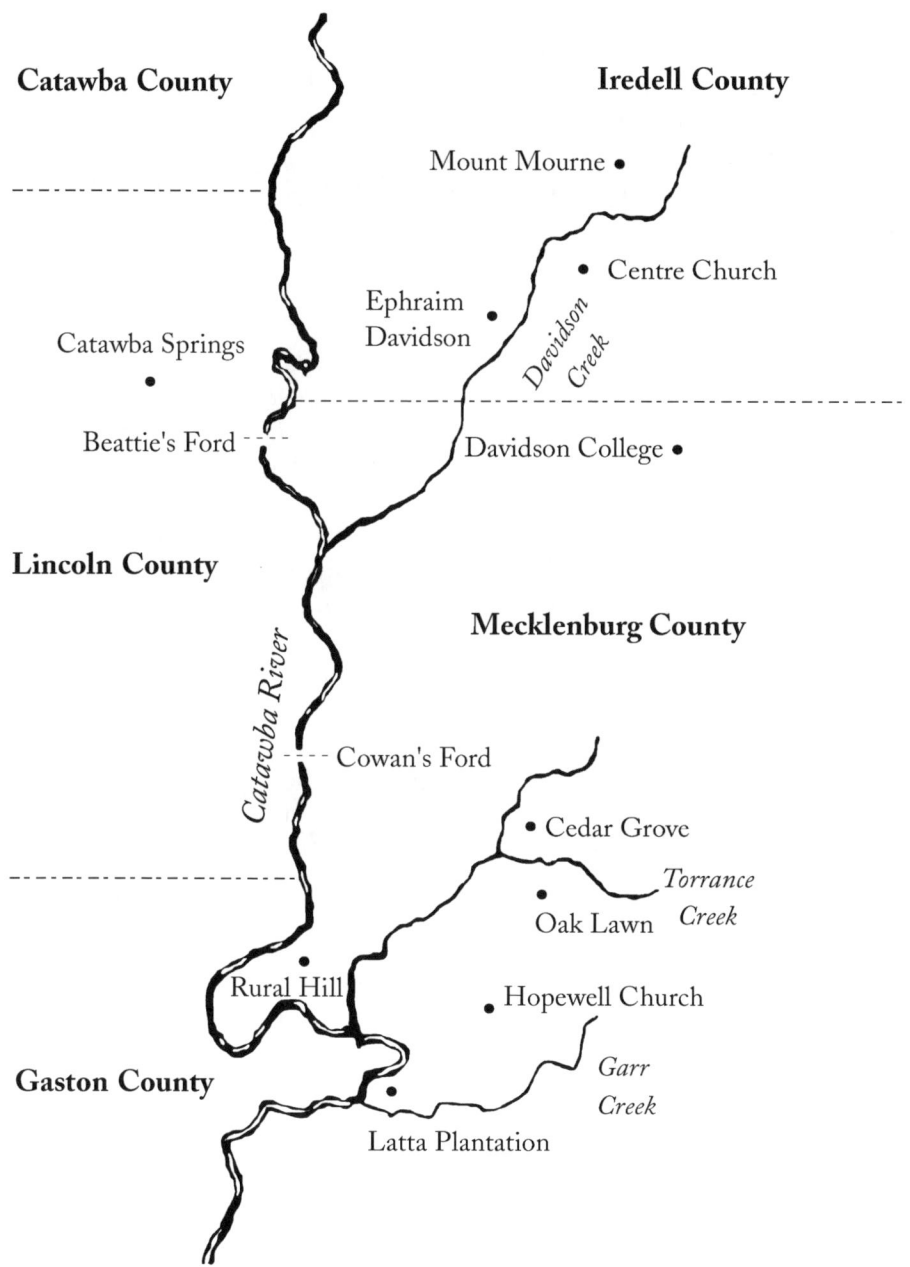

Torrance Neighborhood
before creation of the Catawba River lakes
and the formation of modern towns

Family Life

In the eighteenth century most marriages were arranged, usually as economic unions. Love followed more often than not, but there was no guarantee. By the turn of the nineteenth century people were beginning to choose their own mates, especially in the backcountry where patterns of settlement made the old way impractical. Nevertheless, the economic parameters were still important among the elite. Birth and death rates were both very high. Large families created by a succession of marriages were commonplace as were repeated intermarriages among the same families. In a sparsely settled area where social class was important, there were often few choices.

In spite of the way families were formed and blended, their relationships were close and affectionate. Never do we see the words *step* or *half* applied to a parent or sibling, and rarely is *in-law* used. A stepmother became "Ma" and was always addressed as such. This was a convention of speech and does not in itself connote affection, but the letters reveal that the bonds of blended families were deep and strong. The mere act of calling a relative acquired by marriage "sister" or "uncle" may well have strengthened those bonds.

Families lived in intimate quarters and seemed to prefer it that way. After all, they came from a long tradition of living in one- or two-room houses where privacy was unknown. Cedar Grove is a large house of over five thousand square feet, yet it has only four bedrooms that were shared by up to a dozen family members and frequent visitors. Loneliness and despair over family separation is a common theme in the letters.

It was often the custom for first-borns to be named for their grandparents and successive children for their parents. The paucity of surnames among these intermingled families often meant that several individuals were given the same or similar names. For this reason it was common to refer to one another as "Uncle Frank" or "Brother Frank," and pet names abounded.

To compound the confusion James Torrance twice changed the spelling of his name. As a youth he spelled his name "Torance" as his father had. In early adulthood he changed it to "Torrence," then later to "Torrance." He supposedly made the changes to avoid being confused with his cousin and other Torrence families in the area. For the sake of simplicity "Torrance" is used throughout this story unless another spelling occurs in a quoted document.

Slavery

Because the story is told from the point of view of antebellum slave owners, the concept of human bondage emerges in a fairly benign, matter-of-fact manner. Slavery was the underpinning of the agrarian economy and the lifestyle enjoyed by the Torrances and their neighbors. The people in the story, black and white, were born at a time when the system was well established, and they knew no other way of life. In modern times we have dispelled the romantic myth of the happy slave eager to please his master and replaced it with as nearly an erroneous idea that all slaves were constantly beaten and tortured. The institution was indeed odious, but it does not follow that all within it were treated with equal inhumanity. In fact, there was a broad continuum of circumstances under which Negroes lived.

The most horrid situations were generally found on enormous plantations owned by absentee landlords along the coasts and river deltas. These plantations consisted of thousands of acres worked by hundreds of Negroes managed by unsupervised overseers who had no particular interest in their well-being. The overseer's aim was to turn a profit for his employer by any means at his disposal in order to have his contract renewed. His efforts were frustrated by erratic cotton prices and the difficulty of working in one of the most disagreeable, malaria-infested climates on earth. Many of these men were excessively cruel, although some of them recognized that healthy laborers were more productive than starved and injured ones. Unfortunately this mean and chaotic situation was the experience of most blacks and very few whites.

Somewhat more benign was the experience of slaves on midsized plantations such as the one owned by James Torrance. These holdings ranged from a few hundred to a few thousand acres and from about thirty to one hundred fifty Negroes. The most important differences were that the owner lived on site, and the black population was small enough that he knew each of them. If an overseer was employed, he was strictly supervised. The owner not only knew his people as individuals but also saw them as an investment to be nurtured. It would be wrong to infer that cruel acts never occurred on midsized plantations. In a time when harsh punishment of children and the beating of wives was perfectly acceptable behavior, why should anyone be surprised that some men thrashed their Negroes? The level of abuse on midsized plantations was probably a reflection of the temperament of the owner more than anything else.

The kindest situation of all was experienced on small farms or in households where twenty or fewer people were owned. The smaller the slave population, the more likely bonds formed between black and white. It was also somewhat likely that the black and white families lived in similar houses, ate the same food, and worked side by side at the same chores. This was the experience of the fewest Negroes and most slave owners. The vast majority of white people, especially in the backcountry, owned no slaves. Most white people were poor and slaves were costly.

In all of these situations the slave populations were demographically familial. In general about half of one's Negroes were adult or teenage laborers; the rest were small children, the elderly, and women excused from hard work during the months surrounding childbirth. Approximately one-third of any population were children under ten. A large number of blacks on a plantation did not preclude work by the white family. Management of the business and the people took considerable energy and skill. The letters speak of the need to be on the land from first light to last. Although the Torrances lived extremely well, they did not simply sit back and count their money.

It is doubtful that James Torrance ever entertained the idea of freeing his slaves—if he had, he would have immediately dismissed it. He could not have turned a profit from his land with paid labor when all of his competitors had slaves. It asks a lot of a man to give up his livelihood and thrust his children into poverty to satisfy his convictions, and there is no evidence that James had such convictions. The Latta family, who lived nearby, were much intertwined with the Torrances by marriage and commerce. There is anecdotal evidence that Jane Latta, mistress of the Latta plantation, despised slavery and wished to free her people, but a brief passage in a letter from the 1860s contradicts this. We know that she was deeply religious and for that reason might have taught black children to read a little of the Bible. Presbyterians of that time believed that everyone should be able to read from the Bible to protect themselves from being led astray by errant ministers. Teaching Negroes to read was a thorny issue among the pious, and surely the law of God was above that of man. However, the instrument which saved one's soul could lead to insurrection.

The word "slave" is not used in the narrative. It almost never occurs in regional documents of the period. Whether this was an attempt to temper the shameful nature of the institution or simply the common vernacular is unknown—it is likely a mixture of both. In documents as formal as court records and as personal as letters, the recurring words are "Negroes," "black people," "hands," and occasionally "servants." The terms "Negro family" and "black family" occur frequently. In some letters one must read for a bit to discover if "our family" is the one the writer belongs to or the one he owns.

The lives of the Negroes are woven into the story with as much accuracy as can be determined by the documents. There is every indication that the Torrance Negroes were cared for adequately and humanely. Field workers received plenty of water and rest in the heat of the day; and all of them received food, clothing, and medical attention—the latter they would have been better off without. They were often given money and whiskey at Christmas and were probably given small amounts of money and liberty at other times evidenced by their shopping for personal items on another plantation. There was also genuine sorrow expressed at the death of Negroes. A very businesslike letter James received concerning cotton commerce ends with the following lament: "My respects to your family, my friend I have met with a great loss up in your neighborhood my old wagoner Bob died at Wm Montieths."

Negroes were generally regarded as simple, childlike creatures in need of much supervision and moral guidance. This attitude was certainly not lost on them and had to be demeaning. On the other hand, white people considered such treatment kind and appropriate. It probably never crossed their minds that the Negroes were not as happy as nature intended them to be. None of this is offered as an excuse or apology for the institution of slavery; it is simply an attempt to add some perspective from the time and place. Captivity is deplorable under any circumstances.

The Families

The Torrance and Latta family trees on pages 8 and 9 aid in understanding these two complex families. Key family members important to this story are shown in bold type. The simple family trees use the names the individuals were commonly called. The appendix contains a complete list of these and the other families in the story. It includes full names, expanded birth, death, and marriage dates for the important characters (when known), and more details of the family relationships. As previously noted, James Torrance changed the spelling of his surname several times. Technically his older children should be "Torrence" and the younger ones "Torrance," however the existing records (including gravestones) are rife with inconsistencies. For simplicity the last spelling is used throughout this narrative.

Dates come from a variety of sources and also contain inconsistencies. The dates used here are based on the best evidence that could be found, and discrepancies are noted. Graveyards were visited whenever possible and, if legible, considered reliable for death dates. They are somewhat less reliable for birth dates, especially if the person was elderly. Some gravestones tell the person's age at death and is the sole surviving record.

The dates used in the appendix for the major figures are complete (month, day, and year) when known. For the minor characters only the year is given unless the date is a significant event in the story.

There are puzzles that may never be solved. The only records found state that Lettitia Torrance was born November 1828, and her sister Mary, February 22, 1829. This of course is not possible. Nothing could be learned from their gravestones (they are probably both buried somewhere in or near

The Torrance Family

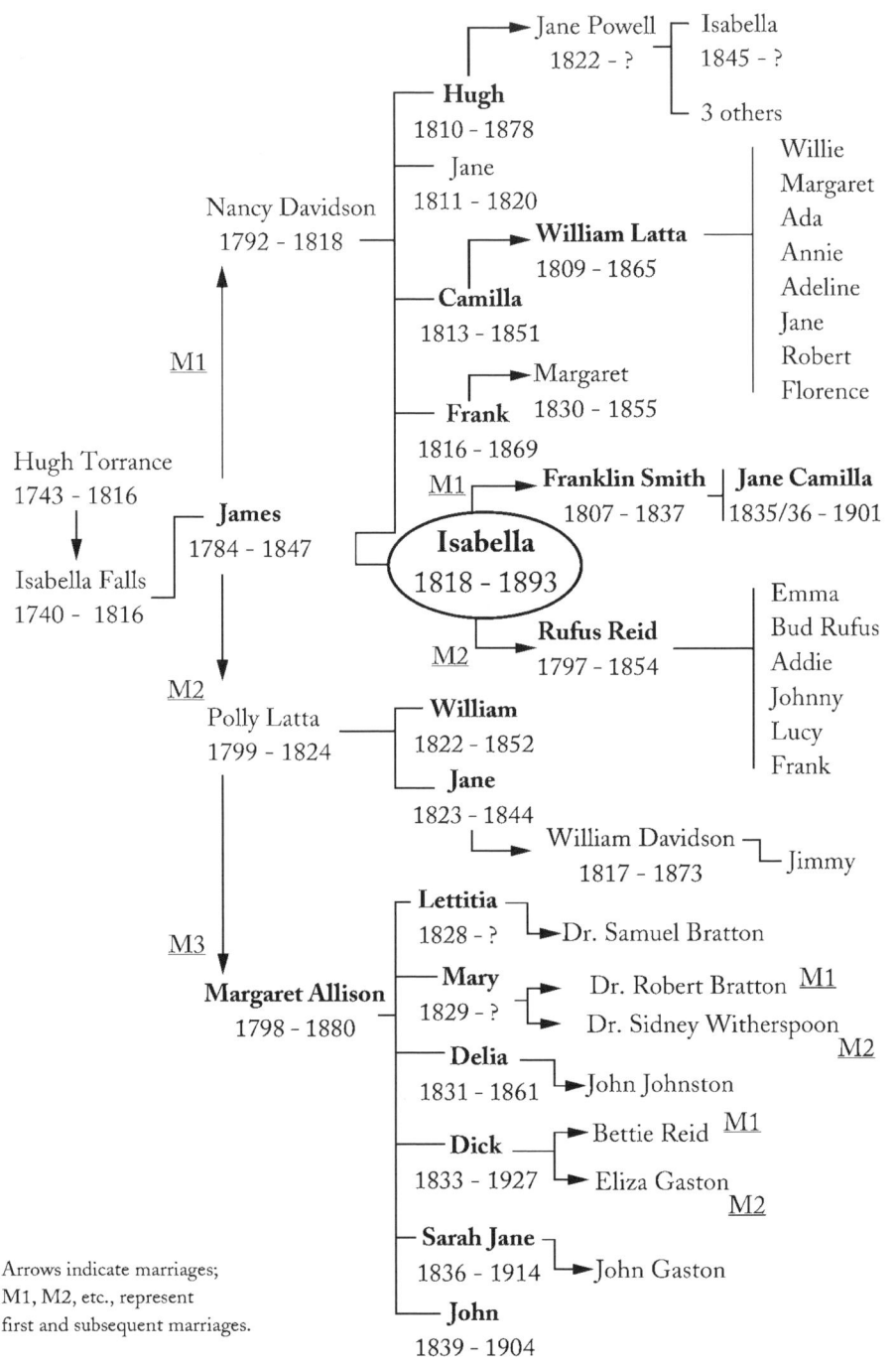

Arrows indicate marriages;
M1, M2, etc., represent
first and subsequent marriages.

The Latta Family

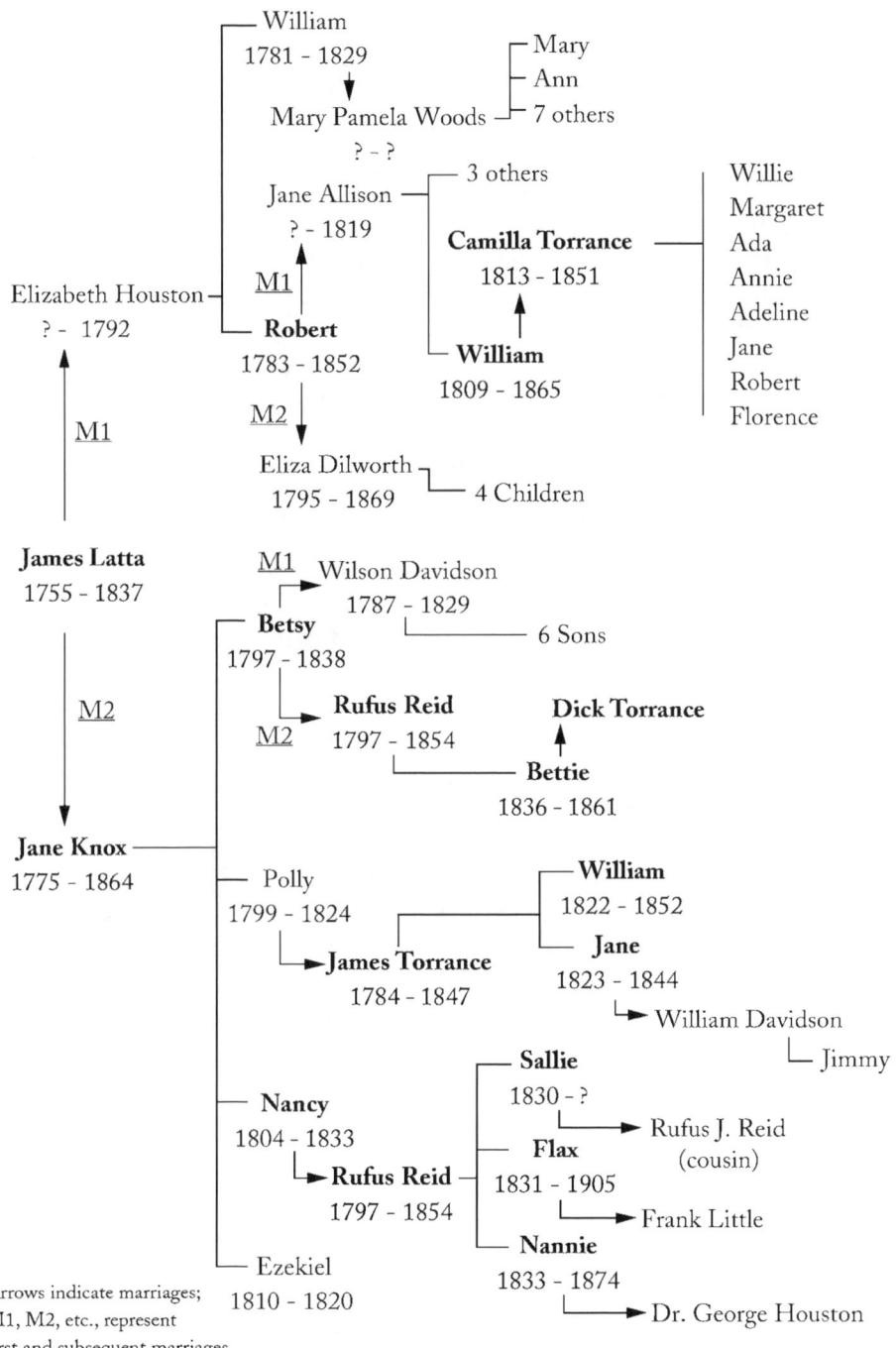

Arrows indicate marriages;
M1, M2, etc., represent
first and subsequent marriages.

Atlanta), and no wedding date (just the year) has been located for their mother. Mary's record seems more consistent, so Lettitia may have been born earlier in 1828. It is obvious from the letters and other records that they were very close in age and did nearly everything together, including marrying brothers.

The Ephraim Davidson family of Mount Mourne in Iredell County and the John Davidson family of Rural Hill in Mecklenburg County were probably unrelated when they came to North Carolina. Ephraim's grandfather arrived in North Carolina about 1748. John arrived as a small child about 1740 with his sister and widowed mother. They were all Scots-Irish Presbyterians who came by way of Pennsylvania, which can be said about most of the early settlers of the area. They have long since intermarried.

Margaret Allison, James Torrance's third wife, came from a large Allison family who lived near Statesville, North Carolina. The extensive genealogy of this clan gives no hint of a relationship with the South Carolina family of Jane Allison, Robert Latta's first wife. More extensive genealogical information is provided on many of these families following the epilogue.

The Letters

Most of the letters were written to James Torrance by his children, the greatest number from Isabella and her brothers when they lived in Mississippi. Unfortunately no letters have been found that traveled the other direction. The vast majority are in excellent condition, containing only a few tears, smears, or indecipherable words (most of the unreadable words are names of people casually encountered and have no bearing on the story). In this book the letters have been set in a distinctive font. With rare exception they are quoted in their entirety and have been edited with the lightest possible hand. Only two or three of them were in poor enough condition to require an editorial leap. Brackets enclose words that might have been where a tear or smear now exists; often partial words or letters give a clue. Ellipses are used when the lost material does not appear to interfere with the flow or context of the letter. Parentheses and dashes are those of the original letter writer.

The unconventional capitalization and punctuation have been retained. Names of people and places were always capitalized, other proper nouns and the initial letters of sentences, only randomly. Commas and periods are used less often than in modern writing, colons and apostrophes even more infrequently. It is sometimes difficult to distinguish between a comma, a period, or a random drop of ink, which is not surprising considering the writing tools available. Dashes are commonplace, but often the space between words is the only indication of a pause in thought. Keep in mind that these were written family conversations; they were never intended to endure editorial scrutiny.

Language

Do not infer from the unconventional spelling that the letter writers were poorly educated or sloppy. Their high level of literacy is evidenced by their sophisticated vocabularies and elegant turns of phrase. They placed great importance on schooling and penmanship, owned extensive libraries, and subscribed to newspapers. They were exceptionally well educated considering the time and place in which they lived. During the early nineteenth century there was a movement afoot led by Noah Webster to Americanize the English language, and Webster's first dictionary published in 1806 proved to be a helpful reference. Many of the unusual spellings can be attributed to the fact that these people were schooled before Webster's reforms were complete. Most of us are familiar with some of the old spellings (still used in England) such as *colour* or *plough*. Others are less familiar such as *musick, waggon, affraid*, and *bagg*. Nineteenth-century people were not bombarded by the printed word at every turn; their language experience was much more aural than visual. The confusion of *two, too*, and *to*, or *some* and *sum* can be forgiven.

Contractions were beginning to enter the language during this time period (with a few ancient exceptions such as *'tis* and *'twas*). In the letters from the 1830s, they occur rarely and without apostrophes. Letters from the 1850s contain many contractions, although they are punctuated inconsistently. Written language conventions generally grow out of speech patterns. Personal letters are perhaps the most informal of written language formats, yet they are not as casual as conversation. The letters offer a valuable insight into nineteenth-century language evolution.

The text contains words that might be unfamiliar to modern readers and several that are now used somewhat differently. A brief glossary follows.

&c - Abbreviation for et cetera.

apoplexy - Nineteenth-century term for a stroke.

bacon - Any sort of smoked or cured pork. Most of it was probably more akin to modern-day ham than bacon.

bagg, bale - The terms are interchangeable for bundles of cotton packed for market. Bagging is the cloth they were wrapped in. A bale was not yet a unit of weight; all bales or baggs were weighed individually, and the weighing charge was deducted from the price paid to the seller.

black choler - Extreme mental depression supposedly the result of excess black bile, rather than yellow, in one's system.

breaking, broken, broken up - Being without funds, or broke in modern slang. The terms do not refer to a dissolved partnership.

country, county - County, when uncapitalized, can mean a specific county, or the general area. Uncapitalized, country takes the latter meaning, comparable to countryside. Both are used as synonyms for neighborhood or region, and it is sometimes difficult to tell which word the writer intended.

ell - A French measurement of forty-five inches. It came to be used by tailors, seamstresses, and cloth sellers in England and America.

farm, plantation - In general, farm implies sustenance agriculture with little left over to sell or barter. A plantation was a larger holding on which cash crops were raised. The amount of acreage devoted to cash crops is immaterial. A plantation owner wishing to appear modest often called his place a farm, and a bragging farmer might speak of his plantation.

freshet - A flood, especially a flash flood due to heavy rainfall.

Governor - Sometimes used as a polite form of address for an important man, not necessarily an elected leader.

improve - Used most often in reference to academic achievement. It is used less often to refer to a betterment in health or prosperity.

inst. - An abbreviation for instant, meaning the present month.

lay by - The final cultivation given to a young crop. After the crops have been laid by they generally need little attention until harvest.

miasma - Unhealthy air or aura arising from swamps or other fetid places. Miasmas were believed to be the cause of all sorts of fevers and illnesses.

neat - In financial transactions, net or profit.

note, notes - IOUs. Notes were often traded for goods or services as if they were hard cash. To lift a note is to pay off the obligation. The signature was often torn, or partially torn, from the rest of the paper to indicate the debt had been settled.

security - A cosigner who assumes responsibility for a note if the original debtor cannot comply.

since - The most common meaning, which has been lost in modern times, is ago, as in "I received your letter three days since." It also expresses the contemporary meaning of elapsed time as in "It has been raining since Thursday." It was not used to mean because or therefore.

swept yard - A common feature of the nineteenth-century rural domestic landscape. The dry soil was swept neatly and sometimes in patterns. For modest homes, this was typically the yard immediately in front of the house. In the context of a plantation, however, the swept yard was usually the work area surrounded by slave cabins and outbuildings such as smitheries, tanneries, washhouses, carpenter shops, etc. Feathers, bones, wood shavings, and other by-products of labor accumulated there, so it was swept or raked daily to keep it clean. It was also the social center of the slave community.

ultimo - A Latin word meaning last month.

Your Affectionate Daughter,
Isabella

1 Mecklenburg 1825

Salem N.C   Nov. 27th 1825

James G. Torrance Esq.
  Dear Sir.
    I have the pleasure to inform you that your dear daughters Catherine and Isabella have continued in good health since they made their abode with us; and that they are perfectly satisfied in their new situation. They are very good children and pay due attention to their studies. Their improvement will I hope be equal to what you can reasonably expect from the[m]   It will remain our constant endeavor while they are in our care to promote their best interest as far as we are able   Your daughters are affectionate and well disposed children who give attention to the precepts of their purposes. They both desire their love to you, and will write themselves soon. Wishing you health and prosperity
      I am dear sir
              Yours respectfully
              Benj. Reichel
              Inspector

*All our pupils are
in good health*

That was good; the girls were safe. It had been two long weeks since James had enrolled them in the Salem Female Boarding School. He was avid for their comfort and hoped they were not troubled by homesickness. As he reread the letter he wondered if Inspector Reichel knew the girls well enough to make so astute an assessment; he seemed not to have realized that his older daughter was called Camilla, not Catherine. Perhaps his German formality or Camilla's shyness kept her from voicing her preference to a man of such imposing authority. And why should they be homesick? Home of late had been steeped in sorrow and unpleasantness, unlike the secure nest of earlier years. He had been warned that his girls were too young to be sent so far away; Camilla was eleven and Isabella only seven. Some predicted that the little one would be rejected for her youth. The Salem Female Boarding School was a prestigious institution and could afford to be selective of its pupils. Nevertheless James pled for its aid in shoring up his crumbling

15

domestic situation, and the kindly Moravians had indeed accepted his daughters into their fold, probably because of his hardship.

James Torrance had married the girls' mother sixteen years before, when all he touched seemed to turn to gold. His father had been a hard-working and able businessman, who during James's youth had amassed an impressive plantation and mercantile enterprise. When James reached his twentieth year, his father entrusted him with the mercantile interests, and four years later his hand was accepted by the lovely Nancy Davidson. Although Nancy was only seventeen, she was the daughter of a prosperous and important man and well suited to the place the Torrances had carved in Mecklenburg's red clay hills. James felt that the sun and moon were his and his alone.

Life was good. In ten months' time Nancy presented him with a son who was named Hugh after James's father which was the custom in their family. Hugh was soon followed by Jane, Camilla, James Franklin (always called Frank), and Isabella. Early in 1816, the year of Frank's birth, both of James's parents died, ushering in the malignant decade. In November of 1818, Nancy was violently attacked by typhus fever. James held little hope for her recovery as nearly all who were afflicted succumbed. She mercifully died on the eleventh day of that month, free of delirium and torment.[1] Isabella was less than a year old. Two years later little Jane died at the age of nine.

James began seeking a wife. Being widowed with young children was a dire hardship for both men and women. Many marriages were inspired by the urgency of earning a living while caring for a handful of children. It was a job God had designed for two. Of course he wanted to marry again into the socially elite of the community. He had placed his children on that path; it was important for a new mother to be able to guide them along its way.

On April 14, 1821, he took Polly Latta as his bride. She was a daughter of James Latta who owned a nearby plantation, and who also sought prosperous marriages for his family. This wedding day was a joyous occasion celebrating an excellent match.

Perhaps marriage overburdened his new wife. Polly was twenty-two and had led a pampered life. She was now a mother of four children ranging from three to eleven years old, and she had no experience in child rearing. Her brother, who had died the year before at the age of ten, had been a quiet and sickly child. She was ill prepared for a house full of rambunctious youngsters which immediately increased. William was born eight and a half months after they were wed, and Jane followed the next year. Polly never had the opportunity to take advantage of her own careful upbringing and education. Overwhelmed by responsibility, illness, fatigue, or perhaps all of them, she died on November 26, 1824. She was twenty-five, and little Jane was fifteen months old. Once again James was a widower with a house full of children, one of them an infant.

More difficulties came to James in 1825. Since his father's death, cotton had become more and more profitable. As he increased his land holdings and put more acres under the plow, he found that it demanded nearly all of his energy. Soon after Polly's death, his uncle and mentor Albert Torrance passed away. James had practically grown up in Albert's home. His death was as harsh a blow as that of his parents and his two young wives. James closed his mercantile store which had served the community for twenty years. There was no joy in it with Albert gone, and he had little need for it in the new economy. Still, the demands of family and his remaining business interests were pulling him in diverse directions. The familiar longing for a feminine mind to share his responsibilities crept in upon him, especially in regard to his children.

He glanced once more at Reichel's letter and prayed he had done the right thing for his daughters. Polly had also been a student at Salem (although she entered at the grand old age of thirteen). She had spoken glowingly of the Moravian community and its academic excellence dispensed with great warmth and love. She had certainly been the most literate and knowledgeable woman he had ever known. He dearly missed her quick wit and affectionate companionship.

Surely his girls would be well cared for over the next two years; he must have confidence in that. Now to find tutors for Hugh and Frank. Many of the local families were pooling resources for schooling their children. Then there would be time to concentrate on business and the babies, a respite he needed to make his home calm and safe for all of them.

As he folded the letter its date caught his eye, one year and a day since he lost his dear Polly. November seemed to be a time for dying, and he had had quite enough of it. By God's grace perhaps the grim reaper would leave him be for a while. He tucked the letter away in a pigeonhole of his secretary. It would be there when he needed a reminder of his daughters' safe harbor. James was a keeper of letters.

2 Salem 1825~1827

The school seemed huge and bustling to Isabella. An array of neat brick and half-timbered buildings surrounded a green square, and even more buildings sprawled down the adjacent streets. She soon learned that they comprised an entire village, and each one had its purpose. In addition to the girls' school, there was one for boys, various workshops, stores and businesses, a house for the Single Brothers, and one for the Single Sisters. There were also homes for families built closely together along the cobblestone streets. Imagine, living right beside another family that you were not related to—how odd! On the plantation only the Negro families lived in such a fashion but not in such attractive houses. At home most visiting took place at church or involved quite a bit of planning. The closest plantation to her father's was Aunt Betsy's, and that was nearly a half hour's walk. In Salem one could cross the threshold and be talking with neighbors.

Many years before, the Moravians began coming to America from the Bohemian and Moravian regions of central Europe. They came seeking religious freedom. In America they created settlements where they could practice their rather unusual Protestant faith. Salem was such a community. They relied on the guidance of God in the drawing of lots for important decisions. When a decision needed to be made, a parishioner approached a church Elder who would reach into a bowl and, without the aid of his eyes, select a reed. The color of the reed would tell the faithful that God's answer was yes or no or the matter deserved further prayer and study. The drawing of lots guided the selection of land for villages and cemeteries. A young man might seek such counsel before proposing, yet the young lady always had permission to refuse.

Although families lived together, nearly every other aspect of Moravian life was carried on in one's choir. The choirs were grouped by age, sex, and marital status. There were separate choirs for children, older boys, older girls, Single Brothers, Single Sisters, married men, married women, widows, and widowers. The pews in the church and the plots in the cemetery were arranged by choir. They worked communally, although each person kept his own wages. They did not engage in warfare, nor believe in the private ownership of land. Their faith was deep, and the church governed all facets of their lives. They were hard workers, excellent at crafts, and good at business. Working together, they farmed the rolling fields that surrounded the village. In spite of their communal lifestyle, they lived harmoniously with their fiercely independent Scots-Irish neighbors.[2]

The Moravians established a school for boys and one for girls. Their doctrine placed great value on education for everyone. The younger children attended day classes, and the older ones, while often taking meals with their families, boarded at the schools. When their education was complete, the young men and women moved on to the Single Brothers or Single Sisters House where they learned and practiced various crafts and trades for the benefit of the community. The needs of the society always came before any individual's wishes.

~   ~   ~

Moravian education was greatly admired around the countryside; when the girls' school was opened to outsiders, it was immediately popular. It was a costly and pious institution, an odd combination that appealed to prominent families. Most non-Moravian congregations provided little or no education for their girls. Some even believed the idea to be dangerous. In Mecklenburg County, James could have found lessons in music, deportment, and plain and fancy sewing to complement the basic reading, writing, and catechism of a Presbyterian education. Only in Salem could his girls learn history, geography, mathematics, and philosophy.[3]

"Miss Isabella, what can I do for you today?" The kindly gentleman behind the counter at the school store found her page in the great ledger book. He dipped his pen and wrote the date on the next line, December 19th, 1825.

"Shoes, sir; I need a new pair of shoes."

"New shoes?" He glanced at the earlier entries on the page. "Why, it has not been three weeks since you last bought shoes. Do you not take proper care of them?"

"But sir, look at the soles; they have gone all awry. The holes fill with pebbles, and my feet are scratched and dirty. I know that Papa would want me to have new shoes." A tear welled in her eye and her lip began to tremble. "I have not walked on cobblestones before; perhaps I don't know how it should be done."

"Now, now, Miss Isabella, I only meant to tease. Of course you shall have some new shoes, and I will take the torn ones to be mended. The Sisters are always complaining that our shoes wear out too quickly. Sit here on the bench, and I will find a sturdy pair for you and send the old ones off to the cobbler." She felt better as she wiggled her stockinged toes while he searched for her size. This school was not such a frightening place after all. [4]

Isabella and Camilla shared their room with two other girls who were both Camilla's age. When their whispering and giggling shut out the younger child, Camilla took it upon herself to bring her sister into the play. Camilla had some memories of their mother, and she knew that Isabella had none. Mother Polly had been the only mother in Isabella's life; both girls had grown to love her dearly. Now Camilla felt that she must become a little mother to the child. [5]

The girls quickly made the acquaintance of Mary and Ann Latta who had entered school the previous summer and were nieces of Mother Polly. Ann was Camilla's age and Mary was a year older. They lived some distance away in South Carolina but had on rare occasions visited their Latta grandparents which gave the four of them common ground. They were quiet and skittish girls but pleasant enough companions. James had sternly insisted that his daughters befriend them; after all they were cousins. What James could not explain was that their father was a man of ill repute. [6]

There were no other boarders as young as seven. Isabella took her classes with the day students and was making new friends. She needed fewer books and less writing paper than her sister. She spent much of her time with needles and thread and scraps of cloth. Learning one's stitches was as important for young ladies as learning from books. A yard of cloth or a piece of ribbon purchased every few weeks were the tools to learn the various stitches, seam finishes, buttonholes, hems, and dress trimmings that she would use to clothe her family for the rest of her life. Never again would a needle and thread be far from her fingertips.

At the end of lessons Isabella joined the boarding students to take her meals. Most of her free time was spent in the company of older girls. Camilla's classes, appropriate for her age, required not only more books and papers, but silk threads and embroidery supplies for fancy stitching. In both of their classrooms there were books, maps, and globes for the use of everyone. A few books had to be purchased; each girl on her first visit to the school store bought a copy of *Murray's Grammar*.

The library, at first stern and forbidding, became a tranquil place. As the days grew short and crisp, the library with its smells of paper, ink, and leather enticed them with burning lamps and a fire in the ornate tile stove. Camilla especially liked the library—so many books, so many things one could know. She often opened a book to find the printing all in German. It looked as if little birds had stepped in ink pots then danced across the page. Many of the Moravians still spoke German in their homes, and she would sometimes hear the strange tongue in the village shops. Thank goodness their lessons were all taught in English. Her father had lots of books. Perhaps that was the lure of ink and leather—its aroma reminded her of home. And it reminded her of her promise to be strong and to take care of the little child.

Frequent visits to the school store became a delightful adventure. Isabella had had no experience with money on the plantation. Until recently her father had operated a store in the building next to their house. She had seen the neighboring farmers and their wives exchanging coins for sugar, or spices, or nails, or coffee, but she had no part in such commerce. After all, her father owned the store, and he supplied all her needs. Now she could simply tell the kind man behind the counter what she wished, and he would write on her ledger page and get her the books, or stationery, or toothbrush, or whatever she requested. The necessities of schooling, some grooming items, and a seemingly endless supply of shoes and cobbler services could be found at the school store. But its most exciting feature was the distribution of pocket money. When she asked for pocket money, he would give her some coins and on the ledger sheet add their amount to her purchase. In the end he would send the total to her father and he would pay—as simple as that! With coins clutched in her palm she could race to the village shops for all sorts of sweet and pretty things. The Winkler Bakery was right around the corner. Its yeasty aura overlapped with ginger and cinnamon was always tempting; a lot of pocket money found its way to the bakery.

Camilla often paid for postage along with her purchases at the school store, and about twice a month she wrote to her father to report on their improvement. Isabella was new at writing; she added her own brief notes to her sister's letters. Some of the letters requested an increase in their allowance of pocket money.

Isabella managed to embarrass herself on one occasion over that very matter. She and Camilla had gone with the Latta girls for supplies and, as usual, had requested coins. Isabella turned to her cousins and said, "Ask him for some money and we can all go for a treat."

"There is no pocket money in our account," said Ann.

"Then you must write your papa and tell him," said Isabella.

"Papa does not fill our account; Grandpa Latta does. Ma told us not to ask for extras," Mary mumbled the uncomfortable words, her eyes affixed to the floor. Isabella began to ask if that explained the patched and threadbare nature of their clothing, but before she got three words out Camilla gave her a rough pinch on the shoulder.

"We have more than enough," said Camilla. "Come along and we shall all share in a treat." Isabella was learning to hold her tongue.

As the winter wore on, the girls became accustomed to Moravian life. The simple cooperative community was a sharp contrast to the lavish, isolated, self-sufficient plantation. The loving care and attention of the Sisters eased the transition. The women of Salem dressed a little oddly, a bit old-fashioned. At home the young ladies had taken up the latest styles, and their gowns were soft and graceful. Most of the women in Salem, young and old, dressed in drab work clothes, just like Grandma Davidson. Camilla was especially curious about their caps. They were made of white linen like the ones worn at home; but they had a handsome pointed design stitched right over the forehead, and they were tied under the chin with ribbons of cherry, or pink, or blue, or white. A Sister explained that the style indicated their faith, and the color of the ribbon denoted their choir.

In 1826, the glories of spring were spoiled by illness. A fever spread through the school, and the sick girls were confined to their rooms. The Sisters took on the task of nursing and when necessary called in a doctor. Early in April, Camilla fell ill; a week or so later Isabella was also feverish and coughing. Dr. Keel was called; he examined the girls and prescribed a remedy. Isabella recovered first and returned to her classes; Camilla soon followed. Camilla was usually taken harder by illness and was always slower to recover. Their routine finally resumed, and on the first of May, the day Dr. Keel's bill arrived, they were both at the school store seeking pocket money.

There were no summer recesses at Salem. (Such an idea was impractical since some of the girls lived as far away as Tennessee.) However, James would visit them whenever possible. He sometimes had business in Salem or nearby, and he would use these opportunities to spend a day or an evening with his girls. There were special activities to break the tedium of study during the hot season. Camilla and Isabella were both treated to exhibitions, pleasure rides, and other diversions. In the fall, studies once again became serious. The school year culminated in December with celebrations and public examinations where students presented elocutions and musical recitals so that all could admire their achievements. In 1826, James took his girls on a brief excursion following their examinations.

The new year was much like the previous year, except the girls moved to higher classes, and new girls came in to replace those who had completed their studies. Among their number was Sally Ridge, the daughter of a Cherokee Indian chief. Her tawny complexion was framed by the blackest of hair, and her prominent cheekbones were regal. Isabella thought she was beautiful. "Is she a princess?" Isabella had asked.

"Of course not," replied Camilla, "she is the same as any other girl." But she was not the same. She was elegant and moved like a ribbon of silk.[7]

In addition to academics, they learned order, neatness, and absolute obedience. Obedience was solicited by kindness, respect, and a desire to please God, never by punishment. They were quickly becoming well educated and accomplished young ladies.

Isabella escaped the springtime illness. Camilla was more seriously afflicted than she had been the year before. This time Dr. Shuman was called and Isabella was worried. First her own mother, then Mother Polly, and now Camilla was so very ill. For as long as Isabella could remember she had clung to Camilla as her very own anchor in life. Dr. Shuman made several visits and dispensed medicines including a quart of wine. By the end of April, Camilla had recovered and rejoined her classes. Isabella had offered special prayers.

Music was included in Camilla's curriculum. In addition to academics she was acquiring the skills that would be desired by a gentleman planter.

Isabella was still too young to take advantage of all the school had to offer. She would leave school with a good basic education but little in the way of refinement.

It was in 1827 that Camilla burst into their room flushed with excitement, "Isabella! Isabella! We have a letter from Papa! You will never believe his news; Papa is taking a new wife!"

Isabella froze; the color fled from her face.

"What ever is the matter with you?" asked Camilla. "Papa is going to be married. When we go home we will be a real family again, a pa and a ma and all of our brothers and sister!"

"I do not want a ma." Isabella's voice was barely audible.

"Of course you do. Her name is Miss Margaret Allison. Her people come from a plantation near Statesville. And listen to this, Isabella, her cousin went to this same school when she was a girl. Pa says they were more like sisters than cousins, being nearly the same age; Miss Allison knows all about our school."

"No." Isabella's wind had returned, and now she shouted, "I will not have another ma, never! Papa does not need a wife; he has enough Negroes to care for the house and the cooking. I will have nothing to do with her." Now tears were falling between her words. "I shall not go home. At the end of the session I shall simply stay here and become a single Sister!"

"Now, now, come to me dear Isabella. You know that is not possible." Camilla was astonished at her sister's outburst. What could be upsetting the child? "I thought you would be happy for Papa; whatever is the matter?"

"My mothers die. They always do. I cannot have another ma. We must write to Papa and tell him not to marry, for if he does, she will surely die."

"Oh, you poor thing. This time it will be different; I know it will. Papa says he has very tender feelings toward Miss Allison. He says she is much younger than he but old enough to be a full woman. She has passed the age when our Ma and Mother Polly died. That proves she is strong and healthy."

"I do hope you are right, Camilla, but I cannot help being frightened. Why is it all my mothers die? When you were last ill, I was so afraid God was going to take you too. I'm scared, Camilla; I am so frightfully scared." Her voice had once again dissolved into a soft whimper.

Camilla cradled the child in her arms. "You have no memory of our mother; you were much too little. There was a great deal of typhus fever in the neighborhood. Many were ill, and Ma was not the only one to die. Papa was quite worried for you. He was afraid you might become ill from her milk. Do you remember your wet nurse? It was Papa's good fortune that one of our Negroes had milk. He put the two of you in a room alone to keep you well. Jane and I had to share our room with Hugh and Frank and I can promise you that was no fun! You see, it worked. Ma was simply too ill to recover, but the rest of us survived. Papa loves you; he would never do anything that might hurt you."

"I remember; Flora was my wet nurse. She took care of us until Mother Polly came."

"Yes, she did; her own baby, Peggy, was not much older than you but old enough to be weaned. [8] It was not our fault about Mother Polly. She was not of a strong constitution. It was probably too much for her to care for all of us when her own babies came so quickly. God gave her those babies, Isabella; it was not of your doing."

"But I was the youngest of our mother's children. I made her work too difficult."

"No, no, no, Isabella, you must not think that. All of it is God's way, and we are not to understand his mysteries. We cannot know why he took Mother Polly or our sister Jane. Papa says Miss Allison is very strong and about the same age as Mother Polly would be. Do you suppose, Isabella, that Miss Allison could have visited her cousin when Mother Polly was here? Perhaps they were acquainted."

Isabella's eyes brightened. "Yes, do you suppose?!" Her sense of adventure was pushing aside her fear. "Oh, Camilla, wouldn't that be grand! Some of the Sisters might remember; let's go and ask. Perhaps they can tell us what she looked like."

"What a fine idea, Isabella. I do hope someone can recall her. We must ask if she is as sturdy as Papa says."

The rest of the term went quickly. The girls made plans for their commencement and their last public examinations. They gleaned a sense of their new mother from their father's letters and the chatty notes she always added; they were beginning to feel that they knew her. On the first of November, Isabella purchased materials to sew a gentleman's pocketbook. Fancy stitching at last, and a Christmas gift for Papa! Her cheerful nature for the most part had returned. The Sisters soothed her occasional sad moment. "There, there, Miss Isabella, you must not worry about your new mother. I know she is a fine lady. And your papa is a very good man. He loves you greatly and will always take care of you. You come from a very fine family, Isabella, a fine family indeed."

3　The Beginning

James had told them often about their fine family. He had told them of their grandfather Hugh and his many adventures. Four brothers—Hugh, Albert, James, and Charles Torance—were born in County Tyrone in the north of Ireland. Not long after the middle of the last century, still hardly more than boys, they sailed the Atlantic as did thousands of other poor Scots-Irish to seek their fortunes, as the fairy tales might say. Like most of their countrymen, they settled in the southern part of Pennsylvania pressed against the eastern foothills of the Appalachians. They lived there six years or so, working, saving their money, and learning the mercantile trade. They were astounded by the vastness of their new land and enchanted by the stories of those who traveled the trading paths and wagon roads. They heard of riches and fertile fields and peaceful southerly lands where the native Indians were not mongering war.

Early in the 1770s, Hugh and Albert bid their brothers farewell and headed south on the Great Wagon Road. Many hundreds of Scots-Irish walked the length of the Shenandoah Valley alongside their wagons heaped with all they owned. These were the people who settled the backcountry of Virginia and the Carolinas. Hugh and Albert ended their journey in Salisbury, North Carolina, the largest town in the western part of the state, a fitting place for a pair of merchants. Albert seemed content to establish himself there; Hugh was not yet shed of his wanderlust. He traveled around the neighboring counties in North Carolina and up and down the wagon roads—buying, selling, bartering—sowing the seeds of his fortune.

In 1779, Hugh bought land in Mecklenburg County, a fine piece of land, over six hundred acres at the confluence of two creeks. No longer a youth at thirty-six, he had found land to his liking and was ready to make a home. His time was divided between the log house on his new land, Salisbury and nearby towns, and the longer journeys required by his trade.

The War for American Independence, which had dragged on far too long, had come to the southern colonies. The character of the Scots-Irish led them naturally to the side of the American patriots. They had had no use for the monarchy for as many centuries as anyone could remember, and fighting came to them as easily as drawing breath. In 1780, Hugh joined the light cavalry militia company of Captain Galbraith Falls, and for the next two years was in the business of war. Settling down would have to wait a bit longer. Captain Falls was a casualty of the Battle of Ramsour's Mill, and in 1783 Hugh married his captain's widow, Isabella. Hugh was forty years old, and the widow Falls was forty-three, the mother of eight children.

The newlyweds first lived in Salisbury. Hugh's log house had been a handy place to throw his bedroll in his bachelor days, but it was hardly suitable for his new large family. Isabella would require a necessary house and, eventually, a smokehouse, a kitchen, and a place for their black family. She brought into their marriage five Negroes named Binah, Ned, Nell, Phebe, and Phill, along with a large assortment of furniture, household goods, livestock, farm equipment, and her brood of children. There was much to do to turn Hugh's land into a working farm.

On the nineteenth of November in 1784, Isabella gave birth to their son James Galbraith Torrance. He was called James after Hugh's father, and Galbraith seemed a fitting choice. Hugh's brother, Charles, had married a Galbraith, and they could both appreciate the virtuous sacrifice of Captain Falls. Isabella, at forty-four, had borne her last child.

Three years later they moved to Hugh's land in Mecklenburg County. The log house had been covered in handsome beaded clapboards and painted white. A room had been added for Hugh's inventory, and the loft had been outfitted as a dormitory for girls. Fields had been cleared, and the outbuildings were in their proper places. Hugh's many years of hard work were coming to fruition.

The forests and fields of the Piedmont were an ideal place for James's early years. Walking with his father down rows of tender plants introduced him to the rich possibilities of agriculture. He rode with his father from farm to farm, the wagon loaded with necessary goods and exotic trinkets, unaware he was absorbing lessons in trade. There was plenty of time for play between these childhood lessons. The woods abounded with imaginary adventures. He spent hours at the big rock that bolted up from the earth near his home. Sometimes he pretended to be Hugh, fighting the ferocious Shawnee in Pennsylvania so many years before. He hid behind the rock with his musket at the ready (he had carved it from a branch) waiting for the faintest crackle of a leaf under the soft step of a moccasin. "Bang, bang! Got 'em!" Then off, running through the woods, now chasing a bear. "Bang, bang!" Or he would climb to the top of the monstrous rock, which in the game had become Kings Mountain, and point his wooden weapon to the ground below. "I got you, Major Ferguson; I got you and all your Loyalist scoundrels! Bang, bang, I'm the king of the mountain now!" Hugh had told him all the war stories, and now the battles were being fought all over again by a single boy soldier joyously romping through leafy woods.

Isabella's two oldest children were sons; they were nearly grown when she married Hugh and out of the nest by the time they moved to the log house. Her six daughters fussed over James and were always there to help her care for him.[9] James never wanted for female advice in his younger years; no wonder he so enjoyed time with his father and the telling of war stories.

Life was good to Hugh, and as he continued to buy adjacent plots of land, his farm grew into a plantation. A new crop was just beginning to effect a monumental change in the South—cotton. In the old days the only cotton which would grow in that climate was nearly useless. Its seeds stuck tenaciously to its fibers; no number of hands could produce a profit from it. Cotton cloth, made from an old-world variety, was mostly imported from Europe. It was highly desired but its price was dear. The invention of the cotton gin and the beginnings of industry turned the useless upland cotton into white gold. Everyone hungered for this soft luxury fabric; now it could be had even by those of modest means. There was much money to be made in cotton. Hugh was there when it all began, the perfect spot for a merchant farmer.

$\sim$ $\sim$ $\sim$

In 1796, Hugh built a fine brick home just to the west of his log house. He stood in front of it and admired his accomplishment. For nearly as far as the eye could see fields were cleared of trees and plowed. Brick houses were rare in this part of the world. All who rode by could see that Hugh Torrance was becoming an important man.

Meanwhile James was growing quickly, and his father had become concerned about his education. The carefree boy, the pet in this house full of women, would someday have the responsibility of Hugh's domain—he needed to be prepared. Rural Mecklenburg offered few opportunities for book learning, so James was sent to his Uncle Albert in Salisbury where he spent many of his formative years. [10] Schools were close by, and Albert's fine store in town was a more fitting apprenticeship than Hugh's itinerant business scattered across the countryside. At first James was not happy in Salisbury; he missed his farm and woods and even his sisters. His parents sometimes visited him, and whenever possible he went back to Mecklenburg for brief delightful interludes.

Salisbury 14 July 1801
Dear father and mother
You have not written to me since I have come to this place and I would be very glad if you would by uncle concerning how long you are a gowing to keep at this plais and to appoint the time wheather it be long or short sow that I may not think long to git home, and acquaint him ove It and I am thinking gowing home at Christmas and I want you to send fur me so that I may stay home all holidays
Mr Bitz ac/ is 2..17..6
James G Torrance

Hugh smiled at his son's clumsy letter; clearly his education was not yet complete. Of course he had written since James had been at "that place," but not since his last visit home. He promised himself to write more often.

James grew accustomed to life in his Uncle Albert's home and gradually developed a deep respect for him. He learned the importance of structure and hard work. Salisbury was a sophisticated town. Albert's customers expected more than mere necessities. Where could a merchant go for books, and clocks, and bolts of silk? Would silver candlesticks sell or tie up his capital? How to find a fair price? One had to be careful when buying goods for pounds and shillings then selling them for dollars and cents. Each state had its own currency; who would accept whose money and at what rate was a constant puzzle. He learned to keep meticulous records; both the mind and the pen had to be sharp.

In time James returned to his father's home; he was now a man. He spent many hours with his father as their wagon bounced and heaved over the rutted clay roads carrying goods from farm to farm. They used this time to develop a plan. "It has become more and more difficult to find the time I need to tend the crops," said Hugh. (By now his plantation exceeded thirteen hundred acres.) "Cotton has proved to be a fine thing, but to make the most of it I need to be in the fields managing the hands. Yet I am not willing to give up the merchant trade; it's greatly needed, and it pulls in a good profit."

"You seem to be saying that you should be two men," laughed his son.

"Ah, yes, two men indeed. What I want is for you to be one of them." This was no surprise to James. He had always assumed that he would take up business alongside his father. That was the usual way with fathers and sons, especially when there was only one son. "There is much more to my plan; listen and see if it suits you. Mecklenburg is growing. There are many more farmers now, planting many more acres. They are planting crops to sell, not just to feed themselves. They have money, James, and they want to spend it on fine things. I have come to resent the hours I spend rattling around in this old wagon. It is a very poor use of my time, and the wagon hardly holds enough to satisfy my customers. I could sell cloth from twenty different bolts, five kinds of tea, and tools of every shape and size; but such a variety cannot fit in this conveyance, and a larger one could not navigate these deplorable roads."

"So what is it you propose?" James could see where his father was headed with this and he was pleased.

"I would like to open a store, something like Albert's, and I would like for you to be the storekeeper."

"That is a fine idea. I seem to have been keeping store since I could see over the counter. Do you have a place in mind?"

"Yes—the log house."

"But the overseer lives there."[11]

"That is part of the plan: if I can devote my energies to the farm, I shan't need an overseer. I have long felt resentment at paying that man to do the job that I should be doing. And I certainly could not trust someone outside the family to drive this cargo around the countryside; it would be an invitation to thievery."

"Should I continue living with you and Ma?"

"I would prefer to fix the log house to include living quarters. As a man, you should have a place of your own. Times have changed here, James; the merchandise is becoming more and more valuable. It would be an asset to have you living on the premises." Hugh had thought of everything.

By now they had reached James Latta's plantation, and Hugh turned the rig into the yard. Mr. Latta had lived in the neighborhood for as long as James could remember; his sons, William and Robert, were close to his own age. They had often played together as children when they accompanied their fathers on business. Mr. Latta was also a merchant farmer, and the two men traded with one another frequently. After Sunday services at Hopewell Presbyterian Church, families shared their boxed dinners and visited, for work was forbidden on the Sabbath. James had many fond memories of Sunday afternoons gamboling about the churchyard with William and Robert, tending to the rough-and-tumble business of boys.

Mr. Latta had come to this country some years ago, leaving behind in the north of Ireland his wife and the two boys. His wife died before he had an opportunity to bring his family here—if that had been his intention; he had gone about it slowly enough. He did not speak of that part of his life, and it would be impolite to inquire. In any event, after her death the boys arrived in this country to live with their father. William was about thirteen and Robert eleven when James first encountered them at the Hopewell Sunday dinners. He and Robert became immediate companions, being nearly the same age.

William was different. He was shifty-eyed and always carried a chip on his shoulder. At first James thought the older boy did not want to appear associated with the younger ones, but over the years he came to know William as insolent and filled with discontent. Robert had been an infant when Mr. Latta left Ireland and had scant memory of his leaving. He accepted his new home and his father's open arms with enthusiasm. William, on the other hand, seemed to have never forgiven his father's abandonment. There had been a palpable wall of distrust between William and Mr. Latta for as long as James had known them.[12]

"Good afternoon, Hugh, James; I am pleased you could come by. I'm eager to see the newest wares you have to offer." Mr. Latta had heard the approaching wagon. He put down the hoe he was using in the kitchen garden and greeted the men.

"And good to see you sir," said James. "I had heard about your fine new home but had not seen it until now. My, you have outdone yourself. It is indeed a handsome place."

"Why thank you. We built it about four years since, but you've been in Salisbury most of that time. I fashioned it after a style I admired in Philadelphia. I suppose it looks out of place set down here among the fields."

"Not at all, it suits this place perfectly." James did indeed admire the tall and narrow white frame house. It had two ample stories plus a full garret. Like a tall man, it possessed authority. The two merchants stood by the wagon discussing its contents while James walked around the house. On all sides were numerous windows, resplendent with sunlight. In the winter the house would be bathed in warming sunshine. Mr. Latta had the good sense to place his house on a jut of land between the Catawba River and Garr Creek and locate the windows to take full advantage of the river's cool summer breeze.

A little girl of about five ran out of the kitchen toward the wagon. Mr. Latta had married Jane Knox several years after his boys had come to live with him; once again he had infants in his home. James joined the group at the wagon.

"Papa, Papa," said the little girl, "Ma says dinner is nearly ready!"

"Thank you, Polly, tell Ma that I will be there in a bit. James, meet my little daughter, Polly. Polly, you remember Mr. Torrance; this is his son, another Mr. Torrance."

"Good afternoon, Polly," said James. "I am pleased to meet you." She politely lifted her hand to his, giggled, then retreated behind her father's coattails. "Mr. Latta, tell me the news of Robert and William; I've seen so little of them in recent years."

"Well, I am happy to report that Robert is turning out to be a fine young man. He spends part of his time in our home but most of it in the Yorkville District of South Carolina.[13] It seems his eye has been caught by a young lady in that country. I would not be surprised to hear of a wedding once he has found a suitable home. Both of my sons are following me in the mercantile trade but by very different means. While Robert strives to better himself, William seems content to peddle a wagonload of trifling stuffs. I hear he causes offense to everyone whose path he crosses." William apparently had not mended his ways.

"James, we need to be moving along if we intend to complete our rounds before nightfall," said Hugh as he secured his load in the wagon against the jolting ride that lay ahead.

"Coming, Pa. Good-bye, Mr. Latta. I am home to stay now, so I am sure we shall be meeting more often. Good-bye, Miss Polly, give my regards to your Ma." He waved to the pretty child with the bright smile—having no idea that many years later he would take her as a wife.

On the journey home Hugh and James continued to discuss their plan. "Pa," said James, "I have been thinking about the living quarters you mentioned earlier. I like the look of Mr. Latta's home. Perhaps we could borrow some of its design."

"Ah, I'm sure he would be flattered. I supplied Mr. Latta with some of his building materials, and I know the craftsmen who performed the work. What was it that especially drew your eye?"

"I think its high and narrow shape gives it an air of importance, and all of those windows make it bright and inviting."

"Imposing and inviting at the same time; that is a rare combination. I doubt there is any way to make the log house high and narrow. I learned many years ago not to interfere with its structure. I cut through some logs to enlarge the garret and nearly lost the whole building in the process." James remembered that story and was quite familiar with the huge turn-buckle and tie rods that spanned the garret. "However," Hugh continued, "perhaps we could add a wing to one side that would fit your vision."

"That would be splendid. I also took note of Mr. Latta's brick chimneys. They frame the house quite well, one at each end, accentuating its height."

"You certainly have an eye for tallness today. We've done our share of brickmaking on our place. Digging up clay makes for better fields, as well as houses." He paused to gather his thoughts. He still had not broached the best part of the plan.

"This is what I would like for you to do, James. I have saved quite a bit of money and made lists of the finery that is in demand these days. I would like for you to go to Philadelphia and buy goods to open the grandest store that Mecklenburg has ever seen. You will have to be shrewd with those men. They will first take you for a naive boy from the backcountry, but I will give you letters of introduction. I think you have been trained to deal with them as equals." James beamed at the suggestion. He was twenty years old and he knew that his father considered him a man. That was the highest compliment he could ever be paid.

4 The Store 1805~1825

Philadelphia was a cornucopia of delights. James arrived in the afternoon of the twenty-sixth of May. He secured lodging, sent his driver Phill to the livery with the horses, and now was free to walk about the city. He had never before seen such a place. Streets, lively with people and horses, were lined on both sides by houses and stores built closely together. As he walked he studied the list of merchants provided by his father and Uncle Albert, hoping to spot some of their stores. Today was for finding his way around; none of the shops would be open on the Sabbath. He hoped he would be forgiven for traveling on that day; but the evening before, with his goal in sight, the temptation to complete his journey could not be resisted.

He was pleased that his father had permitted Phill to come with him. He needed another man to help with the heavy work and greatly appreciated the companionship. James and Hugh had discussed the issue at length: "Phill will be a good man for you to have," Hugh had said. "Being that he is forty-five years old and has a family on this place, I doubt he would be tempted to join the free men in that city."

"I think you are right, Pa," replied James. "I've never known him to be disloyal or to look for another way of life. And Binah would surely protest if she thought there was any chance of her husband not returning."[14]

"You must be very careful of how he is perceived in the north. Many in Philadelphia strongly disapprove of owning Negroes. Treat him at all times as a hired man. The fact that he is a mulatto should work to your advantage. His color will raise fewer eyebrows than a purely black man. I would suggest you bring him around to help pack and load the merchandise after the deals have been made. And give him some coins to spend on his own. He deserves some pleasure."

"Where shall he stay?" asked James.

"At the livery where he can tend the horses. That is the proper lodging for a servant, free or otherwise. I am not asking you to participate in a lie, only to refrain from boasting about your ownership."

"You shall have no worry on that account. I've known Phill all my life and feel almost the affection for him as I do family. I only regret that I have to take him away from you during this season of the year."

"We will make do. The cotton is all in the ground, and I have enough hands to tend to the young plants. I trust you will both be home before the hard work begins."

Indeed James did want to accomplish his mission quickly. This magical city was full of excitement but so was the prospect of opening his store.

He continued walking the streets and making note of the city's geography until dusk; then he returned to the hotel, had a light meal, and retired to his room. By the lamplight he read over again the extensive lists of goods provided by his father and uncle. Could a whole caravan of wagons bring all of these things back to the Carolinas? And would he have enough money? In his pocketbook, kept close to his person, was over four thousand dollars—more money than he had ever dreamed of holding in his hands at one time. He had been taught to be very careful about guarding his money, as well as spending it. Tomorrow he would begin testing his lessons.

On Monday the adventure began.[15] The streets were once more filled with people, but now they were scurrying about with a sense of purpose. Yesterday all of the shop windows had been draped for the Sabbath; now he could look inside and see an array of goods never before imagined. He entered those shops which seemed most promising, sometimes only to look, sometimes inquiring about merchandise and prices. Most of the tradesmen were cordial. If they could not help him, they referred him to someone who could. By the end of the day he was beginning to form an idea of how to go about his business. Only one purchase was made that day: at Joseph Sprenger's he bought several hundred yards of assorted laces, ribbons, and edgings. Most of Mr. Sprenger's goods were measured in French *ells*, rather than yards, but he was one of the few merchants who priced his wares in dollars rather than pounds—that simplified the calculations. Uncle Albert's lessons in reckoning were coming to good use. He spent $66.94½ at Mr. Sprenger's shop; he hoped it was money spent wisely.[16]

The next morning the exploration continued. It was difficult to keep from being distracted by enticing baubles whose price was too dear for resale in the backcountry. He peered into the window of John McAllister's tack shop and was drawn inside by the finery he saw. This was not tack for farmers, but for gentlemen. He selected a few handsome whips; if they could not be sold, they would serve as fine gifts. Then a stylish cane with a beautifully wrought head caught his eye. He must have it! He paid for the purchases and left the shop with the whips wrapped in a bundle under his left arm and the cane perched properly in the fingers of his right hand. He would be a fine figure of a man when dealing with the merchants of Philadelphia.

At the end of the day he had dealt with only one more tradesman. From Ensworth and Jolley he bought rasps and files, augers and saws, dozens upon dozens of table knives and spoons, spectacles, scissors, needles, thimbles, knitting pins, and all sorts of sundry goods. By the time he had made his selections and arranged for their packing, the day was gone. It was going to take some time to spend four thousand dollars.

On Wednesday he bought some shoes and yarn, then spent the rest of the day revising his plan. He decided to make lists to be left with the

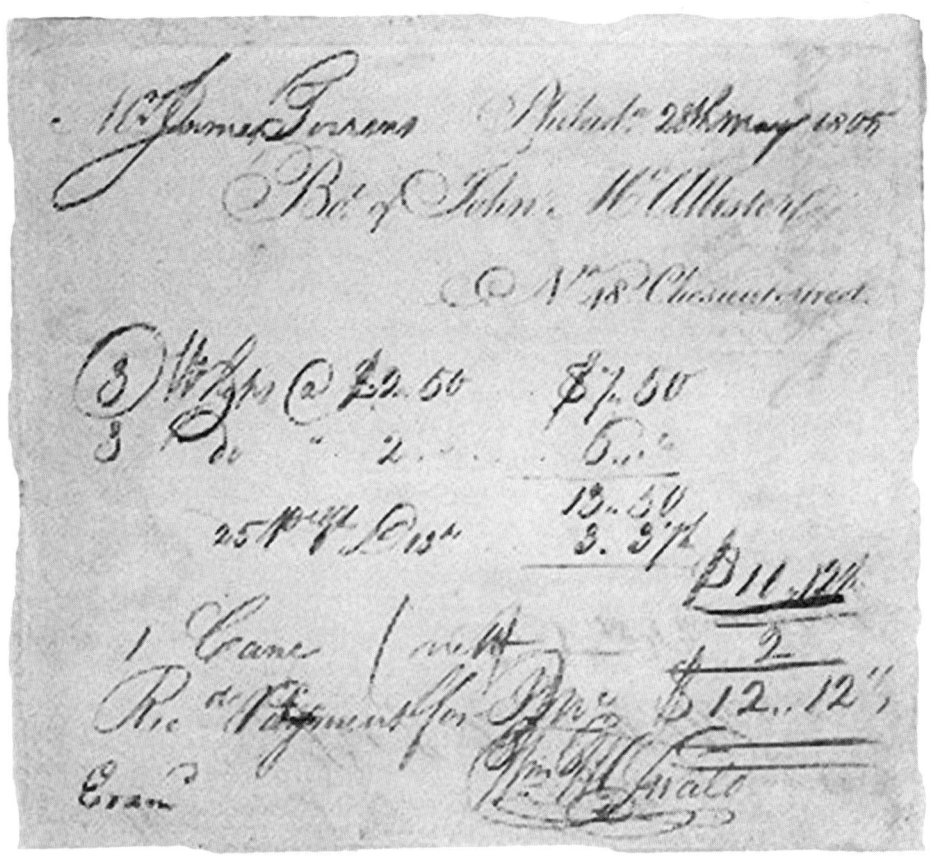

merchants for each sort of goods. He would describe the things he needed, the price he could pay, and put trust in their judgment. There were not enough years in a lifetime to examine everything for sale in Philadelphia.

The next day was more productive; he managed to do business with four merchants. He was efficient at buying shoes but had some trouble at the dry goods establishments. He wanted to handle every bolt of cloth and imagine the gowns that could be made for his mother and sisters or fine suits for himself. His eyes lingered on fancy embroidered handkerchiefs and ivory combs. It was nearly closing time when he reached Beck and Harvey's apothecary and spice shop. Mr. Beck was happy to take his list and promised to fill the order within a day or two. James wished he could have tarried longer; he would make an effort to keep his store fragrant with nutmeg and cloves.

He checked regularly with Phill who was assembling crates, ropes, and other supplies for the homeward journey. Phill was having his own adventure walking freely around town spending his coins. James hoped Phill was not overly enchanted and was relieved to note that he had bought gifts for his wife and children. James stayed up late that Thursday. He needed to work more on the efficiency of the thing. The lists were revised once more, and on Friday he vowed to stick to his purpose.

Nine merchants were visited that day, and a list was left with each. On lists both long and short, some items were not available, at least not at the price he was willing to pay; the lists were constantly under review. He left a very long list at the shop of William Albert. Mr. Albert dealt in dishes and pottery of every kind. They discussed the styles that James thought would suit his neighbors and arranged for packing and crating. He seemed to be buying enough crockery to outfit every table in Mecklenburg County, but he knew some of it would be jolted to pieces on the long journey home.

Saturday the first of June was the most ambitious day yet. Again he visited nine merchants, but this time all of his lists were long. Three of them were dry goods stores where he requested hats, gloves, pins, needles, thread, stockings, blankets, and hundreds of yards of cloth. He must trust Mr. Gibbs, Mr. Potter, and Mr. Henry to make the proper selections. On to Wiltberger's for hardware, tack, and kitchen utensils by the gross. Then to Peersol's for steel, Blakely's for weights, Morgan's for pocketbooks, and Catherine Brooks' for gloves. He had not dealt with a woman store owner before; the experience was pleasurable.

The last stop was a bookseller, John Conrad and Co. Here he requested several hundred volumes, mostly schoolbooks, Bibles, essays, hymnals, and other religious titles. The citizens of Mecklenburg were going to be faithful as well as educated—he was determined about that. He also bought a daybook and ledger to use in his store. As he paid for his purchases he noticed on the shelf a handsomely bound copy of *The Pilgrim's Progress*. It would be the perfect gift for his father. On the counter were brightly colored tin boxes of wafers. He bought a one-pound tin for his mother. She would be very pleased.

On Sunday he reflected on the week and felt proud of his accomplishments. Later he would take stock and prepare for the week ahead, but first he felt the need to refresh his soul. Although Philadelphia was a cosmopolitan city and had citizens of many faiths, a large proportion of its inhabitants were Quakers. James had heard often about these gentle people and was curious to know them. They could be recognized in the city by their plain style of dress. They were warm and welcoming and quite tolerant of people of other faiths. In several conversations James learned that strangers were always welcome at the Friends' Meetings. James took the opportunity that Sunday to attend one. The meeting house was built in a simple but elegant fashion, unadorned with any distraction. It was painted white inside and out, and its windows admitted copious amounts of sunlight. As he entered by the men's door, he was amazed by the brightness of the interior; it seemed aglow with an aura of purity. He followed the example of others and took a seat on a wooden bench. He looked around him for the pulpit but could not see one. As the people entered the building, they took their seats and sat quietly in still reflection or prayer. There was not a word of greeting or conversation, simply quiet, somber silence.

After what seemed to be a very long time, a gentleman rose and began to speak. He spoke about a passage in the Bible and how it had helped him to resolve a conflict during that week. There was more silence, then a woman rose. She talked of illness in her family and how her faith in God was helping her through the distress. And so it continued for several hours. There was no minister, and there seemed to be no leaders, although several older men in the front row were always deferred to. This was a very strange church indeed: no singing, no preachers, no structure that he could see. At the same time it was one of the most peaceful experiences he could remember—that is until one of the men rose to speak adamantly on the evils of African bondage. His voice swelled with passion using Biblical passages to illustrate his point: no one should own another. James was somewhat uncomfortable. He knew the arguments well, yet he could not imagine getting a profitable crop from his father's land without their black families. Those in Mecklenburg who had no hands could barely manage to farm a hundred acres and struggled to feed themselves. Their cabins were as humble as Negro dwellings, and their everyday lives were similar to the Negroes' in every detail except freedom. The Quakers clearly did not consider freedom a detail. James understood the gentleman's protest but was in a complete quandary as to what could be done about it. He would give Phill a few more coins and seek the counsel of Reverend Caldwell when he returned home. He would also tell Caldwell about the lack of preaching and women speaking before the congregation. Perhaps what was transgression in one faith was not so in another. [17]

The next week was as busy as the last. He made return visits to several shops and sought out a few more that were new to him. One was William Smith's apothecary where he bought bottles and vials of remedies for all human ailments: Bateman's Drops, British Oil, Seneca Oil, and Godfrey's Cordial. He smiled as the box was being packed; he could not imagine that he should ever need slumber salts. On Wednesday he visited Mr. Sommer and bought two boxes of window glass for twelve dollars and twenty-five cents each. He hoped some of his neighbors craved the sunshine as he did. Most of the week was spent packing, crating, and arranging transportation for the goods he could not carry himself. As he went over the lists for what seemed like the hundredth time, he saw that he had nearly all his requirements and many other things he hoped would please his neighbors. He and

Phill took the wagon from store to store picking up some orders, and finalizing the arrangements for the rest.

On Friday the seventh of June, he prepared to leave Philadelphia. However, there was still a little money burning a hole in his pocket. Several times he had passed the shop of Taylor and Newbold but had not gone in as the goods appeared to be quite expensive. Today he would give in to the temptation. His eyes grew wide at the sight of cloth fit for kings and queens. He bought small amounts of taffetas, velveteens, cassimeres, and other exotic fabrics. For seventeen pounds sterling he bought a chest of Hyson Shin Tea weighing eighty-three pounds. James and Phill had finally completed their tasks and began the long journey home.[18]

～ ～ ～

As the wagon turned onto their land, James could see with new eyes how the two-story addition was beginning to resemble the architecture of Philadelphia. The changes to the log house were well under way. The squarish log portion, which had been slightly elongated so many years before, had now taken on an **L** shape, as if a smaller brother of Mr. Latta's house had been appended to its right shoulder. The oldest part of the building had been divided nearly in half by a new board wall, complete with matching crown molding and chair rails. The larger room had been fitted with shelves and a counter for storekeeping. The door between the two rooms had windowpanes at eye level so that shoppers would never be neglected. The slightly smaller room would be the dining parlor. Here a ceiling had been installed to cover the rafters, and a richly carved mantel had been placed above the old fieldstone fireplace. This building was not as elaborate as Mr. Latta's home but quite satisfactory for a young man.[19]

By August he was ready for business. Over the next weeks and months word spread about the new store. People came from around the countryside to buy, sell, trade, and visit. At the Torrance store one could find wheat and nails, calico and salt pork, hammers and brandy, and all the latest in news and gossip—a veritable treasure trove satisfying everyone's needs and wishes. Some paid with money, some by barter, and some settled their accounts by hauling cotton to market and bringing back goods from Charleston or elsewhere.

Gradually James became the leader in both the family businesses. Hugh was growing old and was pleased to see his son assuming responsibilities. The living quarters attached to the store were quite spacious and served James well after his marriage to Nancy Davidson and the coming of children. Hugh and Isabella were close by in the brick house. By now all of Isabella's children from her marriage to Captain Galbraith Falls were grown.

All had established their own homes, except for one unmarried daughter, also named Isabella.

As the Falls children matured and left his home, Hugh gave each of them approximately one hundred pounds. This was their share of their father's estate which he had held in trust for them, augmented by the natural growth of its value. Isabella Falls had only received twenty-five pounds of her portion; since she was supported by Hugh, she had everything she wanted for a decent and comfortable life. He would have paid the rest to her at any time had she called for it. Hugh assumed since she did not, that she had no need for the money.

Early in 1816, both Hugh and Isabella became ill. Isabella died on the first of February; Hugh followed her two weeks later. She was seventy-six and he, seventy-three. James took some comfort in knowing their lives had been long and productive. He gave nearly all of their household goods to his sisters, keeping for himself only a few chairs and tables, two cupboards, a clock, a secretary, and a bed. By May he had inventoried his father's remaining property and found himself the owner of a fourteen-hundred-acre plantation, a large quantity of livestock, an impressive collection of farming implements, plenty of grain, salted meat, and cotton. He also inherited thirty-eight hundred acres of land in Tennessee that Hugh had bought some years before. He had carefully listed on the inventory the names of the Negroes. There were fourteen males and nineteen females, thirty-three in all. Ned, Phill, and Nell, who had once belonged to Captain Falls were among them.

James, Nancy, and their three children moved into the brick house. They suggested perhaps the time had come for Isabella Falls to seek residence with one of her married sisters. Isabella, at forty-one, was not pleased to leave her home of twenty years. It was not long before the entire Falls clan descended on James like a plague of locusts. They were not satisfied with a few pieces of furniture. They had been cheated! James explained that the hundred pounds they had each received from Hugh was nearly twice as much as the Captain's estate settlement had decreed. That was not the point, protested the Falls, their raucous voices clattering in his ears. They claimed that Hugh would never have become a rich man without the wealth their mother brought into that marriage. They had no use for the land and no desire for livestock, plows, or wagons. James's new wealth had ignited their avarice, and it was directed toward his Negroes.

"Father paid for them," shouted James. "I have the receipt from the Captain's estate sale." He shook the paper before their haughty noses. "Look, see for yourselves; he paid 142 pounds for Binah, 150 for Ned, 136 for Nell, 200 for Phill, and 70 for Phebe. Altogether it totals a great deal more than Ma's widow's share. Pa bought them and they are mine."

"Flora's name is not on that receipt of yours. Therefore she belongs to our portion of father's estate. We only left her on this place to serve our dear mother, may she rest in peace."

"Flora was not yet born when the estate was settled," said James. "She is the increase of Binah and Binah was Pa's. You have no claim!"

They shook their heads and took their pouty faces home, but soon they were back again with another dissonant tune. "You are wrong," they said. "We have studied father's records and found that Flora was born in 1784. Some of us remember her birth in the winter; it must have been February."

"The estate was settled in May of that year," said James. Perhaps she was not born until December. That was thirty years ago, how could you possibly remember the month of her birth? No matter, if she was born she would have been a babe at Binah's breast. No one would sell a nursing infant away from its mother. She came to my father as part of Binah, born or not."

The Falls continued to insist that Flora and her increase were theirs. Flora was the mother of six children. Since the importation of slaves had been prohibited some years ago, increase was a very important factor in plantation economy. Increase came from the female line (paternity was often unsure) and was frequently stipulated by wills and other documents. Captain Falls had no will; his estate had been settled by law, and increase was not mentioned in the receipt James held. And furthermore, they claimed that Hugh had promised them Flora and her children, and they were here to take them. James had never heard of such a promise, and was not letting go of his Flora and her little ones. He was glad that Binah, now dead, could not hear the uproar.

In April of 1817, all eight of the Falls heirs filed a lawsuit against James for the recovery of their alleged property. He fought long and hard to keep his Negroes. Flora was essential to Nancy who had given birth to Frank in 1816 and then Isabella two years later. Sam, John, Mindy, Sollomon, Melisa, and Peggy would be important to his plantation's future. For ten long years the suit dragged from court to court until March of 1827; the supreme court of North Carolina ordered James to pay $1069.13⅓ to the heirs of Galbraith Falls. At least James still had his Negroes. Who knows what abuse they would have suffered from that disagreeable tribe. Dividing seven Negroes among those eight quarrelsome heirs would have required the wisdom of sages. For the rest of his life James would have a strong distaste for the courts.

It was during this protracted struggle that James's Nancy had died (thank goodness Flora's youngest was old enough to leave her breast), his daughter Jane had died, and he had married, then lost, his dear Polly. Of course there had been good times. He had fond memories of his two wives and was surrounded by six strong and healthy children; Polly had given him William and a second little Jane. His plantation continued to grow (he had added nearly a thousand acres over the years) and provide abundantly for his family. A water mill had been constructed for the grinding of grain and the sawing of lumber, beneficial in convenience and income. He regretted having to close the store after Albert's death, but there was no way to justify his time there.[20] Among the last entries in the ledger book was for a tombstone for Polly. On July 7, 1825, it was purchased from John Robertson of Charleston for forty-five dollars.

After taking his daughters to Salem, he began seeking lessons for Hugh and Frank. In 1826, Alexander Gordon was retained as a tutor for the sum of ten dollars. Later James joined with a group of neighbors to form a subscription school. The dozen subscribers paid two dollars per scholar to Robert Sadler to teach orthography, reading, writing, arithmetic, English grammar, geography, and surveying. They agreed to provide Mr. Sadler with boarding, washing, a suitable house to teach in, and firewood when required. At last James felt his life was well ordered.

5 Home Again December 1827

The first week of December unfolded crisp and sunny, shimmering with excitement. Camilla and Isabella had spent weeks in anticipation of their last public examination, anxious to please Papa and their new ma. One of the Sisters fluttered into their room and announced elatedly, "Your parents are here, I have spotted their carriage! Come, come, I know they are eager to see you." Camilla ran ahead with great glee. Isabella followed, but not too closely as she was still unsure of the wisdom of Papa's marriage. From the front door they saw their father helping a woman down from his carriage. That would be Ma, and she did seem to be sturdy. Camilla ran to her father and flung her arms around him. He kissed her fondly, then grabbed Isabella who had caught up to them.

"My dear girls," he said, "I am so pleased to see you and especially glad that we will all be going home together after the exercises. I want you to meet someone very special. Margaret, these are the young ladies you have heard so much about, Camilla and Isabella."

The girls had hardly begun their curtsy when Margaret knelt down to their level and placed an arm on each girl's shoulder—not so tight as to smother, but firm enough to imply genuine affection. "At last I have the pleasure of meeting you both, although I feel as if I have know you for quite some time. I have read all your letters and find you the topic of conversation everywhere I go. Your Aunt Betsy is especially eager to have you visit. I believe she was a bit jealous of me, going to Salem to fetch my girls. Certainly she wrote you that she had her fifth little boy last spring; I think she will welcome the company of girls. Now, let me look at you." She stood up and took a step back, all the while keeping a hand of each girl in one of hers. "You are pretty things, just as your pa said, not that I would have doubted him. I've heard so much about you without an idea of what you looked like."

"We are pleased to meet you," said Camilla, "and thank you for writing to us."

"What are we to call you?" inquired Isabella.

"Why, 'Ma', would be fine; that is, if it suits you. I could never replace your own ma in your hearts, but I hope to raise you as she would have. Your brothers and sister have taken to calling me Ma." It would suit. Isabella could see that this woman was strong and kind. The letters from Grandma Davidson had spoken highly of her. If Grandma Davidson was willing to trust their care to Papa's new wife, then it must be a sound idea.

James and Margaret took lodgings in town and spent the next several days tending to the girls' activities. Many parents had gathered for the public examinations, an opportunity for all to admire the students' accomplishments. They presented dramas, read essays, recited poetry, and performed musical pieces. Camilla played the pianoforte with great pride. After all, her father had paid forty dollars extra for eight quarters of music instruction. Isabella listened politely; she was too young for music.

Mr. and Mrs. Latta had come to witness the achievements of four granddaughters, both the Torrance girls, and Mary and Ann Latta. William Latta sat at the back of the hall, and Isabella stared at him wide-eyed when she realized he was father to her cousins. His clothes were those of a common farmer, stained at the knee and frayed at the wrist. This disheveled costume was complemented by an unsightly stubble across his face and red-tinged eyes. When the ceremonies were over he remained in the background until his daughters had bid their grandparents farewell and apologized for their mother's absence. Their Negroes had been sold to settle debts, and she could hardly leave six children at home unattended. When they were done, William gathered the girls and their few possessions into a barnyard wagon and whisked them quickly away.

At the Inspector's office James made the final payments on the girls' accounts. Altogether he had paid a little over four hundred dollars to educate Camilla. Isabella's fees were seventy dollars less; they did not include music nor ornamental needlework. Margaret helped her new daughters pack their belongings. Several pairs of tattered shoes were to be left behind; not even the Negroes could make use of them. Finally there were hugs and tears exchanged among the students, along with addresses and promises of letters. They had all become writers of letters during the past two years.

~ ~ ~

Back home on the plantation Isabella and Camilla began to adjust to their new routine. To Isabella, now nine years old, the brick house looked both strange and familiar. Gradually the things she remembered and those forgotten began to blend comfortably and become home. The word "Ma" was beginning to slip more easily from her tongue.

Margaret was proving to be well suited to her situation. She was twenty-nine and a spinster when she married James, an age when a lady should begin to worry about being a lifelong burden to her family. It was natural for her to feel gratitude toward James, but she also had a great affection for him. She had been raised to value hard work and to abhor frivolity and self-centeredness. It was her deepest desire to devote herself completely to the care of James's children and the creation of a tranquil and pious home. Their marriage was an ideal union of their needs and abilities.

The strange and familiar of her family members were also blending for

Isabella. Hugh had spent most of the spring and fall at boarding school in Charlotte and now, at seventeen, was beginning to work with their father in the management of the plantation. James had let go the overseer he had hired during those turbulent years when his house was filled with motherless children. Now, Isabella watched her father and brother laughing and talking together almost like equals; Hugh had become more like an uncle than a brother. On the other hand Frank was only eleven, closer to her own age than any of the Torrance children. She and Frank quickly resumed the fond kinship they had shared as youngsters. Now, being two years older, they had more freedom to romp and play. Isabella was not delicate like her sister. She enjoyed the out-of-doors and vigorous activity. Camilla, at thirteen, preferred the world of adults. She kept close to home and helped Ma with the little ones. William was five and Jane, four. They had been babies when she and Isabella had gone to Salem; now they were fine children with personalities all their own.

The holiday season, with land lying fallow, had always been a time for visiting. Margaret seized the opportunity to reacquaint the girls with their relations. The first call was indeed paid to Aunt Betsy, whose plantation was so close to theirs. All of the children except Hugh clambered into the wagon, but only the girls reveled in the novelty; the others were frequent and familiar visitors. Betsy was James Latta's oldest daughter, sister to Mother Polly. She and her husband, Wilson Davidson, lived in a most handsome home called Oaklawn. As the wagon rolled up the long farm road with oak trees flanking both sides, Isabella could see why the name had been chosen.

Inside, the parlor was spacious and boasted fine moldings and wallpaper depicting tropical scenes. Such elegant appointments seemed out of place in a room so populated by boys. Robert, the oldest, was not quite Isabella's age, and Aunt Betsy had a babe in arms. Like clockwork she gave birth to a boy every two years.

"Girls, girls, do come in," Betsy had flung open the door to greet them. "My, how you have grown! You are even prettier than I remembered. I've had some tea and cakes prepared, but I know they will not be as tasty as those from Brother Winkler's bakery. Did you enjoy your schooling? I certainly did when I went to Salem."

"Yes ma'am," said Camilla. "We were very well treated. I especially enjoyed the music instruction. I have learned to play the pianoforte and hope to be able to continue my lessons somewhere in the neighborhood. I understand that you play quite well."

"I'm afraid I am out of practice; as you can see I have my hands full with all the little ones."

"I was not old enough for music," said Isabella, "but I have made Papa a pocketbook for Christmas."

"James and I are always looking for tutors," Margaret chimed in. "We were quite pleased with the school that he and Wilson helped to organize last winter."

"As were we," said Betsy. "I was so disappointed that Mr. Sadler would only remain with us for three months. Perhaps he was afraid that his scholars would disappear once the spring farm work began."

"Keep us informed if you hear of another situation."

After their refreshments Camilla stayed at the tea table with the women, while Isabella joined Jane and the boys in play. She had forgotten that she had so many relations and enjoyed getting to know them again.

Another day they visited their Latta grandparents. The hectic pace at Salem a few weeks before hardly allowed for a proper visit which Isabella was eager to have. If there was any advantage to having three mothers, it was the extra grandparents. James Latta had reached his seventy-third year and had eased away from commerce into cotton but was still an active man. His only concession to his age had been the hiring of an overseer two years before. Perhaps it was his wife, twenty years his junior, who kept him young. Jane Latta had set a lovely tea table in the parlor. Her cook had prepared a lavish assortment of tarts which Jane had artistically arranged on tiered sweetmeat dishes. Isabella marveled at the array of colorful fruits and jellies glistening in little pastry nests. Sprigs of boxwood and tiny lemons were set between the tarts for decoration, and mounds of sugared almonds filled the cups at the top of each dish. At the center of the table was a fat plum pudding speckled with currants and nuts. Dainty cups of tea and delicate stemmed glasses of syllabub completed the spread. It was obvious that this household was not as blustery as Aunt Betsy's nor as devoted to simplicity as those in Salem.

"Oh, my!" exclaimed Isabella. "I've never seen such as this. Is it real? I mean, can it be eaten?"

"Oh, yes," replied her Grandma Latta, "every bit of it. We wanted to have an extra special treat for your homecoming and in gratitude to you, Margaret, for taking on my grandchildren. My heart is relieved to have them in your care. I consider all of James's children as my own grandchildren; I know Polly loved them all."

"Why thank you, Mrs. Latta," replied Margaret, "I aim to raise them as well as I can. Your table is lovely; the tarts look almost too festive to eat!"

"But eaten they will be," replied the older lady. "I trust the rest of my family will be joining us soon. Here, let me pour you some tea."

There was a rustling of crisp silk in the doorway. "Nancy, there you are; come and join us." Jane Latta motioned to her youngest daughter who had just entered the room. Though Nancy was twenty-three, she was still unmarried and lived with her parents. "I see you are wearing your prettiest gown, my dear," continued Jane. "You have made quite an effort for a tea party."

"Mother," Nancy blushed, "I told you I was expecting a visitor later in the day."

"But of course—Mr. Reid again if I remember correctly. We've seen quite a bit of Mr. Reid lately."

The children and ladies chatted as they enjoyed the refreshments which were nearly as tasty as they were beautiful. Presently Mr. Latta poked his head into the room. "Can an old gentleman join in the festivities?"

"Mr. Latta," replied his wife, "do come in. I believe there is plenty here for you." He shook hands all around and pulled up a chair.

"My dear, this is delightful." He cradled a teacup in his hands, absorbing its warmth. "What a reward at the year's end, to be surrounded by a capable wife, children and grandchildren, and tasty morsels fit for the gods. Mrs. Torrance, please tell your husband that I made an excellent crop this season. The cotton has been sold, baled, and sent to Charleston. Yet I have never before seen such a pathetic price; I only received nine cents per pound. At least the volume of my harvest was sufficient to keep the wolf from the door."

"I will pass along the news," answered Margaret. "Our experience was the same. Mr. Torrance says too many farmers are vying for the same market. He is already clearing more land to put under the plow."

"Ah, yes," said Mr. Latta, "my plans are less grand. I shall probably plant about the same acreage as I did last year. We have all that we need for a comfortable life. As you can see, I have only one more daughter to marry, then I can truly be a gentleman of leisure."

"Father!"

"All in jest, my dear," chuckled the old man. "I will gladly support you for as long as you desire. But I have noticed that young Mr. Reid has become a fixture around here of late. I understand that he is quite enterprising in business, a desirable trait in a suitor." Nancy seemed to have been stricken with blushing all afternoon.

Presently there was a knock at the door, and one of the Negroes ushered a gentleman into the room. Mr. Latta rose, "Mr. Reid, do come in. You know Mrs. Torrance and some of her children, of course, but do you remember her young daughters, Camilla and Isabella? They've just returned from school."

After shaking hands with the boys, one by one Mr. Reid greeted the ladies by taking a hand in his and bringing it nearly to his lips in a sweeping bow: first the little girls, then Mrs. Latta, Margaret, and finally Nancy, only this time the hand and the lips touched. Isabella had never seen such elegant behavior; Nancy was not the only one who blushed. As they rode home Isabella reflected on the afternoon: sweet tarts of cherries and figs, candied almonds, creamy syllabub, kind and dear grandparents, and Mr. Reid. He was the most handsome and dashing gentleman she had ever seen. Aunt Nancy was the most fortunate girl in the world to have him for a beau.

The journey to the Davidson grandparents was more arduous. It was half again as far as the Latta plantation, but the visit could be completed in a day if one started early. This time the whole family was loaded into the wagon, and several of the Negroes went along to do the driving. James had selected the Negroes for their musical ability; he knew that General Davidson would have planned an entertainment. It would be a Christmas treat for his Negroes to visit those of another plantation and join in the musicale. Visiting among Negroes on different plantations was normally prohibited; Sundays and the Christmas season were exceptions.

General Ephraim and Jane Davidson were both in their sixties and were also leading more leisurely lives. Their son, Frank, lived with them and was beginning to share in his father's business. It had always been important to James that Nancy's children remained close to her parents. He arranged visits with them as often as the distance would permit. Isabella cherished these visits. She would look into her grandparents' faces and imagine what her own mother had looked like. She liked to hear her grandpa tell war stories. He had fought in the Revolutionary War and shared his tales with his grandchildren, just as James's father had done a generation before.

Mrs. Davidson had overseen the preparation of the midday dinner, and the whole family feasted on pork, goose, cabbage, potatoes, onions, and beets, followed by an assortment of cakes. Afterwards Uncle Frank and Hugh supervised the children's games, while the others visited. Uncle Frank had been a child when James and Nancy married and was only five years older than Hugh. He had grown up in the company of the Torrance family; since he reached adulthood James had begun to confer with him on business matters, almost as if he were a son.

In the twilight of the afternoon came the entertainment. Half a dozen Negro men with fiddles and tambourines gathered in front of the house to sing and dance. The rest of the Negroes swayed and clapped along with the rhythm and joined in the songs. Most were spiritual in nature; some seemed to be poems of nonsense. The leader would sing out the first line, and the others would respond in tropical harmonies which twined like vines, their passionate voices rhythmed by flailing arms and tapping feet. Many years later Isabella was to learn that these plaintive chants were often a code known only to the Negroes in which they sang about freedom or made mockery of the white people. "Steal Away, Steal Away to Jesus," and "If I Get to Jordan Before You Do" were partly about salvation and partly about escaping to the mysterious lands of the north where black men were free. Oh yes, oh yes!

It was dark when they began the long journey home. Isabella fell asleep in the wagon musing over the day spent with her relations. She had a large and loving family; becoming reacquainted was the best Christmas gift of all. There was no call on the Allison grandparents; they had died several years before. Margaret had brothers and sisters in the Statesville area who were frequent visitors at the Torrance plantation.

～　　　～　　　～

The observance of Christmas was accomplished with very little ceremony; the day itself was regarded as an extra Sunday popped into the middle of the week. The Negroes were allowed a holiday, and on Christmas morning James made the rounds of their cabins with small gifts of clothing, or whiskey, or coins. Afterwards he read to the family from the Bible, and holiday treats were given to the children: oranges, or sweets, or something Margaret had been secretly sewing during the previous weeks. The oranges, so sweet and juicy, had come all the way from the islands.

Isabella presented the pocketbook she had made at school to her father. It folded in thirds to keep his money safe, and the outside was wrought in Irish stitch with brightly colored silk thread. The Sisters had helped her until every stitch was perfect; blue, yellow, and brown threads all marched together uphill and down to form the flame-like design. She was proud of her handiwork; she hoped Papa was pleased.

Then Camilla handed her gift to her father. He unrolled the scrap of cloth and saw that her lessons had not been wasted. It was a sampler, and a very fine one. She had used blues and greens, browns and gold to stitch all the letters of the alphabet, both large and small, and all of the numbers to twenty. Below that was a pleasant grouping of motifs: flowers, birds, baskets, and trees. The whole was surrounded by a square garland which met perfectly in the corners. A smaller garland, surrounding some of the motifs, also had perfect corners. Her name and the date had been stitched between the two alphabets. The silk threads shimmered on the creamy linen.[21]

"Camilla, this is beautiful," said Margaret. "I remember my school sampler. I thought my fingers would be worn away before my teacher was pleased. It was well worth the effort; my father hung it in the parlor insisting that it would attract a suitable husband."

"We were told the same thing. I had hoped you would want to display it in order not to have an old maid on your hands."

"We'll not have to worry about that for a few years yet; however, it took long enough for my sampler to appeal to the right man! I've kept it all these years; I must show it to you later." Margaret noticed that all of this sampler talk was bringing a pout to Isabella's face. "And the pocketbook is simply lovely, Isabella; that is quite an accomplishment for someone with no classes in ornamental work. As soon as I hear of a school for needlework nearby, I will see that you are enrolled." Camilla had also made a gentleman's pocketbook. She would give it to Hugh, privately.

James hugged his daughters to him. "One needlework to snag a son-in-law, and another to keep my money close to afford a dowry; I am indeed blessed to have such affectionate daughters."

6 Changes 1828~1833

For Isabella the new year began routinely enough with chores, tutors, lessons, Sunday sermons, and family visits. But that routine was to be swept away by the capricious wind of change. Once again their family was growing; Ma gave birth to her first child, a girl named Lettitia.

In December, Aunt Nancy married her handsome Rufus Reid. It was a small wedding and served perfectly as a family holiday celebration. For some reason Uncle Wilson did not approve of the match. He attended the ceremony but left immediately afterwards declining to partake of the festivities. It was rumored that Reid's faith was in question.

Mr. Latta's younger son, Robert, and his family had come all the way from Yorkville, South Carolina, for the occasion. Robert was a tall and wiry man who never displayed a sense of humor. It was unclear if he disapproved of frivolity or simply had no use for it. His reputation as a miserly, close-fisted curmudgeon was undeserved. It was true that he took business seriously and saw debt as something to be collected posthaste. But anyone in genuine need was treated with a quiet and ample generosity that he preferred not to display. James and his old boyhood friend had much to talk about. Robert had also prospered as a merchant-planter and had built an impressive three-story mansion in the middle of town. Both men, now in the prime of their lives, had far exceeded their fathers in wealth.

Death had been no more a stranger to Robert than it had to James. Robert's first wife, Jane Allison Latta, had borne four children; she and three of them were now gone. The last born had died in infancy, followed several years later by Jane. In 1824 his eleven-year-old daughter (also Jane) had died at boarding school in Philadelphia; then several years ago his older son had died at eighteen. Only William remained. Robert was now married to Eliza Dilworth Latta, and they had two small children. They had been joined in a Quaker ceremony in her native city of Philadelphia. Although his parents adored Eliza, they prayed that such a union was valid in God's eyes.

William had just turned twenty and was the object of admiration from the young ladies in attendance. Two years before, he had gone with his family to Paris to buy furnishings for their elegant new home. William was entertaining them with fantastic tales of the ocean voyage and life in a luxurious French hotel. Camilla at fifteen seemed especially smitten by him. She had never before heard of someone so near her own age crossing the Atlantic and dining on Parisian delicacies. Isabella watched them in the corner of the room whispering and giggling while nibbling at cake. She wondered if this behavior was inappropriate and should be reported to Ma. However, thought

Isabella, Camilla was nearly a grown lady, and perhaps it was best to keep quiet. Isabella was growing jealous of her sister's blossoming figure and the effortless way she mingled in the company of adults. Later, as they were leaving, she was sure she saw William squeeze Camilla's fingers tightly in his own. William was nice looking enough, but the fairest gentleman in the room was Aunt Nancy's new husband, Mr. Rufus Reid.

～　　　～　　　～

The Latta family saw even more changes in 1829. In February, as surely as clockwork, Aunt Betsy produced another baby boy; but before the year was out, Uncle Wilson became ill and died leaving poor Betsy with six sons to raise. Fortunately, Grandma Latta was still young enough to be of help to her. In August, William Latta, James Latta's older son, passed away. Mr. Latta had had little contact with that errant child for many years. After his death it was revealed that William's widow and brood of nine (the youngest an infant) were living in South Carolina in dire poverty. Camilla worried about Mary and Ann and how they would fare. She had heard little of them after leaving Salem. Grandma Latta spoke of them occasionally but never in the presence of her husband. Rumors were bandied about that William had been a wanderer and a drinker and made little effort to provide for his family. He was obviously at home often enough to give his wife a new baby every year or two; beyond that his pathetic life was a mystery. Mr. Latta's anger toward this wayward child did not extend to his daughter-in-law and grandchildren. With William gone, he continued to see that his grandchildren were educated.

The Torrance household was much more placid that year. Another baby, Mary, was born, and James took pride in nurturing his land and the community of families that was growing around them. He followed his father's very active role in the Hopewell Church. Every Sunday, unless the roads were impassable, the entire family was loaded into the wagon for the three-and-a-half mile journey. The outspoken and flamboyant Reverend Caldwell of James's youth had been long gone, much to the relief of the more somber parishioners. Reverend Williamson had been the minister since the year of Isabella's birth. The congregation seemed content both with his personality and his solemn manner during services. His wife taught school at the church. The Moravian education of James's daughters was supplemented by Mrs. Williamson's Presbyterian touch. James served on a number of church committees and was treasurer for nearly thirty years.

In 1830, Camilla turned sixteen and plans were made to further her education. All spring and summer there was a flurry of activity: letters written, stagecoach and steamboat schedules consulted, lodgings secured, and clothes made. Camilla was going to Philadelphia to attend Mrs. Sarazin's school for young ladies. Two of her acquaintances, Mary Laura Springs and Mary Ann Irwin, were also going to Mrs. Sarazin's. Whenever possible the girls got together to talk over their plans.

An indignant Isabella felt left out of this activity. "What do you mean, I am not old enough?" she asked her father.

"Just as I said," he replied; "Isabella, you are twelve years old and much too young to be so far from home."

"But Papa, I went to Salem when I was seven!"

"And you were too young for that as well. If you had had a mother I never would have let you go at such an age. Jane is seven now; you do not see me getting her ready for Salem."

"So you would rather keep me with Jane who is just a baby than let me go with my only true sister."

"Isabella! I'll have none of that talk. All of my children are your brothers and sisters, and you are never to forget that."

"Yes, sir." She left the room with tears in her eyes and feeling very much alone. Frank was spending most of his time at the Hopewell school or working with their father. The childhood romp and tumble with Frank was a thing of the past, yet she was not old enough for Camilla's circle of young ladies. Isabella supposed she would remain at home for the rest of her life taking care of the babies that Ma was popping out every year. She overheard Camilla talking to Ma, telling her "Mary Ann said this," or "Mary Laura said that." Mary Laura was from the Yorkville district. She probably knew that haughty William Latta that Camilla was so silly over. Isabella could imagine them spending the whole year at Mrs. Sarazin's tittering about sweet William.

Camilla was not blind to the plight of her younger sister. Isabella was the headstrong child, quick to stamp her foot or thrust out her lower lip. It was that same jaunty temperament that whetted her hunger for adventure. Camilla, on the other hand, was the dutiful child. She fitted perfectly into the current trend of girl-rearing. They were being raised to become subservient, but civilizing, helpmates to their husbands and to create homes of domestic tranquillity. Her frequent bouts of illness intensified her desire to be cautious and obedient. Camilla would never feel entirely free of her girlhood responsibility, taking care of the little child.

"Isabella," she had said, "I'll only be gone for a year. I will write to you often and be home before you know it."

"If you go without me, I shall be all alone."

"Alone, in this house full of people?! Now don't be silly. You know perfectly well that you will need several more sessions with Mrs. Williamson before you will be ready for Philadelphia. I was three books ahead of you last session, and I am just barely prepared. Hugh has been teasing me that the only purpose of Mrs. Sarazin's school is to learn to catch a husband; surely you are not interested in catching one at your age, are you?"

"Is that what you'll be doing?" Isabella could not imagine how this school would be organized; it sounded like a game of tag, not at all like Salem.

"Of course not. I will study French, English, music, and drawing. They say that men are attracted to ladies who know those things; it is probably an excuse to make us want to improve. Isabella, can I tell you a secret? In some ways I am very frightened about going away so far from home."

"Frightened? Camilla how could you be frightened? You're going to have an adventure."

"I do want to go. I know father expects it of me. He has given us so much, and it would crush me to disappoint him. I am looking forward to the company of the other girls and being treated like a lady. But I have never been so far on a stagecoach nor even seen a steamboat. Papa says Philadelphia is an enormous city. What if I should become lost or ill?"

Isabella hugged her sister. "Camilla, I've never known you to be scared. You always appear so calm and at ease. You will be well chaperoned on the journey; you need not worry."

"I know you are right, but the mere thought of a steamboat sends my heart leaping to my throat. Remember, this is our secret. I will be calm for Papa, for that is what will please him. Now, I do not want to hear another thing about your being alone. You are needed here to help with the children. I do not know this for sure, but I suspect Ma will have another mouth to feed before I get home."

Of course Isabella would not be alone, but she would be lonely. She had not been separated from Camilla since the day she was born; she could not say that about any of the others.

In September, Camilla was dispatched on her way. Her father had sensed her trepidation and had made every arrangement possible to ease her journey. Instructions and money were sent to Mr. Reeves Buck, his agent in Philadelphia, who promised to see to everything. James was confident that she could travel safely with the Irwin family. They planned to arrive in Philadelphia about a week before school commenced (one always allowed extra time for the vagaries of transportation) and to board with Miss Abalone during the interim.

"When you have settled in with Miss Abalone," James had told her, "I want you to buy what you need for that place. Mrs. Irwin will stay a few days; she and Miss Abalone can give you good advice. I remember my first time in that city. I arrived feeling tongue-tied and awkward; it was the purchase of a two-dollar cane that gave me the confidence of a man. I want you to be as well outfitted as the other young ladies, so do not hesitate to pay for dressmaking or whatever is needed." He knew he would not have to warn Camilla about extravagance.

It was not long before her letters began to arrive. Camilla wrote that the journey was indeed an adventure; the stage route took them through numerous cities and towns. She had not imagined that the country was so huge and so filled with people. The night spent on a steamboat, tossing and rolling across the Chesapeake Bay, would never be forgotten. The day after their arrival at school they were joined by Mary Laura Springs who had made a similar journey; Mary Laura's party had done some sightseeing along the way. She said, according to Camilla, that in the city of Washington "we spent half of the day in viewing the market and other public buildings. The first was the President's residence, but we had not the pleasure of seeing the interior or the President himself. The other most important place was the capitol, which is situated on quite an elevation, indeed, I think it the most magnificent edifice I ever saw. A gentleman conducted us all through the building." Mary Laura had also spent a night in Salem and had a brief reunion with some of the Sisters who "when they recalled me they seemed delighted and pleased with the idea of my coming to school again. When they found I was for Philadelphia, they laughed, saying they supposed I was going to get the polish." [22]

Isabella smiled; the Sisters were correct. They had provided academics; Mrs. Sarazin's school was merely polish. Camilla seemed to be satisfied in her new situation, and secretly Isabella was glad to have remained at home. She would have relished the steamboat, but all of the attention to dressmakers seemed tedious.

~   ~   ~

After the busy scramble surrounding Camilla's departure, James began to take inventory of his life. Cotton had been good to him, as had his livestock and crops of wheat and corn. It had been wise to diversify his agriculture; the price of cotton and the cost of getting it to market varied greatly from year to year. In 1816, when cotton was still new to the area, he got as much as 30¢ per pound for his crop. That year the crop was small; he sold only three bales whose weight totaled less than 900 pounds. Since then, as more and more farmers devoted more land to cotton, the price had fallen dramatically. James kept pace by increasing his planting. This year he had sold nearly 20,000 pounds. Prices were beginning to rise again; each pound had brought 10⅜¢ last May. The future looked fair indeed. He had provided well for his family; very little was out of their reach. Margaret persisted in raising the vegetables herself and selling the butter she made; this was done of her need for industry, not money.

Hugh was nearly a man and Frank was fourteen. They were being groomed to join their father in operating one of the largest plantations in all of Mecklenburg. James stood in front of his house and surveyed his land. He owned well over two thousand acres, and ninety-two Negroes. Hardly any planter of his acquaintance owned more hands. In front of him for nearly as far as the eye could see were tidy fields burgeoning with cotton ripe for harvest and the stubble of gathered corn. The cotton was especially pleasing. The bolls had been heavy with their fruit, and upon bursting, the creamy contents had spilled over their shoulders. Acre upon acre of billowy clouds of cotton lightly speckled with brown seeds and bracts lay before him as if the sky had gone down for a nap. Off to the southwest there was still forest. Under its canopy the water wheel turned in the creek-fed mill pond, providing the milling of lumber and flour to farms for miles around and a bounty of fish for his black and white families. Between the forest and the house lay pasture for the beasts. Several dozen plump hogs nuzzled one another for a space at the trough; cows grazed, their fat udders full of promise; sheep filled their bellies, innocent of their only requirement: to replenish their coats.

James called the family together to tell them of his plan. "I think the time has come to build us a new house."

"A new house?" asked Margaret. "Whatever is the matter with this one?"

"Not much. But we are getting a bit crowded the way our family keeps increasing," he smiled at his wife who was indeed expecting another child. "Margaret, dear, I want to do this for you. I have given the children the best schooling I could find. And I have bought land to increase my own wealth. Now I want to build you the finest home in the countryside. I want everyone to see you for the gentle and privileged lady that you are."

"Where are you planning to put this new house?" asked Hugh.

"Right here on this very spot. My father was quite confident that this rise in the land was the perfect place to oversee his holdings. I've thought about it and determined he was right. I want to build a house with one porch facing south and another north, so that I can have an eye on all of my property."

"Are you thinking to tear this house down?" asked Isabella.

"That I am. It is the only way to have a new home with a view from this hill. This house is not so fine that it would be worth much if left standing."

"But where are we to live?" asked Frank.

"I believe we can make do with the log house for a while; it suited me once before. Hugh, you've lived in that place; do you remember it?"

"Not very well, I was barely six years old when we moved into this house. I well remember the store there. You pressed me into service on many occasions during the last several years of it."

"But Papa," said Jane, "how can we live there? It's filled with dusty old things, and I know I heard a rat scrambling around not so long ago."

"Jane!" gasped Margaret. "You know you're not to play over there; one of those 'dusty old things' could fall on your head and give you quite a whack."

"I'm sorry Ma, I went exploring with William." William gave a sharp tug to her hair.

"She has a point, James," continued his wife. "The log house has become a refuge for every worn-out implement on the place, as well as necessary storage for wool and cotton."

"Now listen to my plan," he replied. "We need not move from this house for some time yet. I've spoken to a master mason who comes most highly recommended. With the hands that I can spare, it will take nearly a year to make the bricks needed for the house I have in mind. I would like to start right away. Next I will make inquiries about master builders, carpenters, and joiners, and have the lumber prepared. Then craftsmen need to be found for the interior. There is no need to tumble this house down until all of that is well under way. This will provide us with ample time to clean the log house, perhaps even give it a fresh coat of paint. No doubt we shall be cozy there, but it will only be for a short while."

The plantation became a beehive of activity; further schooling for Isabella was postponed for a time. She cared for the babies and did what chores she was assigned, while her mother supervised work at the log house. Smoke from the brick kiln hung heavy in the air and mingled with the tang of freshly cut lumber. James became occupied with builders and craftsmen and obtaining supplies. Hugh oversaw the more ordinary autumn chores: gathering and baling cotton and getting it to market, drying the corn, and slaughtering and curing the meat. The making of sausage, work in the log house, and the tending of children exhausted Margaret by the end of each day. She was pleased to see that Isabella was teaching William and Jane their lessons.

Preparations for building continued at a feverish pace over the winter, and by May over twelve thousand bricks had been made, enough to begin. At last the family moved into their snug quarters, and construction commenced in earnest. James, Margaret, and the babies established themselves in the same upstairs room he had shared so many years before with Nancy and his older children. Isabella and Jane took the small room adjoining that of their parents. Hugh, Frank, and William had the run of the loft, formerly the lair of the infamous Falls daughters. Isabella and Jane made it abundantly clear that their brothers should make use of the trap door and ladder installed by their grandfather more than fifty years before. There were to be no boys galloping through their room and that of their parents to reach the staircase of James's handsome addition.

In the room below the loft, where James had once kept store, the business of building was being conducted. It was a large room that could be entered from the outside and shut off from the living quarters, an ideal place for the meeting of carpenters, joiners, and masons. On long tables were spread drawings and plans and the latest books on architecture. The only drawback to this arrangement was the room's lack of light; two small windows and one door were often insufficient. James and his band of builders frequently gathered their papers and drawing tools and set up shop outside; or in bad weather, they took over Margaret's well-lit parlor.

James had not lost his eye for architecture, nor his love of tall buildings and sunlight. Enthusiasm leapt from his face as he shared the evolving plans with the family. "The cellar will be half underground and half above, with windows all around. In that way it can be put to good use as a work place for you, Margaret, and your Negroes; you may even use it as a winter kitchen if you wish. Above that will be two floors of living space, each more than twice as tall as a man. We shall have plenty of windows; each will begin about thirty inches above the floor and extend nearly to the ceiling. There will be four large rooms on each level. The rooms above will be our bedchambers; downstairs will be four parlors."

"Four parlors!" exclaimed Margaret. "My goodness, James, whatever for?"

"For whatever you wish." He carefully unrolled the sheets of paper so that all could see. "Look, it's all here on these drawings. Here is a central hallway running north and south through the house with a door to the outside at either end. On each side of the hallway are two good-sized rooms. Both the east parlors and the west parlors are separated by sets of folding doors that can be thrown open so that on either side of the hallway you may have one very large room or two merely generous ones."

"What is this to be?" She pointed to a boxed-in area in the northeast corner of the hallway half surrounded by radiating lines.

"That, my dear, is a spiral staircase. I've found a plan for it in one of my architecture books. It shows how it can be cantilevered to be well supported, yet appear to be gracefully floating in air. It will be one of the many elegant features of your fine new home."

Margaret continued to study the diagram to get a sense of its proportion. "If that represents the staircase and these are the doors, then how wide is this hallway? It looks quite generous."

"And it is. I expect the hallway is a bit wider than the parlor in this house."

Margaret saw the size of the rooms emanating from the hallway and began to grasp an idea of the grand scale of it. "Oh my," she said, "the new house may be the rival of Major Davidson's Rural Hill."

"Yes, my dear, it might be at that."

Hugh and Frank did not know what to make of the growing opulence. They were accustomed to hard work and more comfortable in the fields than in fancy parlors. Tea cups and finery only brought out their awkwardness. Isabella stared at the drawings and tried to reconcile them with the huge hole that had been dug on the hill and the neat courses of brick that were rising from it. She imagined a *polished* Camilla squeezing fingers with sweet William before an elaborately carved mantelpiece. Where will I fit in? she wondered.

"Will I still share a room with Camilla when she comes home?" she asked.

"Of course you shall," replied her father. "The house may be large, but our family is larger. We'll all be sharing rooms." He smiled at his wife who was nursing their new daughter; Delia had joined their family that spring.

James rolled up the papers and carefully returned them to their case. He had forgotten to mention the garret, nearly as tall as the other floors, and the stepped chimneys that would rise grandly on each end of the building. He remembered the conversation with his father all those years ago when they had planned the improvements to the log house. Imposing and inviting at the same time—it was quite a trick and he believed he had mastered it.

By the end of the summer of 1831, much progress had been made. Until now James's expenses had been minor. The clay and the lumber had come from his land, the labor performed by his Negroes, and the sawing done at his mill. The time had come to pay the professionals who directed the work and buy materials he could not produce, such as the walnut for the spiral staircase. He inquired of the Salisbury Branch Bank about the requirements for a loan. Farmers were accustomed to buying on credit since harvest income was received only once or twice a year, but this building project threatened to demand more than his creditors might be willing to bear. The bank replied with terms that were agreeable. The first of three equal payments would be due in ninety days; by then a good portion of his cotton would be sold. In spite of his confidence in his ability to repay, James decided to pursue the loan only as a last resort. He still had some unsold cotton from last year, and the new crop looked promising. He arranged for six wagons to take his old cotton to Camden, South Carolina, and hired drivers to haul it. He guessed its weight to be about thirteen thousand pounds; surely the price would be fair and he could avoid the bank. Very little was as dreadful to him as the prospect of debt.

Late in September, he went to New York and bought twenty-eight boxes of tin, thirty-eight sheets of copper and ten of zinc, pound upon pound of fine nails and cut nails, brads and screws, and sundry building tools. He also bought blankets and linens requested by Margaret. On the first of October he arrived in Philadelphia to bring Camilla home from school. First he settled her bill with Mrs. Sarazin; he had paid a little over five hundred dollars for her year in Philadelphia.

"My, you are a pretty picture," he said as he greeted her. She did look quite grown up dressed in a gown that was fashionable, yet demure. "I'm pleased to see that you have not adopted the fashion I saw on some ladies in New York. The poufs of their sleeves were large enough to hold bird cages, but the birds looked to be nesting in their hair!"

"Papa, I can hardly believe that you are really here!" She kissed his cheek, then stepped back and twirled on her toes. "I wore this gown especially for you; I'm glad you approve. Those ladies were wearing leg-o-mutton sleeves; I'm afraid its a style I don't fancy."

"No sheep on my farm has so fat a leg. The inventor of it must have had a brain-o-mutton is what I think."

Camilla laughed and glowed with happiness at pleasing her father.

"Now let me see you smile," he said. "I paid Dr. Gardette a fine sum to fix those teeth of yours." She opened her mouth revealing a space where the offending tooth had been extracted and three spots of gold where others had been repaired.

"Dr. Gardette instructed me on how to take better care of my teeth and supplied me with a box of dentifrice. I suppose I had been negligent. I am thankful that a bad toothache was the only illness I suffered this year. Philadelphia must be a healthy place."

"Indeed it is. There are still a number of things I need to buy for our new home; I hope it will suit you to remain here a few more days. I would like to surprise your Ma with the proper tableware to use for entertaining," he said. "And I need the help of a lady, preferably a lady with a sophisticated education, such as you, Camilla."

"I would be delighted to help." She blushed at hearing her father call her a lady.

"Now let me tell you what I have in mind. The china pattern must be fitting for our new home, and there must be enough dishes to serve some number of people. The families of our neighborhood are growing almost as rapidly as our own. Had you heard that your Aunt Nancy is expecting her second child soon? Now you know how your Ma dislikes gaudy extravagance. Can you help me select something stylish, yet simple, that will suit her fancy?"

"I think it can be done. Tomorrow we can visit Mr. Cauffman's shop. I hear Philadelphia's most prominent families are his customers. He will know the fashion, and you and I know what will please Ma."

"With that settled, do you suppose your landlady would object if a gentleman were to take his fashionable daughter out for a bite of supper?"

"I imagine she expects as much." Camilla drew a soft French merino cloak about her shoulders. She was as well dressed as any of Mr. Cauffman's clientele.

The next day they chose a set of brown-trimmed dishes consisting of one hundred and thirty-two pieces. There were three dozen dinner plates, two dozen smaller ones, and two dozen six-inch plates, numerous serving dishes of various sizes, and an assortment of soup and sauce tureens, custard cups, soup bowls, pickle dishes, and so forth. They also bought a tea set, pitchers, tumblers, wine glasses, and chamber pots. Entertaining would not be the only function of the new house.

They visited other shops for hats, books, and more hardware, then dropped in on Reeves Buck to collect the items James had ordered through him. Among them were 5⅓ dozen shutter bolts. James had never lost his love of windows.

They made one last stop before leaving for home; he bought a nine-inch front door lock for nine dollars.

~　　~　　~

Back at home Camilla squeezed herself and many of her belongings into the tiny room Isabella shared with Jane. Their father had insisted that the boys reserve a portion of the loft for the girls' trunks. Removal of the younger girls' summer frocks and the gowns Camilla had acquired at school would provide them with a bit more space.

"You expect them to keep their clothes in our room, while we are forbidden to pass through theirs?" asked Frank. "That hardly seems fair."

"Your loft is three times the size of their room; I imagine the girls don't find that very fair to them. It won't hurt you to give up a bit of space, and I doubt the girls will come rummaging through their trunks until spring. But more to the point, young man, it will profit you nothing to expect fairness in this life. To do so is to beg for disappointment." Frank at fifteen had grown to be a diligent, though sometimes reluctant, worker. His health was often frail, and he was quick to worry about that and all other difficulties he encountered. The unfairness of life would plague him all of his days.

Late in 1831, James received a letter from his cotton factor in Camden:

Camden   19 Oct.   1831
Mr. J G Torrance
D Sir
We have recd by the six wagons forty-nine square bales cotton which we think it would not be advisable to sell in this place as old cotton of that quality would not bring over 5 or 5 1/2 cents. And therefore will ship it to Henry D. Conner & Co. by the first opportunity as directed by you. Above you have bill of salt which we hope will please and the amounts paid each wagoner at 75 cents per

100 lb. New cotton ranges from 6 to 8 1/2 as in quality and but very little coming into market.

Very Resp^t Yours

Shuman McDowall

This was very bad news. McDowall could only promise about half as much as last year's crop had earned. James had held on to those forty-nine bales hoping for a price increase. It had been a gamble and now a loss. In addition he owed the man nearly one hundred dollars that had been paid to the wagoners, and eleven dollars for salt. He wrote McDowall and agreed to have the cotton sent on to Mr. Conner in Charleston. He would have to husband his resources and find ways to sacrifice in order to complete his home.

He directed his hands to harvest and bale his new crop as quickly as possible. But labor devoted to the land was labor lost to his home. Everyone was complaining of the cramped quarters and eager to become situated in the beautiful brick building. Even his own bedchamber, which had seemed ample last spring, had become a maze of trundles and cribs, impossible to navigate after nightfall. He sat his family down for a harsh lecture:

"I have become more than weary of the carping and angry voices that have become commonplace around here of late. No one is comfortable in this place, and the harder we work, the sooner we will be out of it. I intend to avoid taking a bank loan if at all possible, and I expect it will take the income from the current crop as well as next year's to complete our home. Now, if all of you will work as hard as you are able, more of the Negroes can be freed up to harvest and build. Hugh and Frank, I want you to continue to oversee the farming, and put your own shoulders to the plow whenever possible. I am not calling for cruelty, but I want you to tolerate no idleness. Surely the black people want this behind us as much as we do. Camilla and Isabella, you are to take instructions from your mother to be charged with cooking, sewing, and child care. There is no need for black women inside this house when I have strong daughters who can do that work. William and Jane, you are to perform tasks assigned to you by your mother and sisters; you are old enough to contribute to this family, and I expect you to do your share. Also I think we can refrain from lessons this winter. I want each of you to be so spent at the end of the day that you will not notice how crowded we are. Am I understood?"

There was a subdued chorus of "Yes sir."

James continued, "So far, I have been blessed with ten children, and the Lord has seen fit to take only one of them from me. I can think of no other family of our acquaintance that has been given such good fortune. When you next feel inclined to complain of crowding, you should instead thank the Lord for the good health of our family.

"I'm sorry to be so firm with you, but I must complete this project, and I do not intend to go into debt. Nothing that I could imagine, other than the lawsuit, could make me feel so wretched."

The demeanor of the Torrance family changed that winter: "industry is virtue" and they became a most virtuous clan. The lawsuit, brought before most of them were born and only settled in recent years, had been the nadir of James's existence. When a letter or document concerning the lawsuit had been delivered to his hands, he retreated to the gloomiest recesses of his soul. All but the youngest children had witnessed these dreadful bouts of despair and had no interest in seeing them return. Debt was to be avoided; that was their common goal.

Early in January, James received a check for $573.90. On December 26, Mr. Conner had sold his cotton in Charleston for 4½¢ per pound.

The work proceeded through the winter and into the spring. Frugal living was rewarded, and the crisis passed. He took his carriage to Charlotte to be fitted with new curtains, wheels, and a harness. Cushions were mended and brass polished. He left for Charleston late in March; once again he looked like a gentleman planter as his carriage disappeared down the road, its brass fittings glimmering in the sunlight. Tools and hardware were still needed for building; and he brought home other necessities and treats for the family: yards of fine fabrics, coffee and spices, dyestuffs and medicines, ten gallons each of rum and brandy, Mexican sugar and ginger, and boxes of raisins and almonds. Not a word was said about where these goods would be stored; even Frank had learned to keep his thoughts to himself.

By fall, with the exterior nearly complete, the house stood tall and proud, its stepped chimneys nearly reaching the sky. Inside there was still much to do. The price of cotton had once more begun to rise, and James took full advantage. Plaster was the fashion and they were to have plenty of it—no more board walls for the Torrance family. An expert plasterer was engaged for the work which would culminate in broad intricate moldings. On the third of November, 1000 pounds of plaster of paris and 250 pounds of white lead were sent from Charleston. Silas Rogers hauled it for $2.00 per 100 pounds; Rogers collected $30.60 for his services.

There was some disappointment that the house would not be ready for holiday entertaining; the brown-trimmed dishes would have to remain in their packing crates for a while longer. But James assured them they would be able to move in before the spring leaves graced the trees.

One afternoon after a trip to Charlotte, James came home excitedly waving a slip of paper. "Isabella, come see what I've found," he called. "I've learned of a new school which seems to be ideal for your situation." She bounded down the stairs with visions of steamboats in her head; she was going to Philadelphia at last. "Look, here is an advertisement for a new school; it is to be called the Charlotte Female Academy." He handed her the paper to see for herself, then was perplexed to see the smile fade from her face, and her lower lip engage in its all-too-familiar tremble. "What is it, my dear? I expected you to be pleased."

"Charlotte?! I'm to go to school in Charlotte?" It was not clear to him if this was a question or a protest. "But Pa, I thought I was for Mrs. Sarazin's! Why should anyone want to go to school in such a backwater as Charlotte!"

"Calm down, Isabella. I think this will be the best thing for you at this time. Hugh had good schooling in Charlotte, and there was nothing there for young ladies when Camilla was your age. You know I have put all of my money into the building; I don't have the resources for Philadelphia at this time. You had no lessons at all last year, so I doubt that you are even prepared for Mrs. Sarazin. Perhaps we can reconsider Philadelphia or even New York after a few sessions in Charlotte."

Isabella read the advertisement with downcast eyes. She knew that her education was her father's prerogative, and she would have little voice in it. The adventure would have to wait. "Have you read all of it?" he continued. "They are proposing to have higher studies as well as the common curriculum. There will be classes in drawing, painting, music, Latin, Greek, French, and Italian. This is more than was offered to Camilla; Mrs. Sarazin doesn't teach the classics."

"Where shall I live?" she asked.

"We will have to arrange for boarding with a neighboring family; I hear there are several of my acquaintance who are willing to take in a few girls. A building committee has been assembled, and perhaps in a year or two there will be full boarding facilities. Classes are to commence sometime in the spring or summer, so we will have ample time to make arrangements."

Isabella sighed. School in Charlotte was a bitter disappointment. At least there was music. She would at last learn to play the piano (pianoforte was becoming an old-fashioned word). Camilla would have accepted their father's decision with grace. Isabella vowed to herself to become more like her gentle sister, but she still yearned for a ride on a steamboat.

In the early spring of 1833, the Torrance family moved into their new home. There was some work yet to be done, and well into April there were people finishing the steps and porches, touching up the paint, and working in the garret. Margaret saw that a semicircle of cedars was planted, emanating from each side of the house down the hill to the road below. They formed a perfect frame for the house stretching out like welcoming arms to all who would come to call. From then on the house was called Cedar Grove.[23] James had rescued the brass doorknocker from the earlier brick house his father had built. The ornament had been purchased from James Latta in 1797 for one pound, eight shillings, and one and a half pence, which included engraving. James mounted it neatly on the new front door.

They quickly began to enjoy the luxury of large, well-lit rooms. Margaret and the girls welcomed the return of the Negro women to the household chores, as they were occupied with decorating four parlors. Margaret had another reason to be grateful for some rest; she was expecting another baby.

The white Torrance family was not the only family increasing; little black babies were born in the cabins with great regularity. Then an extravagant gift of six Negroes came to William and Jane from their grandfather, James Latta. The old gentleman was seventy-eight and had nearly ceased the planting of cotton. His children were grown, and he and his wife needed little to keep them comfortably. It was the custom for a man late in life to distribute some of his holdings to his heirs. Over a period of two years James Latta sold or gave away twenty-one of his thirty-four Negroes. His Torrance grandchildren were the recipients of Norfolk, Jerry, Patience, Livinia, Abby, and Martha. All were just barely old enough to be full hands and promised many productive years. William and Jane felt quite grown up to be the owners of such valuable property; of course their father would hold the property in trust until his children were grown. Young William and Jane were perplexed by the Negroes' sad and teary faces. After all, they could see their old master any Sunday if they wished.

During the summer, the Charlotte Female Academy began its classes. Space had been found to conduct lessons, and boarding had been arranged for Isabella. She had been enrolled for two consecutive sessions which would end just before Christmas. James loaded her belongings into his carriage, and they set off on the familiar and mundane twenty-mile journey. She had barely become accustomed to the grand plantation house, and now she would once again live in cramped quarters shared with other girls. In spite of herself, Isabella settled into the academy and soon became fast friends with the other young ladies. Dr. Leavenworth, the school's director, was a stalwart Christian minister whose notion of sin included almost everything other than learning and constant prayer. He was intent on establishing a proper institution for Charlotte's growing population.

On the twenty-ninth of September, Hugh unexpectedly rode up to the house in which she was boarding. "Pa sent me to fetch you," he said. "I'm sorry to be the one bearing bad news. Grandma Davidson died yesterday." Isabella blinked back tears as she packed a few things for the trip home. Grandma Davidson had been solace and comfort to Isabella all of her life. Many childhood hours had been rocked away in the soft lap of her grandmother, listening to stories about her mother. "Tell me again," Isabella had asked, "what did she look like? And what was her favorite sweet?" The old woman drew a portrait in words which Isabella would always cherish. She was a kind and loving grandmother who would be deeply missed.

It was a somber gathering at Centre Church in Mount Mourne. General Ephraim Davidson, at seventy-one, was about the same age as the congregation itself. Hardly anyone in the community could remember a time when Centre Church had functioned without Jane Brevard Davidson's guiding hand. Isabella caught the eye of Rufus Reid. He and his family lived in the Mount Mourne community. His wife, Nancy, did not attend the funeral service; her third confinement was near at hand.

In a few days Isabella returned to school, and in almost no time she received a letter from Ma reporting that on the fifteenth of October, Nancy Reid had been delivered of her third daughter. The baby was healthy enough, but Nancy was weak and ill. Grandma Latta was worried. Once again Hugh appeared in Charlotte to bring his sister home for a funeral, this time at Hopewell. Nancy Latta Reid had died on the sixth of November, three short weeks after giving birth. Isabella's heart went out to Mr. Reid. He looked ashen and bewildered surrounded by his very young daughters. Sallie was three; Mary Jane not quite two; and Nancy Elizabeth Reid, the newborn.

The school sessions ended just before the holidays, and Isabella came home to a more cheerful occasion. On the seventh of December, Margaret's first son, Richard Allison Torrance, had been born. James was pleased to finally add another male to his family. The boy was named after Margaret's father and was to be called Dick.

During the time between Nancy's death and Dick's birth the stars fell: the night sky was lit by a thousand fireballs bursting and spilling sparks to the earth. Many prayed for atonement fearing judgment day had come; others were simply awed by the fiery spectacle. All his life Dick would say he had been born a few weeks after the night the stars fell.[24]

The new house was finally ready for holiday visitors. There were two new sofas shipped from New York and massive made-to-order fire fenders from Philadelphia. The atmosphere was not as festive as usual due to the recent funerals and Margaret's confinement. Grandpa Davidson and Uncle Frank came to stay for a few days. William Latta had no end of excuses for being in Mecklenburg County. Of course he came to offer genuine comfort to his grandparents and Mr. Reid. The fact that Cedar Grove lay between those two homes was an added convenience. William and Camilla seemed to be whispering about marriage.

7 Rebellion 1834~1836

In March, Isabella returned to Charlotte to continue her schooling. The building committee had fulfilled its promise, and now the Charlotte Female Academy was a true boarding school.[25] Her disappointment over Philadelphia had subsided somewhat; there was still hope that she might be sent there next year. Boarding with girls her own age was great fun, even if it was in the sleepy village of Charlotte. Anything was preferable to being at home with four babies under the age of six. Her father had taken her shopping for new shoes before he returned to Cedar Grove. Ma had spent the winter sewing, and her trunk was filled with pretty things. She hoped her gowns would beat any of the new fashions seen in Charlotte. She wanted everyone to know that she was bound for Philadelphia.

At Cedar Grove James had become occupied once more with building. The Hopewell congregation had been collecting pledges for several years to build a new brick church. James had contributed his share and agreed to serve on the building committee. Reverend Williamson had been dissatisfied for some time with the old frame building which was too small for the growing congregation. The sanctuary of the new church, designed to comfortably hold three hundred worshipers, would be surrounded by a gallery for the black people, complete with its separate entrance. James with his recent experience in building fell quite naturally into his role. His horse was seen frequently on the road between Hopewell and Cedar Grove, making many trips to supervise the construction.

By the middle of June, Isabella was home again. She had left school a few weeks early in anticipation of Camilla's marriage. Over the winter William's visits had become more frequent, and James had gladly consented to the union. In fact, James was beaming with joy at the prospect of Camilla married to the son of his dear friend. William showed promise of becoming every bit as successful as his father. There could be no better match for James's most obedient daughter.

On the twenty-fourth of June, friends and family gathered for the occasion. Reverend Williamson performed the ceremony, and afterwards the guests were treated to an elegant feast served on the brown-trimmed china. Mr. and Mrs. Latta were proud to see their grandson marry their step-granddaughter and have their families even more closely united. The elder Lattas had spent a few days at Oaklawn with their daughter, Betsy. They wanted to be nearby to help with the preparations. Betsy had been a widow for about five years, and her six boys were becoming young men. They attended the wedding wearing their finest clothes and best manners. Betsy was an excellent mother. Rufus Reid was also there with his little daughters. He and James were often engaged in business and had become good friends. It was an added delight for Mrs. Latta to have so many of her grandchildren around her.

William's family, of course, had come from Yorkville. Robert and Eliza Latta again had two small children, but not the same two that had attended Nancy's wedding some five years ago. Their daughter had died just three weeks after that event. Little James was now seven and seemed to be a healthy lad; four-year-old Ann had rosy cheeks and boundless energy. Eliza was heavy with another child nearly ready to be born. James prayed for a successful confinement and hoped his friend was done with loss; all the business success in the world could not compensate for so many dead children.

Grandpa Davidson and Uncle Frank were among the guests. The older gentleman was looking forward to the prospect of great-grandchildren; babies usually followed weddings in about a year's time.

Camilla was beautiful. She and Ma had been sewing for weeks, and her gown was stylish, but modest. She and William faced one another and with great seriousness repeated theirs vows. Reverend Williamson must have been pleased.

After the wedding Camilla and William made their home in Yorkville, South Carolina, near his family. William, at twenty-five, had become active in his father's merchant-planter enterprise. However, agriculture interested him more than trade. They owned land at Bullock Creek, about twelve miles southwest of town, and he was beginning to put it under cultivation. It was unusual to live in town and work a farm in the countryside. William hoped he could make a go of it. He knew he could earn a good living from cotton, but he didn't want to give up the social pleasures of living in town.

In August, Isabella returned to school, this time with little enthusiasm. She had scant interest in classical languages or the findings at Herculaneum, and Dr. Leavenworth's constant scrutiny of the status of one's soul was suffocating hers. At Hopewell she had memorized the catechism and studied scripture under the strictest tutelage. She was sure that her faith was as strong as the next girl's, but being somber seven days a week had become tedious. Late in the fall she wrote to her father and begged him to come for her—she was ready to go home.

"I am so sorry, Papa," she said to him when he arrived. "I know I am a disappointment to you, but I have been so unhappy here. I've tried to improve to please you and Ma, but I've had no success at it. I suppose I was not meant to be a scholar."

"It's all right," he said. "There is no need for you to stay here if it doesn't suit. Ma will be glad to have a nearly grown girl to keep her company." He said the right words, but Isabella could tell his heart was not in them.

Camilla would never have done such a thing—but she could not be Camilla. James settled her account which was reduced by eleven dollars for her absence at the end of the term.

~ ~ ~

The next year, 1835, was bleak for Isabella. It brought circumstances she would forever regret, unfortunate matters that were seldom spoken of and never put down in family correspondence. The year began innocently enough. Jane was nearly twelve and had at last been pronounced old enough to go to Salem. Isabella was happy for her sister; she had loved the warmth and serenity of that place. At the same time, she still regretted having gone at too young an age to reap its full benefit. She helped Ma with the preparations, and endlessly filled Jane with words of praise for the school. Jane shared Isabella's high-spirited nature; the two girls became close during this time of planning.

Toward the end of January, Isabella went along with her father to take Jane to school. Nostalgia washed over her as they rode into the little village which seemed not to have changed in the past seven years. They settled Jane into her room which was as warm and familiar as last winter's coat. Later they went to the school store to establish Jane's account; the familiar bouquet of shoe leather brought a lump to Isabella's throat. When they returned to the residence hall to bid Jane good night, Isabella happened to meet one of her former teachers. After they hugged, Isabella asked if there could be a spot for a sixteen year old who already had some education but could use a bit of polish. The Sister laughed. "Why Isabella, you are nearly a woman. God has a plan for you, and this is your time to discover it." Although Isabella's question was in jest, it was something of a bitter irony to be told she had outgrown Salem.

The next morning they arrived at Jane's room to find her laughing and talking with her new roommates, the Johnston sisters. The hallways were alive with squeals and giggles and running feet. Jane would be happy here; this was a perfect place. Before their last farewells, James took his daughters to the bakery for a treat of sugar cake. Another one was wrapped in oiled paper to take to Ma. Its buttery fragrance haunted Isabella all the way home.

Upon their arrival, Margaret greeted them with the news. "You will not believe who has been married!"

"Who?" asked Isabella, expecting it to be one of Camilla's friends.

"Mr. Rufus Reid has married Betsy Davidson, his own sister-in-law."

"Mr. Reid has married Aunt Betsy?!" Isabella was stunned at the idea of it. "How can that be possible; are they not already considered brother and sister?"

"Apparently not. It only happened two days since, but the news of it has spread through the neighborhood," Margaret continued. "I understand it was a quiet affair with not many in attendance. Reverend Williamson was there but declined to perform the sacrament, so a magistrate was called in to officiate. Yesterday I rode by Oaklawn and found Mrs. Latta there with her grandchildren while the newlyweds spend some private time at Mount Mourne. I could hardly get a word out of Mrs. Latta. There was distress all over her face; but you know how she is, she would never utter a harsh word about anyone, especially one of her relations. I know she cares for Mr. Reid, but she did admit that his faith is not deep and pure enough to satisfy her. She expressed gratitude that her granddaughters now have a mother and relief that her own daughter will be raising them. I think she had feared that Mr. Reid would take a wife even more worldly than himself. She said she found comfort in the Reverend's presence. He did not condone the union but neither did he condemn it. It's for the Lord to judge, she told me."

Isabella was surprised at her own thoughts as she absorbed all of this information. She had long admired Mr. Reid, and some secret inner part of her had hoped he would not marry again until she was old enough to catch his eye. Now Aunt Betsy had spoiled everything. Isabella pushed this thought from her mind. What an unchristian attitude to have!

"Well," said James, "that is certainly a merger of two fine fortunes. But I imagine that poor old Wilson is rolling in his grave. I remember that he had misgivings about Mr. Reid's first marriage to Betsy's sister. Now that fellow has taken Wilson's widow and his estate. What did Mr. Latta have to say?"

"I have no idea," said Margaret. "I have not spoken to him, but the rumors indicate that he is not overly alarmed. I think he cares more about Betsy's happiness than the condition of her soul. However, that old man's mutterings grow more incomprehensible each day. I doubt that he truly understands what has transpired." She sighed, then offered her own opinion. "Both Betsy and Mr. Reid have had a hard time of widowhood and deserve contentment."

~　　　~　　　~

The winter dragged on cold and dull for Isabella. She drifted about with little purpose or sense of direction. She helped care for the children, often taking Lettitia and Mary to Hopewell for their lessons. On her way home she sometimes stopped by Oaklawn to visit with Betsy. Her house, as usual, abounded with little ones; her new daughters brought out a radiance in her that Isabella had not seen before.

"Look at this sewing," said Betsy. She held up a workbasket full of tiny feminine frocks and delicate ribbons and ruffles. "Boys clothes need to be so sturdy and practical, and they are constantly in need of mending; these are much more fun. I can't tell you what a blessing Mr. Reid has been to me. As much as I love my sons, I could never guide them properly into manhood. Your brothers have been helpful, but having a father means everything to them. And finally I have girls of my own to fuss over. Isabella, I am having absolutely the best time of my life. Would you like to help with these?"

Isabella took a needle and thread, and Betsy showed her what needed to be done. While they talked Betsy deftly stitched up the seams of a little gown, and Isabella hemmed a ruffle to be attached to its sleeve. Betsy was right, she thought, as she took nearly invisible stitches in the narrowest possible hem. There was deep satisfaction in tidy, well-done work. Isabella was ashamed at her earlier reaction to this marriage. How could she have ever thought ill of this gentle woman?

On the way home her mood of uselessness returned. She could sew frocks for her sisters, but it would not be the same. It was not Betsy's house full of children that she envied, it was her dedication to purpose. Most of Isabella's contemporaries were away at school or lived at too great a distance for visiting. Her father's promise of Philadelphia had been set aside. He insisted she have a solid commitment to education before he made another such investment. She yearned to be in that city, but she had had enough of school.

One of Isabella's chores was to go for the mail. Mr. Alexander, who maintained a post office at his plantation, often brought sacks of mail to Hopewell for distribution in that section. A letter from Jane or Camilla brightened an otherwise dull day. Mr. Reid was planning a large new home in Mount Mourne; his family in one place and his business in another had become a hardship. She dreaded the prospect of exchanging Betsy's visits for Betsy's letters.

It was during that dreary winter that she became acquainted with Franklin Smith. She had met him several years before when he had engaged in business with her father. She was not privy to the nature of this business and, furthermore, had no interest in it. She did have a vague recollection of her father being quite critical of Mr. Smith in some way that involved money. That had been the spring they moved into Cedar Grove, a stressful time in which James was critical of many things. Certainly this charming fellow who was beginning to occupy so much of her time had been misjudged. Although his upbringing was more modest than hers, and their friends were of different circles, Isabella was drawn to him like a moth to a candle. She was flattered by the attention of a man some ten years her senior and was astonished at how she was pleasured by her own womanly response. Otherwise, they had little in common but grandiose dreams and mutual idleness—it proved to be a dangerous combination.

In the spring Camilla came home for her confinement, as it was customary for a young woman to spend several months with her mother surrounding the birth of her first child. Once again there was a flurry of activity in the Torrance household, and Camilla was at the center of it. On the ninth of May, the infant was born and named for his father; he was to be called Willie. Nearly every day someone would come to visit with Camilla and coo over precious Willie. No one seemed to notice how little time Isabella was spending at home.

The grace notes were Jane's letters from Salem. On the second of July 1835, she wrote:

My dear father,

I now take my pen in hand to inform you how I do, I am well at present. I hope you will visit me shortly. I am promoted to a higher room under the care of Miss Lineback and Miss Bagge, who are very kind to me. The school is very much crowded at this time. There was a most severe hailstorm here on Saturday, they were the largest hailstones I ever saw. You must write to me and tell me whether sister Camilla is living with you, tell her she must write to me, and tell me what she intends calling her son. Tell Malvina Graham to write to me and tell me whether she intends coming here to go to school. Tell brother William he must write to me, and I will write to him. Please bring sister Letticia here to go to school. Kiss all of my little sister's and brother for me. Please send me some of your and Ma's hair. The two Johnsons Ann an Jane send their love to you all, they are living in the same room with me. I like to stay in Salem very much, but I want to see you all. My studies are the same as they were when I wrote last. I have had the toothache very bad some days ago an had a tooth drawn, but now another one begins to ache. Give my love to all of my dear relations and request them to write to me. Tell the black people howday for me. Please write to me as soon as you get this. I remain your affectionate daughter,

Jane E. Torrance

P S Please send me a box of cakes and some pocket money, I get some here every month but we buy a good deal of fruit etc that I would like to have more.

Isabella reread the letter replete with childhood innocence; if only she could have hers back! Surely Jane's not asking after her was an oversight.

Late in the summer Isabella announced to her parents, "Mr. Franklin Smith and I are to be married."

"What?!" exclaimed her father. "Have you forgotten the unpleasant dealings I have been drawn into with that young man? I have no intention of giving my consent to this idea."

"I've not asked for your consent," she replied hesitantly.

"Isabella, you are much too young to marry, nor do I believe that Mr. Smith is the right man for you. His family is nothing like ours, and he has not been raised with privilege as you have. Experience teaches me that a life with Mr. Smith will be a life of doing without, which you will quickly come to despise."

"Father, you have not heard me; I am afraid it will be necessary for me to marry Mr. Smith."

By now he was shouting, "I said no and I shall hear no more of it!"

"James," Margaret interjected; she had gotten the drift of this conversation. She had been aware for some time that Isabella was troubled and only now understood the source of it. "She is right; you have not listened to her. I believe that she is telling you that she and Mr. Smith are expecting a child."

"What?!" his voice thundered. "How did this happen?"

"I believe you know how it's done," replied his wife. Isabella was not amused. "Tell me, dear, have I guessed correctly?"

"Yes, Ma, I am so very, very sorry. I never meant for this to happen. Once again I have disappointed you, and I am so deeply ashamed."

James buried his face in his hands. These things did not happen in families like his; they only happened to the lower sort, which well described Smith. He looked at his daughter. She had put on some weight, and her swollen belly was becoming conspicuous. He had not noticed. He silently cursed himself; he had noticed nearly nothing about this headstrong child for some time now. No wonder she had turned elsewhere for affection. He dared not let her see the aching in his soul; that would surely weaken any moral convictions she might have left. She had sinned and would have to pay. It was God's will that he be stern.

"That you have disappointed me is the only thing you have said with which I can agree. Has Mr. Smith spoken to his family?"

"I believe he plans to do so today. We thought you should all be told at the same time."

"You thought! Why in heaven's name have you not done any thinking before now?"

"James, calm yourself." Margaret could show compassion; it was in the nature of mothers. "How long has it been?" she asked. "Do you know when to expect this child?"

By now Isabella was crying. "I have no idea. I know how babies are made and that it was a dreadful sin to give in to my weakness. But I know nothing about confinement. I've only recently determined what was wrong with me; I feared I was taking a fever. I am so terribly frightened. I don't know what to do. I know God has begun his punishment." She had heard often enough the screams of women in childbirth and was terrified of what lay ahead.

Margaret gathered the trembling woman-child into her arms. "Do you care for Mr. Smith?"

"Oh, I do. He has been so kind to me. When I told him of this, he did not turn away but promised to take care of us. We have the same notion of how we want to live. He plans to get a place for us in one of the great cities with theaters and ballrooms and all manner of busyness. I know his family is not wealthy, but they are kind and responsible people."

"That is good," replied Margaret. "It could be much worse."

"I will arrange for a magistrate," said her father. "I doubt that Reverend Williamson will want any part in it. You know that the Session at Hopewell will hear of this, and you might not be welcome there for some time."

"Yes," she replied softly. "I have prayed every day for forgiveness. I will accept any censure I am due."

"I want you to leave us alone for a bit," Margaret said to her husband. "We need to have a little woman talk. There is much she needs to know, and I am certainly experienced in the business of birthing." Margaret would soon be adding to that experience, for she, too, was carrying a child. From the looks of Isabella she judged that they would be having their children about the same time.

James left the room. How could he have permitted such a thing in his household? He stepped out onto the porch, his usual place for contemplation. Had it been only two years ago that Smith had become embroiled in his affairs? When Cedar Grove was nearing completion and money was scarce, Mr. Gorman, the plasterer, agreed to accept a partial payment for his work, the rest to be paid over time with interest. James had paid nearly half of it when Gorman's creditors lit out after them, serving them both with arrest warrants. Smith was an officer of the court, eager to maneuver himself into the practice of law. He had been a minor figure in the ordeal, but had done nothing to prevent its escalation into a great embarrassment. James had regarded him, perhaps wrongly, as a scoundrel ever since.[26] He took a deep breath; the memory served only to fuel his rage, which was not useful. He must give some thought to his share of the blame in neglecting Isabella. With four younger daughters, he would have to give more effort to being a father.

On the ninth of September 1835, Isabella and Franklin Smith were joined in a quiet ceremony at Cedar Grove. They made their home near the Smith family. Several months later Jane Camilla Smith was born—Isabella was seventeen years old.[27]

~ ~ ~

Restlessness crept over Hugh and Frank during the year of 1836. That February, James Latta had been declared mentally incompetent, and the court appointed his son Robert and his son-in-law Rufus Reid to be his guardians. The old gentleman was past eighty and the fog of senility had gradually settled in like plumes of mist obscuring the sun. Now his heirs, who both had profitable plantations of their own, were to manage Mr. Latta's holdings. The Torrance brothers envied their autonomy.[28]

In contrast, James Torrance at fifty-two was increasingly vigorous. He had joined with a group of men to explore the idea of establishing a local college. The Presbyterian churches of the area had grown weary of sending away to northern schools for their ministers. "It's high time we endeavored to educate our own young men to tend to our spiritual needs," James had exclaimed. He and five others had pledged a thousand dollars each toward this end. One of the others, William Lee Davidson, Jr., had donated land and suggested the college be named for his father, General William Lee Davidson, who had given his life in the War for Independence. This was acceptable as the general was revered by all of them.

As James threw his energies into this new activity, Hugh and Frank once again were given responsibilities overseeing the plantation. Labor without pride of ownership held little luster for them. The brothers could not foresee a day when their father would become old and infirm and cede some of his property to them.

They began their mornings before dawn by sounding a horn to arouse the Negroes. Time was allowed for the livestock to be fed and for the Negroes to prepare and consume their own breakfasts; then the horn was sounded again at first light to summon the hands to their labors. Hugh and Frank traveled from field to field assigning tasks and giving close attention that each was performed efficiently. They gave strict notice to the gearing of the horses so as not to injure their shoulders or backs and saw that the plows were in a condition to perform good work with ease to both horses and men. Since no one was permitted to leave the fields, little ones were appointed to go after water for the horses and the hands. Ten-year-old Abram looked so proud of himself driving the pony cart filled with water buckets and his crew of black children. His five-year-old brother, Ezekiel, was the youngest water carrier. Hiram looked forward to the day when Abram would be assigned to the fields. Hiram wished to boss the bucket brigade. Ruth and Harriet were almost in their teens; next year they would be put to adult chores. Boys their age were already behind the plow.

The Negroes were allowed two hours or more to eat their dinner during the hot months and one hour in the spring and fall. They were dismissed from the fields at dusk in the summer and sundown in the winter. They were given strict orders to go directly home and attend to their assigned chores.

The brothers examined each Negro house once or twice per week at night to prevent the people from running about and to look for other men's Negroes who might have entered the premises without permission. Quarreling, loud talk, and profane language were not tolerated.

On wet days they saw that the farming tools were collected in the barns where they were repaired and put in good order. In addition, the brothers directed the care and feeding of the horses and other animals; the maintenance of wagons, plows, and tools; and the activity at the mill. An accounting was to be kept of the livestock to prevent them from being cooked by some of the Negroes. On Saturday evenings two hours or more were given to the women to wash their clothes. Each hand was required to appear on Monday mornings with combed hair and clean clothes unless prevented by circumstances. [29]

James owned some three thousand acres and over a hundred Negroes. The black families lived in one- or two-room cabins surrounding a dirt yard. The families were large, consisting not only of parents and children but also of aunts, uncles, and grandparents. The yard was a social vortex as well as a place for work. Here brooms were made, utensils carved, chickens plucked, and yarn spun. At day's end it was swept clean of the chores' leavings. About forty of the men were full hands, nearly half of them strong well-muscled teens which guaranteed a secure future for the plantation. Narcissus and Ibby were full of vinegar and needed more instruction than the rest. Hugh would soon have them under control. Flora's sons were in their prime and well worth the price that had been extracted from James by the court, both in money and anguish. Jim, in his mid-forties, was the oldest man in the fields. He was frail and weak and frequently ill. Samson, on the other hand, lived up to his namesake; at forty he showed no signs of wearing out.

Nearly as many women were full hands, although half of them were breeding at any given time. Time lost from the fields for breeding was gladly forgiven; future laborers at no cost but their upkeep were a bargain. Livinia had hardly graduated from the water wagon before producing a son, and Martha and Patience were both expecting. Mr. Latta's gift to his grandchildren was proving to be generous indeed.

About half a dozen old ones worked at light chores when they were able. Four of them were taking orders from the third generation of Torrance men. Flora and Minny tended the children of both colors who played together in the swept yard. Barney and Bristol had reached their sixties and were enchanting storytellers. The rest were children who tended chickens and gardens or whatever was dictated by their ages. Nearly twenty black children were still too young for hauling water.

Managing the Negroes was a complex task involving much dancing about to achieve an ideal balance. It was desirable to extract as much labor from each one as possible without causing injury or rebellion. An ill or injured hand could not work and might incur the expense of a doctor. An insubordinate one was a potential runaway who could spread his poisonous contempt to the others. The threat of being sold was often sufficient to correct such a person. None wanted to be separated from his family nor face the prospect of even harsher circumstances.

Hugh and Frank had affection for the older Negroes who had belonged to their grandfather. In that time when the plantation was small and isolated and only a handful of men worked the place, it was common for strong bonds to form between white and black. Now it was different. Both populations had grown and mingled with their own kind. Hugh maintained a friendship with Flora's son, Solomon. They were the same age and had been constant companions as small children. Hugh still remembered when he had been told, at the age of six, that his time spent with Solomon would be limited. Only in the late afternoon when the black boy's tasks were done could they be playmates. That was Hugh's first realization that the color of a man's skin dictated his station. At first he had been angry with his father and chagrined at his friend's struggle with water buckets and swine feed. In time he accepted the twilight hours spent by the creek and later the mill pond as appropriate measures of friendship. Any affection between master and hand was tempered by each one's duty to the other. James understood Hugh's struggle and saw that the black boy was trained as a shoemaker. It was customary to select young men with talent and diligence and train them to trades; James had done so whenever the need arose. This assured value to their masters and respect from their peers. James had trained Samson to run the mill when he commenced its operation in 1825. Specialized labor was essential on a large, smoothly run plantation. Frank had no close Negro companions. The black children who had shared his childhood in the swept yard were all girls. He had paid little attention when they grew into workers.

Illness was a daunting companion of both the white and black families. Agues, fevers, pleurisy, asthma, rheumatism, and many other ailments kept workers confined to quarters. Doctors were summoned to Cedar Grove often to treat more than one sufferer. When conditions were serious, the healer remained overnight. Hugh complained of a troublesome liver, and Frank's skin tended to boils which were aggravated by work in the sun. In spite of illness, drought, and other plagues of nature, the plantation was hugely prosperous, and the brothers wanted for nothing that money could buy. Nevertheless, they felt like unpaid overseers on their father's land.

News began to seep into the community that heightened their restlessness, tantalizing news of land in the west. Rumors scudded about, and newspapers reported tracts of prosperity to be found along the Mississippi River. Land was plentiful, fertile, and cheap; transportation to market promised to be sure and swift. On a steamy day in midsummer, they approached their father. James, of course, had heard of the glorious west. He also knew that tales carried from tongue to ear across the vast land were embellished and embroidered at every campfire along the way. And he could not fathom anyone being dissatisfied with the genteel lushness of the Carolinas. The three of them gathered to discuss the matter in his study, the parlor he had furnished with cases for his many books and a sideboard for brandy. James tried to hide his disapproval, praying that reason would sway his sons.

"I had hoped you would be pleased to work this place until the time came for me to turn it over to the both of you," he said. "North Carolina has been kind to our family. My father began with nearly nothing, and in two generations we have made one of the grandest farms around."

"Which is what we want," said Frank. "We wish to build our own place, just as you and your father did. We want that same challenge of opening up new land." James smiled at his son; Frank always rose slowly to challenge.

"Pa, I'm twenty-six years old," said Hugh. "The time is right to make my own way in this world. With your solid constitution I cannot see you stepping aside for many years yet. Perhaps William—or even Dick—would be better suited to be your successor."

Frank rose from his chair and plucked an atlas from the bookshelf. "I have been studying this prospect, not merely listening to pretty rumors." He opened the volume to a page displaying the entire continent spread out from sea to sea. The whole of the eastern bank of the Mississippi had been carved into states, and a few had been added on its western shore. Beyond them lay mysterious territories stretching to the end of the earth. He pointed to Mississippi; statehood had been granted nearly twenty years before, but it was still sparsely settled. The mighty river curled and coiled against its western edge like a mother snake on a nest of newborns. "The river is the key," he said. "It's broad, well traveled, and fed by a number of tributaries. Getting a crop to market should be a simple matter."

"I will grant you that point," said James. "My land would be perfect if it were connected to a river." The nearby Catawba was riddled with shoals and rapids. Plans for canals with locks had been piecemeal and uncoordinated. James pointed to the northwest corner of Tennessee. "This is where the land is situated that my father bought, some thirty-eight hundred acres. Much of it lies along the Forked Deer River which drains into the Mississippi; perhaps you could farm that for me."

"We would prefer our own place," replied Hugh. "I also have my doubts about the growing season as far north as that land; it may only be suitable for crops we know little about. The reports about cotton in Mississippi are highly favorable."

"Perhaps too good to be believed." There was more than a hint of sarcasm in the father's voice. "Have you considered the route for making such a journey?"

"We have," said Frank. "I've been comparing the newspaper reports to the maps in this book." His finger traced the route as he spoke. "We are familiar enough with the road south to Yorkville and on to Columbia. There we can join a well-traveled road southwest through Columbus, Georgia, to Montgomery, Alabama. In that city we can choose to go by road or river to Mobile. A steamer calls regularly at Mobile bound for New Orleans and up the Mississippi. After we locate some land we can plan the tail end of our journey."

"And how do you plan to buy land?" asked James.

"We were hoping that you would invest with us," said Hugh. "Our work here has saved you an overseer's salary."

"I have provided generously for all of your needs," James retorted, "far more than I would have paid an overseer. No, I am afraid I cannot invest in a project of which I disapprove. I understand the lure that wanderlust has for young men; my experience has taught me it is an infatuation which will pass. You are grown men and are free to leave this family at any time. But I fear that if you pursue this fool's errand into the wilderness you will live to regret it."

Hugh and Frank were disappointed in their father's reaction but not surprised. They understood his devotion to his home, community, church, and now a college. But his passions were not theirs. As long as they stayed in North Carolina, they would be minor figures in his realm.

And the realm was a busy one. Margaret was thoroughly occupied with her houseful of children which now included Sarah Jane born last January. She planned substantial meals around the bounty of the garden and managed the daily chores of the house servants. She arranged the children's lessons and organized the entertaining. At the large dining table places were frequently set for guests.

James, of course, was not entirely absent from the plantation; he took an occasional turn at managing the hands to give his sons the more pleasurable job of going about the countryside to buy supplies and sell their crops. The social aspect of these sojourns was welcome, and they learned more about the mysterious lands to the west.

Jane was back at school after an interlude at home. Her youthful letters were a treat for all. On the seventh of July 1836, she wrote from Salem:

My dear Parents

According to my promise I will now write a few lines to inform you that I enjoy very good health, since I returned. I have been changed into higher classes (viz) Geography, History, and Reading, I *am still living in the same room. I have been anxiously looking for Ann Johnston for the last week but she has not come yet, I do not know the cause of her not coming, she wrote to me while I was at home that she would be here soon. Dear ma, please to send me my cap as soon as possible, likewise some needles and thread the first opportunity you have. I am not as well satisfied as I was before I went home I would rather be at home doing nothing than at school. I am working on a footstool now. My piece in music is the "Bavarian Broom Girl's song". When you write please tell me how aunt Betsy has got as she was very sick when I left her and if Grandpa Davidson is better. Tell M^{rs}. Williamson I forgot to send her the patterns which she told me to send her, but I will get them when I go home, give my best respects to her and her girls. Tell brother he must write to me as he promised to do so. Tell grandma I will write to her soon. Give my love to her and aunt Betsy and all of her family. Kiss my little sisters and brother and tell them I wish to see them very much. Give my love to brother Franklin and tell him to write to me. Give my love to all of my dear acquaintances and friends when you see them. I have nothing more to say but ask you to answer this letter as soon as you receive it. I remain your affectionate and dutiful daughter until death*

> *Jane E. Torrance*

James would write and assure his daughter that Aunt Betsy's health was improving. A little girl named Bettie had been born to her and Mr. Reid the previous March. At last Betsy had a daughter of her own. Grandpa Davidson was doing well for a gentleman of nearly seventy-five years; he would reassure her on that point also.

As the summer progressed Hugh and Frank continued to collect newspaper reports and began a correspondence concerning the availability of land. They inquired quietly about obtaining a loan. They dared not discuss money again with their father. They talked to those in the neighborhood who had traveled to the west or had acquaintances along the way. When the time to begin the journey approached, letters of introduction would be written. Sometimes lodging could be exchanged for news and gossip from back home. Most nights would be spent camped alongside their wagons in unfamiliar beast-filled forests.

When Isabella and Franklin Smith got wind of their plans they were thrilled. Mississippi was the opposite end of the universe from Philadelphia, but that mattered not to Isabella. It was adventure that she craved and a chance to leave the quagmire of shame that had settled around her. She was also anxious to leave the environs of her mother-in-law. Mrs. Smith was a difficult woman. She became overly alarmed at any minor incident and had spells of weeping for no apparent reason. At first Hugh and Frank opposed the idea of carrying an infant across the country. But Isabella's enthusiasm and vitality convinced them to add the Smith family to the expedition.

On the second of December, Hugh and Frank returned home after a brief trip to Rowan County. They had news for their father. "I believe we have made all the necessary arrangements for our move to the west," began Hugh. "We have spent the last several days with Mr. John Campbell who acts as agent for his son and several others of Yalobusha County in Mississippi."

"The gentleman offered us three tracts of land," said Frank, "and we have accepted. Taken together they amount to about two hundred acres. They lie in a vast area that became available a few years since by the signing of the Treaty of Dancing Rabbit Creek with the Choctaw Nation."

"Mr. Campbell's son was among the original purchasers," continued Hugh. "He reports that it is very pretty land. It consists of hilly country good for grazing, flat bottomland for crops, and marshes that carry rich river silt to the fields."

"The place is riddled with creeks and waterways," added Frank, "an excellent situation for farming and handy transportation to market, at least most of the year." Their enthusiasm was infectious, but James remained immune.

"Where is this land situated?" asked James. "Near the port of New Orleans?"

"Quite a bit north of there," said Hugh, "about two hundred miles north, and some hundred miles south of Tennessee."

"And these waterways, I suppose they lead directly into the Mississippi?"

"They do," said Frank. "Our land is about fifty miles east of that river. Mr. Campbell tells us that most crops follow a southwesterly path and join the Mississippi in the vicinity of Vicksburg."

"Two hundred acres is not much of a farm. How can you scrape a living from such shards of earth?"

"We've been assured that land is plentiful, and we can buy more at any time. The country is said to be quite fertile and yields a good deal more than the clay soil here," answered Hugh.

"And does your plan include paying for this property? I don't suppose Campbell is in the habit of giving it away," asked James.

"No sir, he is not," answered Hugh. "Mr. Campbell agreed to a loan of $5000. From that sum, we have paid the landowners $1326, which is half the price of the three tracts. The rest is due in one year's time."

"Where did you find this Mr. Campbell?" asked their father.

"He lives in Mount Vernon," said Frank.

"Mount Vernon?" asked James. "I've not heard of it."

"It's a small place near the Yadkin River about halfway between Salisbury and Statesville," replied Hugh.

"And this perfect stranger gave you five thousand dollars on your word?" James inquired.

"No sir," said Frank; "Mr. Reid is acquainted with Mr. Campbell and arranged the meeting. We stopped at Mount Mourne for Mr. Reid and Uncle Frank who went with us."

"Here is the agreement." Hugh produced a paper for his father to read. "As you can see we have promised to pay interest of three hundred dollars per year beginning in one year. He has agreed to let us have use of the money for as long as we wish. Both of us have signed; Mr. Reid and Uncle Frank signed as security. All the particulars have been laid out, the names of the sellers, location of the land, and so forth. The place includes cabins, so we may set up housekeeping right away. The town of Coffeeville is nearby, convenient for business." James cared little about cabins; it was the money that clutched his mind.

"So it was Mr. Reid's fine reputation that squared this deal. He may be married to your Aunt Betsy, but he is not blood-related. I wish you had not brought him and your uncle into this arrangement. If some calamity should occur, I would be greatly humiliated to have them responsible for your debts."

"We have no securities in our own names, and you made it abundantly clear that you would not finance us. Where else were we to turn?" asked Hugh. "They seemed most willing to put their trust in us, and Mr. Campbell believes he has made a worthy investment."

"It is not your integrity I question but the perilous nature of this scheme." James sat down and heaved a long sigh. The deed was done; their departure could not be prevented. "I suppose if Mr. Reid had not led you to Campbell you would have approached Camilla's husband?"

"The thought had crossed our minds," replied Frank.

"And where do Mr. Smith and Isabella fit into this plan?"

"He has scraped together some money of his own," said Hugh; "I do not know the amount or its source. We will all work together on the farming. You have our promise that we will let no harm come to our sister."

James sat in silence for a while. He remembered his promise to himself to be a better father. His boys certainly displayed determination, if not common sense. He had no wish to know more about Mr. Smith's money—for once it did not involve him. Perhaps Isabella and her blameless infant deserved a life away from the harshness they still encountered. He did not condone this venture, but he could not send them into the wilderness with nothing but Mr. Campbell's money and a half interest in land.

"This is what I can do for you," he said at last. "I will provide you with some horses, wagons, and farm tools. I will also give you the Negroes that I had planned to leave you in my will and have the proper documents drawn up. I ask a few things in return. You are to plan your journey very carefully and see that your sister is provided for. I want you to understand the serious nature of taking on debt. The promise that you made to Campbell is among the most solemn vows a man can take. If you should meet trouble in spite of your best efforts, do not bring Mr. Reid or your uncle into it. I am your father, and you will come to me." At last he relaxed his furrowed brow. "And you must promise to write letters—many, many letters." [30]

8 The Journey 1836~1837

High spirits returned to Hugh, Frank, and the Smith family as they spent the last few weeks of 1836 preparing for leave-taking. A hasty departure was essential in order to have land cleared and crops planted by early spring. Letters were written, wagons outfitted, and documents drawn. They had followed their father's instructions and crafted a detailed plan. The contagious excitement of the travelers spread to the younger children. It was the atlas that grabbed William's attention; after all, he was preparing to attend the new college the minute its doors were opened. But James and Margaret could not manage to shed their misgivings; a trail through unknown lands, the turning of virgin soil, and the burden of debt held no intrigue for them. Margaret, always the nurturing mother, amassed sacks of potatoes, onions, turnips, and other edible roots. From her containers of garden seeds she assembled small packets. She labeled them "peas," "beans," "cucumbers," and so forth and hoped their western garden would be as bountiful as hers. James contributed a bushel of cotton seed, skeptical that the product of his clay hills could find nourishment in the loamy soil of Mississippi. He also gave them as much household and kitchen furniture as would fit in their wagons. Isabella was pleased to see that the kitchen furnishings included proper cooking pots and a decent set of dishes.

They said tearful farewells, never acknowledging that for some this could be their final parting. James promised to visit the west as soon as practical; his children assured him they could easily traverse the land back again after they were settled. In the interim there would be letters. Packets of paper and vials of ink were tucked into the luggage. United States mail was beginning to come with some regularity from the west. This service was supplemented by frontier enthusiasts who crossed back and forth from hither to yon, always pleased to carry letters.

Late in December, the wagons departed Cedar Grove. James and Margaret watched as they disappeared down the hill until only a cloud of dust could be seen, and finally nothing. Hugh, Frank, Isabella and Franklin with their infant Jane, along with about thirty Negroes and a few horses were gone. On Friday the twenty-third of December, the Smith home was left behind; the journey had begun.[31]

Christmas day was spent in Yorkville with Camilla, William, and little Willie. That evening they were served a sumptuous feast in Robert's grand home. By now Robert was reputed to be among the wealthiest men in all of South Carolina. In her excitement Isabella had no thought of savoring this luxury nor any concept of the Spartan conditions that lay ahead.

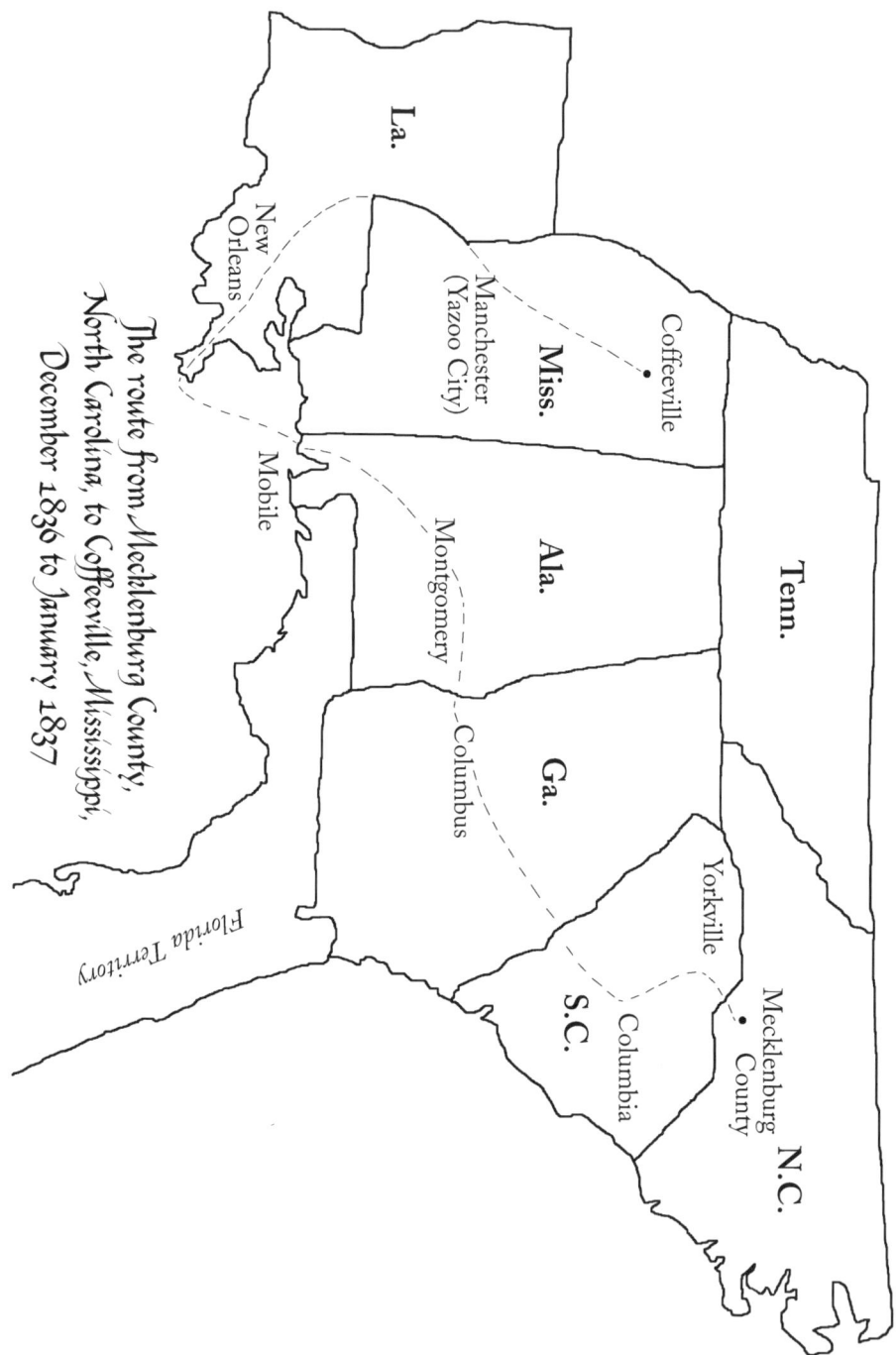

The route from Mecklenburg County, North Carolina, to Coffeeville, Mississippi, December 1836 to January 1837

The day after Christmas they set off in earnest. Camilla seemed a bit unwell, which was not unusual for her. Her good-byes were overly emotional, and she squeezed her sister's hands with such force that her knuckles whitened. Isabella returned the embrace. In spite of her occasional envy and their differences in temperament, she loved Camilla with all her heart. "I will write," she said, "I will write a long letter as soon as we get there and tell you how we fared. And when Mr. Smith buys us a place, I shall write how to get to it. I want you to come for a long visit. Pa said he would come. If William cannot bring you, perhaps Pa will."

Later, in the wagon Isabella hugged her infant close as her eyes absorbed the increasingly unfamiliar landscape. She had tossed the old envies toward Camilla behind in the roadside dust. All of the riches in South Carolina could not match the prospect of Mississippi. Their path led them south to Columbia where they joined a well-established highway on a southwesterly course.[32] As the days passed the climate became milder and the vegetation more lush. Most evenings she and the black women prepared a simple meal of boiled potatoes or turnips, corn cakes, and fish or fowl hunted by the men. Some days they were able to purchase more interesting victuals from farms along the way. On Saturday the seventh of January, they arrived at Columbus, Georgia. They had traveled eleven days and covered nearly four hundred miles. As they had done in each town and village, they inquired of the locals about conditions ahead. The news in Columbus was not favorable.

"This appears to be the place where we must go by differing routes," said Hugh. They knew that separation would probably become necessary but hoped it could be avoided until further along. "The road west from here is said to be very poorly maintained and will be a torture for anyone in our wagons. We can walk quickly enough, but I am afraid Isabella and Jane will serve only to delay us. There is a stagecoach from here to Montgomery which is only about a hundred miles distant. Mr. Smith, I suggest you sell your conveyance. That should fetch enough to buy your transport all the way to Coffeeville. In Montgomery you may continue by stage or steamship to Mobile. Water should be your best route from there. We shall follow the same road to Montgomery with the wagons, the Negroes, and our horses, and inquire there about our best route to Coffeeville." Isabella copied the names of the people they had promised to visit along the way, while Mr. Smith took the horses and rig to the livery. She felt a slight panic at having to part with her brothers—the idea of a steamboat quickly brushed it away.

～　　　～　　　～

It was February before news of the expedition reached Cedar Grove. On the fourteenth of January 1837, Franklin Smith wrote to his father-in-law from Mobile:

Dear Sir

We left home as you no doubt have learned before this on Friday after leaving your house and remained in Yorkville until the succeding Monday evening when we made a fair start for our long journey and after travelling at the rate of from 24 to 30 miles arrived at Columbus Ga on Saturday last not having had a drop of rain on us & much better roads than [we expected.] — at Columbus we . . . determined to dispose of horses [and rig] there and take the stage to Montgomery —

Mississippi with an inset of the Torrance family lands

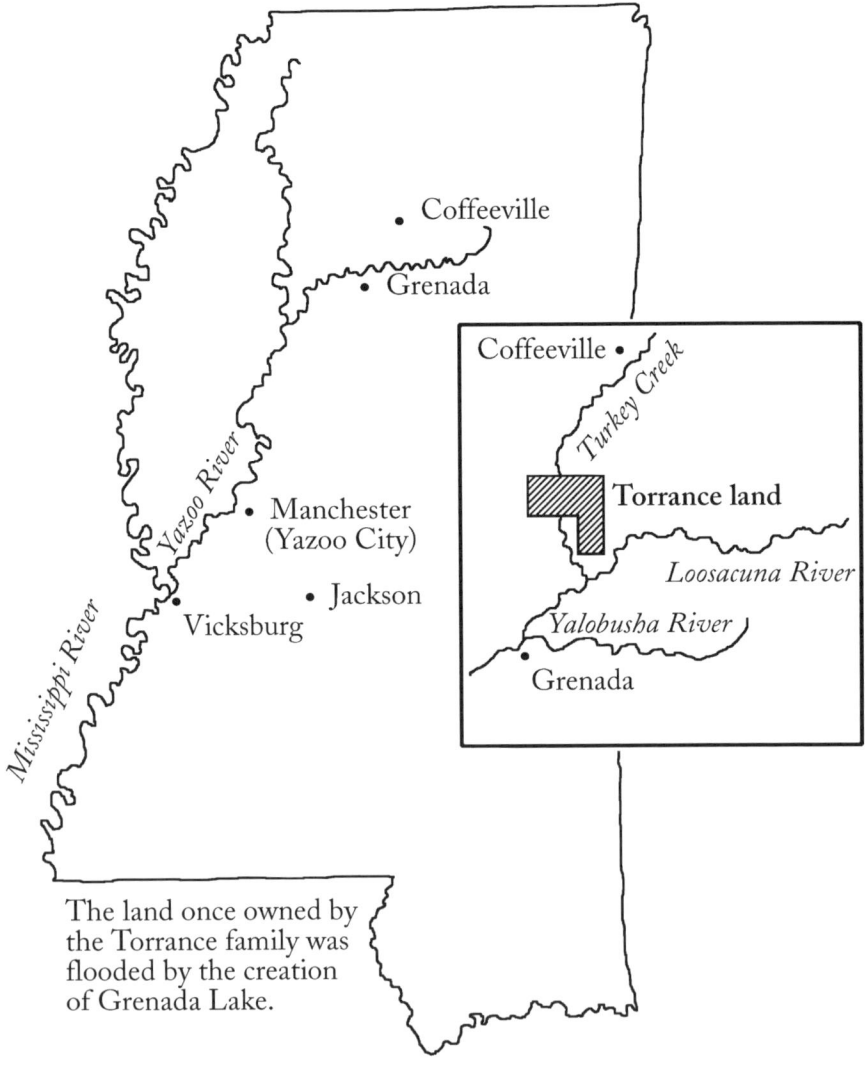

The land once owned by the Torrance family was flooded by the creation of Grenada Lake.

this road owing to the numbers of [wagons] was found in a horrid condition and we were so jolted as to occasion a great deal of scariness & fretfulness in little Jane who had hitherto retained her usual good humor. We arrived at Montgomery on Monday night and remained there until Wednesday morning when we left for this place in a steam boat and arrived here without any accident on Thursday night — We all have colds except which we are all well and Jane has almost entirely recovered from her little spell of fretfulness and laughs and crows with almost as much good humor as when we left home — We had considerable difficulties obtaining lodging here [the town being] so full at the present   [Among] the crowd [we were able to] find many of our old acquaintances among whom was Judge Martin & Lady, . . . R T Wilson, John Irwin &c &c   The weather has been cold and wet since our arrival in consequence of which we have been able to see but little of this town. It appears however to be a place of considerable trade although from a number of circumstances not so much as usual has been transacted this year as usual. Low rivers, the fall in cotton & broken factors have combined to prevent the farmers sending their cotton as early as formerly. Tomorrow we leave in the steam boat for New Orleans which after remaining a few days we will commence ascending the Mississippi & a few days reach our destination. So far Isabella says she is much pleased with the country and with the exc[eption of the] little fear of the [jolting] . . . [we] got along very [well] . . . She would have written herself tonight but has been spending the evening at Judge Martins and has been nursing Jane since her return. We will write again upon our arrival at Coffeeville. Isabella joins me in sending our love to all.

Yours   Franklin L. Smith

James was pleased that they completed part of their journey without accident and hoped to soon have similar news from his sons. He was alarmed, however, to read of the bleak business situation in Mobile. If the cotton factors were broke in Alabama, how could they expect to find buyers with funds in Mississippi? Was it too much to wish that they would abandon this project and return home?

As promised, Isabella wrote to Camilla at the first opportunity. She had finally experienced an adventure, and on the seventeenth of February she wrote her sister an account of it from Coffeeville, Mississippi:

Dear Sister

We arrived at this place a few days since after a long journey of six weeks as safe and well as when we left. Well here I am in a little log cabin with the wind blowing in at every crack (and they are numberless) with a large fire over one side a burning and the other freezing unless you have your cloak on and then your head gets it. After we left you we had delightful weather not a drop of rain on us and the Roads very fine   we went in our carriage as far as Columbus Georgia   there we left it to be sold and took the stage from there to Montgomery passing through the Creek nation over the worst road that I ever saw almost   there we stayed two days and I think it is a very handsome place,   from there we took the steamboat to Mobile we had a very pleasant trip taking us two days and two nights to go down there   we stayed two days but it was very wet and disagreeable so I had very little opportunity of seeing much of the city so I will not pretend to describe it   it does not look like the northern cities that is one thing certain. — We left there in a boat on Sunday about twelve oclock and got to New Orleans about five oclock the next morning where we found great difficulty in getting in   we staid there two days   It was very wet but I made out to see a part of the city any way   I assure you the pavements do not look like Philadelphia they are very muddy and I think it is the dirtiest looking place that I ever saw but I made out to get to the theater one night Caldwells as it is called. I had heard a great deal about it and I was anxious to see it — it is a very splendid building indeed   I cant give you an idea of it but in the centre of it is hanging the splendid chandelier that I had seen so much about in the papers but I must say that I was somewhat disappointed   I need not pretend to describe it to you only that it is so large that they have to have a ladder made of iron to go down into it to light it. After leaving New Orleans we came up the Mississippi on a very fine [boat] and as far as Manchester on the Yazoo and there we had [to] remain two or three days for want of a conveyance   at length a small boat came along and brought us within about forty miles of this place to a landing where we had to ride on horse back through a swamp seven miles through which beat any thing that ever you saw in your life   but through it we came Mr. Smith carrying the baby and me plunging in

*after him sometimes in above the horses knees but we got out safe
to a house on the other side where we staid all night and the next
day. We went to Governor Millers about four miles from there where
I staid until Mr. Smith came here and got brother Hugh's waggon
and came for me (the boys by the bye had beaten us here) I spent a
very pleasant time at Mr. Millers. When I came to the plantation I
found the boys eating out of tin pans without plates or knives and
forks and as happy as lords I intend going out there to live in a
week or two until I can get a house here Tell Minerva that Green
is dead and I expect that Maria will soon follow with the same
disease I have tried everything but nothing will do any good all
the rest are well. I went to a party last night and I never was at such
a place in my life the room was crowded and the greatest fuss and
confusion I ever was in in my life The gentlemen got into what I
call a real frolic while the ladies were there I cant give you any idea
of [it] at all. I sat perfectly astonished all the evening.*

*She grows very fast and stood her journey very well I believe
She is a great favorite where ever she goes. Mr Smith joins me in love
to you and William Kiss Willy for me and Jane Write to me soon
and often. I remain your affectionate Sister.*

Isabella M Smith

She reread her letter then added across the side of the page: "Frank wrote to you a week ago." She so hoped their letters were finding their way to the Carolinas. Of course she had never been to Philadelphia or any other northern city, but she had heard enough about that place to be sure it could not compare to the slough of New Orleans. She regretted having to pass along the news of sickness and death among the Negroes, but Camilla's Minerva would want to know. Thank goodness the rest of them were well.

Their land was in a place called the Loosascuna Valley, about five miles south of Coffeeville. It lay along Turkey Creek near its confluence with the Loosascuna River which joins the Yalobusha and then the Yazoo on its tangled path to the Mississippi. It was indeed pretty land. The hills rose higher than any in Mecklenburg and offered broad vistas of the valleys and farms. It was a great surprise that steep hills and swamps could be so intimately huddled together. Cleared land was covered with a layer of sand and tawny clay, much paler than that back home. But a shovel thrust nearly anywhere brought up soil as black as the heart of Satan. Fine crops could be gotten here. The gnarly oaks of the lower Mississippi had given way to a forest of hardwoods and longleaf pines. The familiar trees imparted a sense of home.

Isabella anticipated the hard work that would be required to clear the land and turn crude cabins into homes, and she expected to be poor for a while. But she had been completely shocked by the lack of civility among the western men and perplexed that the women abided it so well. There was much to learn about her adopted country. She had every confidence that their crop would turn a profit and that Mr. Smith would find them a comfortable home in town. In no time at all they would be influential and prosperous citizens of Coffeeville, and others would learn decorum by her example.

9 The West 1837~1838

In the winter of 1837, the settlers fell to their tasks with zeal, and soon crops were in the ground. Letters from Carolina began to arrive. They gathered like a clutch of hungry hens when they spied one of their number riding home from Coffeeville waving a letter high in the air. James wrote that the spring planting had gone well, but excessive dry weather was hampering its progress; last year's banner harvest would be hard to beat. He wrote of an unhealthy spring at Cedar Grove. Ma had been ill for much of February and March. The doctor had made several visits, sometimes staying the night to watch over her and the afflicted Negroes. He told them that the heavy investment of money and energy into Davidson College had borne fruit. In March, classes had commenced, and William had become the first in his family to attend college.

James quickly developed the habit of complaining about a lack of letters from the west. Were letters being lost along the way, or would no amount of writing satisfy their father? On the seventeenth of June 1837, Frank reported on their progress:

Dear Father

Since I wrote to you nothing of importance has transpired, our crop looks much more promising than it did a week since — cotton crops generally in this, and adjoining countys are rather backward for the season but I am inclined to think that they will be better than was expected a short time since. Corn looks very well, and promises to do well. We shall commence in a day or two to lay by our earliest corn, and cut our oats and then we shall have more time to work our cotton. Corn at this time is selling from $1.00 to 1.50 pe[r] bush[el] and very scarce in this neighborhood. We bought the most of our[s] for 1.00 [to] 1.12 pe[r] bush[el]. Our horses are thin but healthy. We have had but little sickness except bad coals yet and the country is generally healthy. So far we have had a fair season and promised to continue. A Mr. Grier from Steel creek in Mecklenburg spent a night with us a short time since on his way home   he has been looking for a place to locate himself. Dr. Wilson — that married Miss Carr is in this county and I believe he intends remaining here through the summer. Money is very scarce in this county but the presure is not as great at present as it has been — or as great here as it has been below in this state.

Mr Smith and Isabella intend going to Coffeeville to live in a short time. John Smith has gone to Pontitock to live, in the store of McDowell, &co formerly owned by P. Barringer &co. [33] *The news of the county is not such as will interest you   the people in this county as in all other county in this state are particularly fond of using the Bowye knife and fire arms — not less than four or five cases have occured in this county since we got hear in most of which som man has lost his life. I am sorry to hear that Ma has been so unwell but I hope she has recovered long before this. I was in hopes as you had such a dry season that you would have had a healthy one, but I am afraid it has not been the case. I have been confined for several days with a disentary but at present I think I am in a fair way to recover. Tell Ma that we have a bad garden to compare with hers — the bugs has eaten up all our cabbages and nearly every other plant in the garden except Beans and Potatoes and a few peas. we have venison every week and can catch a mess of fish in few minutes — at any time. Turkeys are plenty in the woods — but at present they are not good.*

When you write let me know if Jane is at home and if she intends going back to Salem,   Please let me know how William is getting along at the new colledge. I believe I have written you all that will interest you. Please let us hear from you soon. My love to all the family

Your Affectionate son

J F Torrance

Frank hoped his father would not be overly alarmed by the lack of money in this place. James's eyes were dark and deep set. Dark circles gathered around them when he was displeased. This image always came to Frank's mind when he thought about trouble with money. I told him there was no pressure, Frank thought; surely he should be satisfied. Which reminded him of his father's complaint about letters:

p.s.

I am sorry to see that you have not received but one or two letters from me since I left. I wrote several on the rode and since I got hear I written oftener than I did on the road. I think this is the third or forth since I got here   Your affec—

Son

Isabella vowed not to complain about their crowded conditions. The early weeks were cold and raw which kept them inside too much of the time. Now that the weather was warmer and the days had lengthened, the boys spent nearly every waking hour out of doors and out from under foot. Frank's recent bout of dysentery had been disagreeable; she hoped none of the rest of them would become infected. With Frank up and about she had more time to prepare proper nourishment, keep their clothes mended, and get the kitchen garden into better shape. This situation was reminiscent of the cramped life in the log house when Cedar Grove was being built. And like that time, a new house would be the reward at the end of it. She did not expect anything nearly so grand as Cedar Grove. Even Mecklenburg's more modest homes would look *grand* in Coffeeville. She simply wanted a house that was weatherproof and without beds in the parlor.

In June, Franklin Smith came home with exciting news. He had bought a home for them in Coffeeville where he would try once more to become a lawyer. "I am sure you will be pleased," he had said. "It's a home of generous proportion right in the center of town. The owner has agreed to sell it to me for sixteen hundred dollars, and we can move in shortly."

"Sixteen hundred dollars?!" Isabella was aghast. Such a sum would buy over a hundred acres of farm land, land that would produce income. "How on earth was it paid for?"

"I only had to pay half and took the rest on credit." He was so pleased with himself at granting his wife's fondest wish that she dared not protest further, yet she feared the prospect of becoming a burden to her brothers.

By the first of July Mr. Smith was ill. At first Isabella feared that the dysentery had returned, then his illness began to assume the nature of a mild fever. It was not yet the season for the miasmas borne by night air, but perhaps they arose earlier in this southerly swampy clime. On the fourth day the fever turned from mild to raging and attacked his lungs. Isabella stayed by his bedside with a pail of wet cloths to wash away his delirium. She frequently checked his limbs for rot where they had been scratched by ax and plow, and boiled kettles of herbs to soothe his painful lungs. Hugh went to Coffeeville for the doctor. But the man only bled him briefly and seemed not to have the sense of a fence post. On the sixth of July Mr. Smith drew his last tortured breath, and was finally at peace. They buried him in Coffeeville among strangers. Isabella was a nineteen-year-old widow with a child, a house and lot half paid for, and a six-week journey through wilderness between her and Ma.

Letters crossed paths in July. The ones traveling east carried the sad news of Franklin Smith; those bound west announced the birth of Camilla's daughter, born nine days after Mr. Smith's death. The consequences of Smith's poor judgment gradually began to arise. On the second of September 1837, Hugh wrote:

Dear Father

I received your letter of 11th August by the last mail. I was glad to hear that you were all well. I expected to hear that M^r. Smiths family were much distressed at the intelligence of his death   I am glad to hear that it had no serious effect on his mother. On account of her nervous and hysterical constitution I feared it would produce alarming effects   I forgot to write you in my last letter that it was Mr. Smith's wish that Isabella should return to N Carolina — She has not yet determined what she will do but if she concludes to leave she will not do so until next spring   I shall be very sorry if she goes back to stay — I shall feel lost here without her. It is not my intention to influence her in her decision — I wish her to go or stay as she may be most willing to do. I will do the best I can for her — If she returns I expect to go with her.

I am of opinion that I shall meet with some difficulties in settling the estate. There are more debts than I had any idea of more than there is means to pay without using some of Isabellas property and that I am determined not to do if it can be avoided — So far as I have acertained, there are debts to the amount of between three and four thousand dollars and only two negros to pay it with — except a house and lot in this place which he bought for $1600 half of which is paid   the balance due in one and two years. If his creditors will wait I can pay them all up in the course of two or three years   if they push for their money they will have to loose it unless they can get at Isabellas property by a law suit. I hope you will not say anything about this matter   it may create uneasiness and cause his creditors to press sooner — I will write you more particularly when I have gained all the information I can about the state of things.[34]

On the night of the 21st August we had a considerable storm it commenced blowing about 9 o'clock at night and lasted about an hour   it blew as if it would sweep off our cabins and everything else but we escaped without any damage except that done our crops — the corn and cotton crops so far as I have heard have been a good deal injured some suppose about one third   I do not think that ours is injured more that one sixth   You know that in this country they cut down very few trees on land   that is the reason why so much damage is done by the wind   I intend to begin this winter to cut down the dead timber   the crops will always be injured while they stand in the fields [with trees. We] will make this year forty [or so bales] of cotton and five or six [hundred] bushels of corn. This is a [fine] country for wheet   I know a man here who made 40 bu[shels] . . . This is a fine country for game   Deer [is] very plenty   A company of us went [out] the other day and killed eight. Our hunting company have killed about one hundred since I came here. Give my love to Ma and all the children   Tell William I have two fawns that I wish he could get.

   Your Affectionate Son
   Hugh Torrance[35]

all well

The news of Mr. Smith's death spread quickly through the family. In August Jane wrote from Salem:

Beloved Farther,
   I received your kind and affectionate letter a few days ago and was very sorry to hear of the death of M^r. Smith, the news came very unexpectedly; and also that Ma and aunt Betsy were sick but I hope they are better now. I am enjoying very good health at this time, and well satisfied. The academy was so crowded that we were obliged to take the Chapel for a room. We have now 8 rooms, 16 teachers and 100 girls. I am living in the 4th room (formerly the Chapel) with Miss Reede and Miss Belo. My piece in music is "Marsilles Hymn"   I think it is very pretty when well played. I have been waiting to receive a letter from brother William but have not received one yet, tell him I hope it will not be long before I receive one as he is at home now. When you write to me again, please tell me if Dr. McClain is going to bring Mary Linsey back or not, he said he would be here about the middle of June and he has not come yet. We have Bible questions to say to our teachers every Sunday evening and we go to Bible school every other Thursday and Mr. Jacobson teaches us. I have been expecting to receive a letter from aunt Betsy but have not received one yet, the reason is I suppose that she is unwell. We take

very pleasant walks when the weather will permit us accompanied with our teachers. When you write to me please tell me if you intend getting a teacher or not. Give my respects to M^r. and Mrs Williamson. Tell aunt Peggy Davidson I will write to her soon, give my best respects to her and aunt Sally. Tell Ma to write to me and I will answer her letters with pleasure. Give my love to her. Give my love to Grandma, aunt Betsy, Grandpa, uncle Rufus, and all of my cousins, brothers, and sisters, and inquiring friends and accept the same for yourself   from your Daughter

Jane

And in September, Camilla wrote:

Dear Father
    I have been expecting a letter from you for some time since but still have been dissapointed. I have been so unwell since the birth of my child that I have not been able to write. The news of Mr Smiths death came very unexpected to us and was very distressing, it is a great pity of Isabella. Brother Hugh writes that she is very much distressed they had but a short time to live together. I have not heard from them since we heard of his death, we are looking for a letter every day. There was a little boy died here on yesterday with the hooping cough he was just about the age of Willie (son of Saml Dinkins)   I am very much afraid of Willie and the baby getting it. I have been intending to go to see you, and will go as soon as I am able to ride that distance   We heard here a few days since that Mr Irwin's son Francis was very low with the fever   Mr Irwin sent for Mrs Blare and Mrs Write,   There has been a great many deaths this summer.
    The baby is very hearty and doing very well   we call it after cousin Margaret Smith. Willie is very fat and hearty and talks about going to N Carolina to see his Grand Pa Torrance. I hope you will write to me soon and let me know how you all are. Give my love to all of the family. Kiss the children for Willie & myself

Your Affectionate Daughter
Camilla

She carefully folded the letter, addressed it, and warmed the sealing wax. She dripped wax to hold the letter closed and pressed it with a seal. She would give the letter to William to pass on to his father. Robert Latta was making frequent trips to North Carolina; his father was gravely ill.

James was pleased to see Robert when he arrived at Cedar Grove but displeased to see the pain in his eyes. His countenance was always serious, but now it was overlaid with grim sadness. James ushered him into the study and poured them each a generous tumbler of brandy. "I have come with a letter from Camilla," said Robert, "and I am pleased to find you at home. A visit with an old friend is what I require the most, right now."

"How is your father?" asked James. "I have heard nothing good about his condition for some time now."

"I am afraid he will not be with us much longer; how he has tarried this long is more than I can comprehend. My mother continues to worry if she made the right decision when she moved him to Mount Mourne during the summer so that Betsy could help with the nursing. Father hardly knows who he is or where he is. At home his dementia had so frightened the Negroes that they refused to go to his bedside, and Mother is too slight to care for him by herself. Betsy has not proved to be much help; she languishes in her sickbed as often as not and is having great difficulty suckling her child. Betsy grumbles at me for not visiting enough, Father keeps to his bed staring blankly into the air, and Mother frets that she is imposing. At least they have Mr. Reid when a strong arm is needed.[36]

"Forgive me. I did not come here to wallow in my woes but to deliver condolences. We were so distressed to hear of Mr. Smith's demise."

"Thank you," said James. "We were likewise shaken by the news. I never admired that man, but certainly I did not wish his death."

"Has Isabella concluded to come home or remain in the west?"

"I wrote and offered to go fetch her, but apparently my offer fell upon deaf ears. Hugh writes that he intends to bring her home in the spring. I suppose she is still angry at my objection to her marriage and her leaving home. I grieve for Isabella, even though I am certain God composed this punishment for them. Tell me about Camilla. Has her health improved?"

"Not much. Here, read her letter; I'll carry back a reply if you wish." Robert sipped at his brandy while James read the letter.

"Aha," he said as he finished. "I see she has finally chosen a name for my new granddaughter. Margaret will suit well enough. It took her long enough to come up with it."

"William tells me she is a bit superstitious. She seems to have adopted that old custom of not naming an infant until its survival seems assured. "

"I suppose her own history has led her in that direction. Illness always fills her with dreading the worst," James replied. "Now, how can I be of help to you, my friend? Please tell Mrs. Latta to call on us for assistance. I would send Margaret, but she is too awash in infants to be of much help. Have you visited Reverend Williamson?"

"I have, and he is offering prayers." The men talked for a while longer. James decided not to burden his friend with Isabella's financial woes. The man had enough trouble of his own. Warmed by brandy and friendship, Robert left with a letter for Camilla.

James had no way of knowing his offer to fetch Isabella had crossed in the mail with Hugh's promise to bring her in the spring. It would be months before the misunderstanding was resolved.

On the twenty-sixth of September 1837, Frank wrote:

Dear Father

As the present opportunity has afforded me the pleasure of writting to you again I shall let you know how we are getting on since brother Hugh wrote which was after the receipt of your last. Since that we have had a good deal of sickness in the family and several unwell at this time. I have just recovered from an attack of the fever which confined me about a week. I have been much better since than I had been for sometime before, but have not gained my strength. Brother Hugh has been very unwell today, he has been complaining for several days before, but was not much sick untill today. I believe it is nothing more than his old complaint, (the liver) I think he will be able to be about in a few days. Jane has also been unwell but it was caused from teething   she [is] well at this time

We commenced picking cotton on the 25 of this month (two days ago)   cotton crops is going to [be] very light in this county, this season, if we should have a late frost we shall make something more than half crops   we have a fine corn crop and shall be able to spare about four thousand bushels which will be worth $1.00 per bushel by spring. . . . corn is selling at this time for 75 [to] 87 from the heap. There is considerable excitement in the county at this time in regard to the coming elections, which take place in November   In this state the people elect all the officers from the judge of circuit court down. At this time there is about 30 candidates before the people to fill twelve vacancies.

I received a letter from Jane a short time since and she improves very fast. Isabella says she will write to you in a short time.

The interest on our note with M^r. Campbell will be due about the middle of December and we shall not be able to get there to pay it, and we promised him faithfully to pay the interest as soon as it would become due. We have no funds there and shall have no opportunity of getting it. Unless you would get the sum which will be three hundred dollars and have it paid over to M^r. Campbell and brother Hugh will return it to you when he goes to Carolina next spring with the interest. We would be willing to pay whatever the money may cost if it should be more than the regular percent. If you can make any arrangement to pay the money it will confer a great favor on us and will be gratefully acknowledged. I should be glad to hear from you as soon as convenient and know if you would be willing to attend to it. Hugh would have written to you if he had been able. My love to Mother and the rest of the family. Also my respects to M^rs and M^r. Williamson.

Your most affectionate Son,
James F Torrance

N B   I have been expecting an opportunity to see Mr Davidson to know if he knew anything of the papers concerning your land in Tenn. but have not had an opportunity. When I write to you again I hope I shall be able to give you some information

I have not been able to have the taxes paid for this year, and I am afraid I shall not be, unless Hugh or myself goes up to buy pork for the next year. There is a good many persons passing from here to Tenn., but I have not heard of any going to that part of the state.

Yours
J F Torrance

The next day while in Coffeeville, Frank heard that Mr. John Smith would be in the area any day now on his way back to Mecklenburg. Frank decided to hold on to his letter in the event that Smith would be able to carry it. That method would probably be faster and more certain than the mail. Hugh's health improved, and on the second of October, he wrote a letter to be included in John Smith's packet:

Dear Father
I take the opportunity of writing you a few lines by John Smith who will start in the morning for N Carolina. He would have started on last Thursday but after starting he found that the conveyance he

*had procured to take him to Columbus would not take him there so he
came back — I have authorized John Smith to try to get $300 for us
to pay the interest on our note with Camble which will be due on the
first of Decr We promised to pay the interest every year, if we do so
he will let us have the money for as long as we want it — We can
send no money from this country that will answer the purpose   If
you have the money to spare I will pay you next spring or if you will
borrow the money and give your note for it I will lift it in the spring
— If you can assist Smith in any way to get the money so that he can
pay Camble for us — you will do us a favor that will not be forgotten*

   *Since I wrote you last there has been several cases of fever in the
neighborhood — Frank had a slight attack but has got well   he was
sick only a few days — I have been sick three or four days with an
attack of my old complaint — the first I have had since I left
Carolina — We are all well now   The people through this country
are busy fielding out cotton and pulling corn*

     Give my love to Ma and all the children

       Your Affectionate Son

       H Torrance

The fact that two letters arrived in one packet added to James's discomfort over his sons' affairs. Their crops were only partly gathered and not yet sold, and the money was due. It was common knowledge that money from one state might not pass in another; he had warned his sons, and they had not listened. Perhaps Campbell should bear some of the blame for this sorry condition; he was well aware of the situation in Mississippi. On the other hand, the economy everywhere had taken a hard turn in the past year. James put the letters aside; his mind was on other matters. On the thirtieth of October, James Latta had died in the middle of the night at his daughter's home in Mount Mourne. The long struggle was at last ended. He was buried at Hopewell near his son Ezekiel and his daughters Polly and Nancy. He was eighty-two years old.

In mid-November, Rufus Reid paid a visit to James. He brought with him a correspondence he had received from John Campbell. "Hugh told me that I was to defer this matter to you," said Rufus. "I am not aiming to dismiss my responsibility in it; I will abide by your wishes."

"Hugh was correct," said James. "I did ask him to come to me if trouble developed with this. And it appears my predictions are being realized."

James read the missive:

Dear Sir

Yours of the 6th Instant has been received   the Note alluded to was dated 29th November 1836 so of course one years interest will be due on the 29th instant   the money deposited in the Bank at Salisbury in my name will suite me extremely well   South Carolina Notes has nearly ceased to circulate amongst us   Mr. Torrance will have to pay in North Carolina Notes any time between this and the first of January will suit me —

  Mount Vernon   Nov the 11th   1837

     John Campbell

Rufus Reed, Esqr.

James turned back to his visitor. "How is Mrs. Latta faring? Is she still at your place?"

"She is at present, but she plans to return to her home in the near future. Her faith has been her greatest comfort. She knows firmly that Mr. Latta is with God and at peace. I have never known a woman to dwell so single-mindedly on the Bible and its teachings; now I understand that it was not for naught." Then Rufus began to smile. "It seems that when God takes one life, he gives another. My Betsy expects another child in the spring."

"This will come at a good time for Mrs. Latta," said James. "Nothing brings cheerfulness to a woman like a grandchild. I suggest a toast to a healthy birth with some of that excellent brandy you recently sold me."

James thought long and hard over Campbell's note. Perhaps he should give his sons the benefit of it. A year is a short time to clear new land and get a crop sold. On the twelfth of December, he paid Campbell three hundred dollars. He would keep an accounting; this was a loan, not a gift.

The crop at Cedar Grove was good that year, and James had done all he could from this distance for his children in the west. He was determined to put illness, death, and debt behind him and engage in indulgence.

"Margaret, I want you to go with me to Charleston when I take the cotton to market. Prices are reported to be quite favorable, and 'tis time you permitted yourself some luxury."

"That sounds like a fine idea. Are you planning to take all of us, or is this a journey for you and me alone?"

"We shall hardly be alone. It will take at least four more drivers to get our cotton to that place. The children, however, should be left here. Flora is quite capable of directing their care. We should only be gone a fortnight, not a long journey at all."

Margaret was delighted at the prospect. As much as she loved her children, some respite from their care would be welcome. This was the first time since their marriage that she had been without a babe at the breast or a large one in the belly, and there were plenty of Negroes to help Flora with the little ones. William should be home from college by the time they returned, on Christmas Eve if all went as planned. Jane was unaware of their plans; her letter arrived too late for them to comply with her wishes:

Salem Dec 15th, 1837
Beloved Father,

I have been looking for a letter from some of you for a long time but have not received one yet I will therefore write to you   I am enjoying very good health at this time and hope you all are enjoying the same. My piece in music is "Theres not a word thy lip hath breathed"; I like music very much and will try to improve in it as fast as I can, as well as my other studies; because I know the faster I learn the sooner I will get home. We have a dialogue to recite at Christmas and I have a part in it, I wish very much that you would come to see me at that time if you can. Please let me know in your next letter, when you heard from sister Isabella and brothers Hugh and Franklin. I have not received a letter from any of them in a long time   what can be the cause of their not writing I cannot tell. You must not look for another letter from me before Christmas as I expect the school will be out next week. Please send me some money as I will need some at Christmas to get something then. The weather is very cold and there is snow on the ground at this time. Let me know in your next letter when you heard from sister Camilla and if she is well;

she has not written to me in a very long time. Tell Aunt Betsy and Grandma to write to me oftener and I will answer their letters with pleasure and I hope you will also write to me oftener as you know that I am always anxious to hear from home. Give my best respects to Mr and Mrs Williamson and tell them I would be glad to see them. Give my love to Ma, Grandma, Aunt, brother William and all my friends and acquaintances and accept the same for yourself

Your Affectionate daughter

Jane

December in Charleston exceeded their expectations. Cotton and rice had poured untold sums of money into that elegant city. Church street boasted extravagant homes with enclosed gardens and second-floor piazzas perched to receive the river breezes. They took walks along White Point and admired the splendid homes that overlooked the harbor. Some were old, some new, and some under construction. It amazed Margaret that so many homes as grand or grander than Cedar Grove could be in one place. At the theater she could not decide if the entertainment or the latest fashions delighted her more. Such a concentration of wealth and sophistication was a sharp contrast to Mecklenburg.

Their cotton brought a fine price. In two days they spent over two hundred and fifty dollars on a bounty of goods. They bought silk gloves, silk hose, and yards of silk cloth and other sumptuous fabrics. Margaret bought a lovely watered silk dress for thirty dollars and two cloaks of the softest merino wool that were nearly as dear. Embroidered collars and ascots were the height of fashion—several were purchased. Of course many of these things would be Christmas gifts for the children. Over the years the celebration of Christmas had become more festive and gifts more lavish. Some in the church were not pleased.

On the twentieth of December James made a decision. "Margaret," he said, "with all of this finery, I believe we should go home in style. I propose getting a new carriage. I doubt there are any to be had in Charlotte that are as fashionable as these in Charleston."

"You are determined to display your wealth," she said with a laugh.

"Determined to enjoy it, I say. We both work hard and put up with all manner of inconvenience over which we have no control. We have earned some pleasure."

A fine brass-trimmed chariot was purchased for two hundred seventy-five dollars. At the tack shop they bought a brass coach harness and a horse collar—they would indeed travel in style. As they left Charleston, they

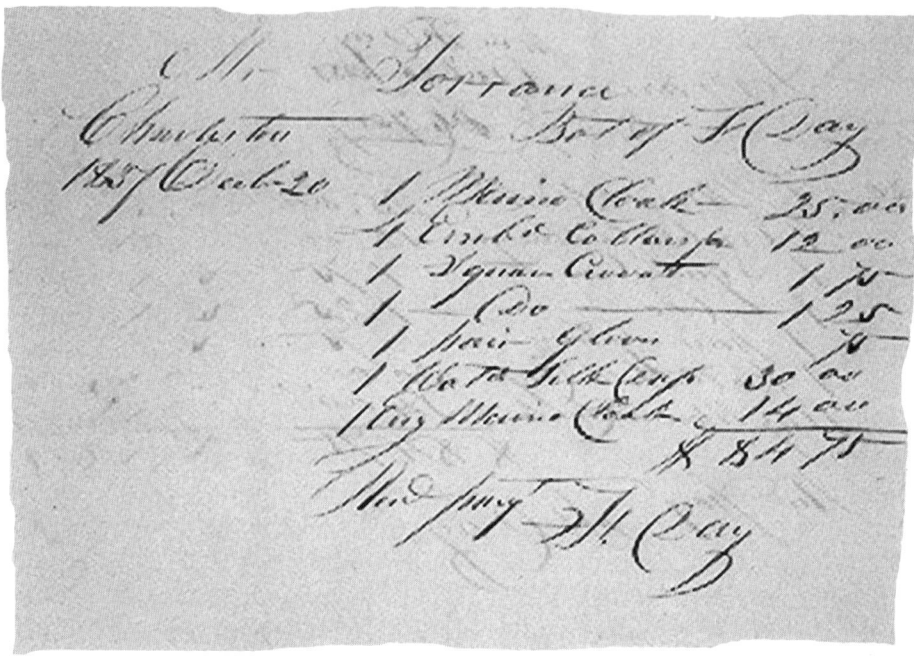

bought two gallons of lamp oil to light their way home, ensconced in the opulent aroma of silk.

~   ~   ~

In the west the idea of such luxury was a faded memory. As the second year in the alien country dawned, the boys still struggled to coax an income from their land. The numbness caused by her husband's death receded, and Isabella realized that her father had not come west because of Hugh's promise, a promise he could no longer keep. Homesickness enfolded her. On the nineteenth of January 1838, she wrote:

Dear Father

I was very much disappointed indeed in the fall when I heard that you had given out coming for me, on the reception of Brothers letter, but I do assure you my dear father that it was entirely a mistake all around. In the first place we received a letter from you stating that you would come for me if it was necessary and before we received that letter from you I had written to you. When brother received your letter (none of us thought that you would come out in the fall) and he asked me what I intended doing I told him that as long as I was here I thought that I had better stay until spring for I thought he could take me then without putting you to any trouble. I do assure you my dear father that it was not because I did not want you to come out here and I hope you will not think so, for I was rejoiced when I received your letter at the idea of seeing you so soon, and had made every preparation for leaving in about two weeks after I got your letter; and now my dear father I hope you will forgive me if I have offended you in any way for I take my Maker to wittness that I did it innocently if I have — I find that it will [be] utterly impossible for me to get to Carolina in the spring unless you will come for me or fix on some plan for me to get home. Times are very hard, money scarce and things high, we have a number of horses to buy besides other things

We lost that black mare you gave Frank, the last day of last year she had been on a decline for some time and nothing we could do for her appeared to do her any good. We are all well and are getting along very well on the farm; we have a new overseer that seems to understand his business very well; we have one field that is clear of trees and it appears to be quite a curiosity here. we have had a very fine winter very little rain or cold weather and no snow but when it is cold it is almost impossible to keep warm no matter how large a fire we have   our cabins are so open that the wind whistles in every direction, but I think it is very wholesome for I have not had even a cold this winter. My little girl grows very fast, and is beginning to talk very well. —

Tell Ma I have been selling some butter and I get as much for one pound as she does for four, half a dollar a pound is the common price, they had a ball in Coffeeville Christmas and had to give that much for all the butter they got. — I have very little to write, I stay very close at home and hear nothing; but I hope you will write to me soon and let me know if you can come for me; tell Ma that I have been looking for a letter from her for some time. Brothers Hugh and Frank join me in love to you and the children. Frank says he will write to you soon. Give the children a kiss for Jane and me. —

I remain your affectionate daughter
Isabella M Smith

In a small way she did not wish for her father to come for her. She knew he would be disappointed in the way they were living, and she had grown tired of being the source of his disappointment. But she could no longer rely on Hugh to take her in the spring. There was too much work and no money for it. She hoped her letter would prepare her father for their circumstances. Any embarrassment was eclipsed by overwhelming loneliness; at least there was no shame in poverty.

On the seventh of February, Hugh wrote:

Dear Father

I received your letter of January 5th a few days ago. I was pleased to hear that Mas health had improved. I hope that by the time this reaches you that she will have entirely recovered — I was also glad to hear that you made a good crop — I think I wrote you what we made 31 bales of cotton weighing an average of 480 and 4000 bu[shels] of corn — We have losed six horses since we came here — Mules suit this climate much better than horses — We have had a very mild winter until within a week — the ground was frozen for four days and we had a little snow but not enough to cover the ground. This weather would not be called cold where you live but — we call it so here — The weather changed yesterday It is now quite warm — We are making preparations for a crop. I expect to plant 150 acres of cotton — I wish you could be here in June to see the crops — If you could I think you would be tempted to leave your clay hills — I am convinced that your negros would make you more here in one year (after the first) than you can make there in three — Our land will produce from 1,000 to 1,500 pounds of cotton to the acre — a hand can work eight acres and will bring about 12,000 pounds if well worked — I have a negro in the woods — he may attempt to go back though I cannot tell. It is Dick I undertook to whip him a few days ago and when I called him up he took to the woods — He is a great rascal — If I ever get him I will sell him — for I believe he will spoil every negro we have if I keep him.

Isabella wrote to you before I received your letter that she would go to Carolina in the spring if you would come for her. She is anxious to return — she has no female friends here and she has a lonely time — We would all be glad to see you here — If you can possibly leave home and come here — I know you will be pleased with our situation We have as fine a plantation as any in this country — You seem to fear that we have forgotten you — I hope you will not indulge that notion — for you may rest assured that you will never be forgotten by any of us while life lasts — I would rather not live than live such a wretch as I know I would be if I forgot my father or my duty to him.

I will write to you again shortly. Frank will write in a few days. We are all well. Give my love to Ma and the children and remember me to all friends.

Your affectionate Son
H Torrance

Isabella read her brother's letter before he took it to town for mailing. His picture was much rosier than hers. She supposed he wanted their father to be proud of their accomplishments, yet that rosy view was not so far from truth in Hugh's eyes. He had little use for creature comforts, and his enthusiasm for the future of this place could hardly be contained. She heaved a sigh of dismay over Dick's rash behavior. Surely the man could not have been so stupid to think that a runaway could find his way back to Cedar Grove. He was certain to be found and sold, probably down river into circumstances she would rather not imagine. Only a cruel or desperate master would take on a known troublemaker. What insanity had gotten into Dick's mind? Isabella, of course, had no concept that Dick longed for his Carolina family as urgently as she ached for hers.

As usual, James continued to complain about the scarcity of letters from the west. This was a source of great frustration for his children; they were trying their best to be dutiful. On the first of March 1838, Frank wrote:

Dear Father

Sum time has elapsed since I wrote to you, but I have no doubt but you have received several letters from us since I wrote or ought to have, if the mails have been regular. Little of interest has occured in this family since brother Hugh wrote. We have enjoyed unusual good health for the season, and are getting along well cleaning up and preparing for another crop. We had a severe snow storm which lasted several days last month and some unusual cold weather for this climate. I believe I felt the cold as sensibly here as I did in the North — the people here ware much thicker clothing than they do farther north, heavy blanket coats are mostly used, or sum other heavy cloath. People of this climate are more subject to coulds and pleurisys than they are further north and the latter disease is generally very fatal. I believe we have as much sickness here in the winter as in the summer, the weather is very changable, indeed one day we may have ice half an inch thick and the next will be warm to do without your coat. Brother Hugh is at Vixburg at this time and will probably go . . . before he returns to collect the money for the notes Mr Smith traded with Mr Springs. [37] *We have collected about half of it and I am afraid we will have some difficulty before we can get the balance, this is the third trip for it. Money is scarce and difficult to get. The banks are discounting very little and will probably discount less before the year is half gone. Cotton has been selling for 10 cts here and from 11 1/2 to 12 in New Orleans. Some of the planters shipped to Liverpool and got about 14 cts neat which is much better than selling in N. Orleans. What little we made we shipped to Liverpool — how long it will be before we get a return is very doubtful. We intended planting a larger crop this year, and as we have our land in better order. I have no doubt but we will make a much better crop. I heard from Charlotte a few days since, which stated your family was well I am glad to hear that you have all got well. I hope it will not be long before we shall have the pleasure of seeing you in Missi. Nothing would do me more good or afford me more pleasure than to see you, and do most sincerely wish that nothing may either happen to detain or prevent you from coming. Isabella has been busy for some time so as to be ready when you come. Jane grows finely and is a great deal of company to us. You will find the road a little rough I am afraid before you get here as we have had considerable quantity of rain of late. If you should come through Tennessee you had better come through Holly Springs and Oxford to avoid sum bad swamps and if you should come from the southern route your best route would be, when you get to Columbus Mi to come direct to Granada and the road from there to where we live is good.*

My love to mother and all the family
Your affectionate
Son James F Torrance

Among Isabella's preparations was the dedication of Franklin Smith's grave. She had ordered a stone for him which had finally arrived in Coffeeville by stage. On a day when the sun broke through, she and her brothers went to town to collect the stone and set it in its place. The cemetery was on a hilltop at the edge of town, and Mr. Smith's grave was near its highest point. If eyes can see from a world beyond, he would forever enjoy the sight of green hills and fertile valleys. They set the stone at the head of his plot. Isabella stepped back and was pleased with her selection. It lacked the grandeur of many monuments at Hopewell, including the mammoth ones of her Torrance grandparents, but it exceeded most anything in this place. The two-and-a-half-by-four-foot slab of granite was carved with crisp block letters: [38]

ISABELLA SMITH
TO THE MEMORY
OF
HER HUSBAND
FRANKLIN L. SMITH
A NATIVE OF
CHARLOTTE N C
BORN JAN. 24, 1807
DIED JULY 6TH 1837

～　　　～　　　～

The news of James's impending visit to the west was broadcast about the countryside. Camilla had given up on going herself; worry about illness had tunneled her mind into a narrow place. On the tenth of March, she wrote her father:

Dear Father

I have been prevented from writing to you on account of my child having the Hooping cough, she had it quite severe for some time, but I am in hopes she is over the worst the changes in the weather affect her very much Willie has escaped so far. We received a letter from Brother Hugh dated 10th of February saying that they were all well and that they had received a letter from you saying that you would be out there in the spring. I should like very much to see you before you go, but I am afraid that I shall not be able to do so. We have had a good deal of sickness here and it has generally been very fatal, there was a gentleman died here about 10 days or two weeks ago, who from all appearances seemed to be a very stout and hearty man he was taken with a chill and it turned to the Typhus fever he gradually got worse every day for about two weeks when he died he left a wife in a very desolate condition he had no children We have had very bad weather for some time and on the first day of

March we had a deep snow   it did not remain on the ground very long. We had some very mild weather before the snow. I had some gardening done the last of February. We planted potatoes and several other vegetables. We have certainly had a very strange winter. Grandma told me that William looked very bad   she said worse than she had ever seen him. I have not heard from Jane for some time. I hope you will write soon and let me know how all are. I do not hear from you as often as I would like   the child grows and Willie talks a great deal [about] his friends in N Carolina   Give my love to all of the family   Kiss the children for Willie and me

Your Affectionate

Daughter Camilla

James knew he should write to Camilla more frequently, but her replies were always filled with unnecessary gloom. He found it ironic that this dutiful pampered child was so steeped in dread, while Isabella could find a cold cabin wholesome and take pride in selling her butter. He would write to

Camilla and assure her that William was again in good health and would begin his third term at the college in another week.

Meanwhile James was having second thoughts about going for Isabella. Frank's information about the swamp was disconcerting; swamps were a source of deadly fevers. His brother-in-law, Frank Davidson, was planning a trip to the west. James tried to convince him to go for Isabella as he would pass near by; but Frank was not eager to do so. He traveled frequently to the western edge of Alabama where he had business interests. He usually went by stage at breakneck speed, covering the entire distance in less than two weeks.[39] Herding a widow and infant back to Cedar Grove did not fit his mission.

James turned a deaf ear to Frank's protest. He informed Isabella of her uncle's plan and suggested that would be her best opportunity for getting home. If by chance, Frank didn't make it to their place, he would come for her in the fall. It would suit him better to travel in a healthier season anyway. James was also unsure if Isabella was truly repentant enough to be welcomed into his fold. Margaret voiced the opinion that it was not for him to judge.

Camilla wrote on the eighth of April:

Dear Father

I received your letter about a week ago and was glad to hear that you were all well. Uncle Frank passed through here on Wednesday going to the west, I was very sorry that he could not make it convenient to go for Isabella as he was going so near to their place, I have not heard from them lately. Uncle Frank onley stayed with us an hour or two. We have had a great deal of sickness here this spring, and several deaths. Mr. Samuel Chambers died here on last Thursday night with the fever he was sick but a short time, we have had a great many instances lately, how short and uncertain life is. You did not mention when you expected to start for the west. I am afraid that I shall not be able to see you before you go to the West. We expect to go out to the place this week I expect to be out there a great deal this summer. I hope you will write to me often, direct your letter to Yorkville. Jim came down on Thursday to see Cintha and I concluded that I would write a few lines to you by him. We are all well. give my love to all kiss the children for Willie and me. I have nothing more but remain,

> *your affectionate daughter*
> *Camilla*

She folded her page, pressed a waxen seal to the overlap, turned it over and wrote, "Mr. James G Torrance, Mecklenburg, NoCa. Per Boy Jim."

Jim delivered the letter that very evening. It was Sunday, and the master was bound to be at home. "Good evening, sir," he said when James came to the door. "I been at Yorkville to stay with my Cintha, and Mrs. Latta asked me to carry a letter to you." Jim handed over the paper with an obliging toothy grin, because smiles were expected of black people; but his eyes were veiled in sorrow, anticipating loneliness. Jim belonged to a nearby farmer; when Cintha had lived at Cedar Grove it had been convenient for him to court and marry her. Cintha was Camilla's now and had been taken with her to Yorkville. Three-day visits every now and again were a luxury in many Negro marriages.

James hoped that a summer spent at the plantation on Bullock Creek would be good for Camilla and improve her outlook. In spite of her gloominess, she was correct that life was uncertain. James did long to see Isabella and his little granddaughter. Perhaps Margaret was right, and it was time to abandon his harshness.

He still held slight hope that Frank Davidson would have a bout with his conscience and decide to fetch Isabella after all. He saw no way he could go himself before fall. He wrote to Isabella to tell her of it. It was a soft moment in which he wrote—he extended forgiveness.

Isabella was overcome by her father's kind words. All the hardships suffered and deprivation endured were trifling compared to the loss of her father's approval. For the first time she felt he might once again grace her with acceptance. She was still insecure about her welcome at Cedar Grove. Camilla had offered to take her in; that might be her best situation if she could only find the means to get there. On the fourth of July 1838, she wrote a letter in which she opened her heart to her father:

Dear Father

I received your letter about a week since and take the first opportunity of answering it, since I received it Brother Hugh has been quite unwell he had a slight attack of his old complaint, this is the second one he has had this summer. I have had a slight attack of intermittent fever the first I have had since I have been in the country. We have had a good deal of sickness this spring but I think it was owing to the water, we have a well now and have not had a case of sickness since we commenced using it. — Pa, if it is at all inconvenient for you to come for me in the fall, I should be very sorry to think that I was the cause of any more trouble to you; and I beg

*of you not to put yourself to any trouble for me. Pa you say that I
have never yet expressed a wish about where I should live, I have not
for I did not know what to do   I have spent many an hour thinking
where it would be best for me to live   I have thought sometimes that
it would be best for me to remain here; but my inclination leads me
back to my native state. You have a large family without me and my
poor child and sister has twice written to me to come and make my
home at her house   but I have never yet written to her whether I
would or not   I thought I would write to you and see what you
would say about it. Dear father you well know how much trouble I
have been to you   I was young thoughtless and headstrong but
thank God I have learned to take things more patiently and have got
more experience in the ways of the world although it has been dearly
bought; you say you forgive me for the past (for which I thank you
with all my heart) and hope that I will bury all bad feelings but I can
say with truth that I bear no ill will against any person on this earth.
I expected to live among my friends in general when I returned and
having but one own sister I thought it would suit us both if I were
to make my home there; but I will abide by whatever you say. and
now my dear father if I have said anything to offend you in this
letter I do most sincerely hope you will forgive me for I assure you it
was not intentional. We have a tolerable good appearance of a crop
although we have had a very backward season   our cotton looks
very well   we found some blooms two or three days ago for the first.
Tell Ma I can beat her making butter   I have made about twenty
five dollars in the last two months selling butter   I get 25 cents a
pound now. — tell Ma and aunt Jane I should be very glad to see
them here. Brothers join me in love to you ma and all the children and
a kiss to them for Jane and me.*

> *I remain your*
> *ever affectionate daughter*
> *Isabella M. Smith*

Isabella found herself surprised at how much she missed Aunt Jane, Ma's
younger sister. She could not imagine her aunt's face without a broad smile
draped across it. She found humor and joy in all she encountered. She was a
frequent visitor at Cedar Grove, being a favorite of Ma's. Letters from Mecklenburg often had sparkling little notes added by Aunt Jane, which always

caused laughter. Her beau, Mr. Carson, seemed quite taken with the idea of moving west. Isabella longed to have such a cheerful soul among them.[40]

It was some time before Isabella had a reply to this plea for peace with her father. It was not James's reluctance to invite her home but his health that prevented his writing. The summer and fall of 1838 gripped James and many on the plantation with one dreadful malady after another. At the apothecary he bought Peters Pills, Epsom salts, castor oil, and Spanish flies, but none of them lived up to their promises. He had been advised to use quinine to keep his asthma in check. He hoped the advice was good, for once an attack began, the treatment was horrid and debilitating, keeping him weak and confined for days. The farming also suffered; his crop that year was only tolerable.

He had also delayed in sending Isabella the intelligence of Betsy Reid's death. Betsy had carried this latest child with great difficulty, having been troubled for some time by an acid stomach. She piled bolsters in her bed to keep her upright, but the bile still rose in her throat and burned it raw. Even the softest pap scraped her throat like sandpaper. She had long since given up nursing Bettie; what strength she could muster seemed to drain away with her milk. Her weak body was no match for the brute force of expelling an infant. On the fourth of May, while delivering a stillborn child, Betsy's abscessed throat ruptured and by nine that night she had bled to death. [41]

Mr. Reid was nearly overwhelmed by the number of children in his care. Betsy's six sons from her marriage to Wilson Davidson were growing up. Several of the older boys repaired to Oaklawn, the grand home their father had built. They declared they could live on their own. Ben, at nine, was the youngest Davidson boy. His Uncle Robin and Aunt Peggy Davidson offered to take him in. They loved children, and God had not blessed them with their own. Robin was Wilson's brother and had remained close to his fatherless nephews. Betsy's mother, Jane Latta, had given up trying to manage her plantation. She had spent much of the past year at Mount Mourne first nursing her husband, then Betsy; it now seemed sensible for her to make her home there and care for her grandchildren. Betsy's middle sons were in their early teens, Nancy's daughters were five, seven, and eight, and Betsy's dear little Bettie Reid was barely two. Jane Latta did not consider it proper to live under the roof of her newly widowed son-in-law. A small house across the road suited quite well.

When some measure of health returned to the Torrance household, James wrote to Isabella explaining himself and giving some hope that he might visit them should he continue to heal. He had never seen the land in Tennessee left to him by his father. He had often longed to go there and see for himself the nature of it. Isabella also received a letter from Camilla stating that she and William planned to visit them in the winter when the crops were in. She looked forward to the journey and seeing their land and prayed daily that poor health would not prevent their getting off. On the eighteenth of October 1838, Isabella wrote to her father:

Dear Father

I received your kind letter a few days ago and take the first opportunity of answering it. I am truely sorry to hear that you have had so much sickness this summer and fall I hope by this time that you have all recovered. We have been very healthy here this year I have not heard of a dozen of cases of fever this year. You want me to let you know what I should like to do   weather go on or remain here   I think as sister is coming out I should rather stay as she will be an entire stranger here if I leave and I know very well the feelings of a person that is a stranger in a new country. I shall be very certain to visit Carolina next summer for I am very anxious to see you all I can scarcely refuse going this winter, but I know so well the feelings that sister would have

My dear father I do hope that if you come to Tennessee you will come down and see us   see how you like our place and how we are fixed, and all about us; I flatter myself with the hope that you _will_ come down and see us if you get that far on the road, we would all be so glad to see you.—

The Methodists held a camp meeting about two miles from us last week but their meeting was conducted like everything else is in this state   no regularity whatever — laughing and talking can be heard during service from every quarter they have very poor preachers here indeed   I wish very much that I could hear one of our good preachers Occasionally we [hear of good] preaching but very seldom near us

Fall seems to have set in in earnest and very early   we had frost here the first of this month to kill the cotton and last year it was not until the 15th a good deal of difference. I am in great hopes that we shall make a fairly good crop of cotton this year   we have about twenty five bales picked out. We are very busy putting up a gin house now   it is rather late in the season but we could not get at it sooner.

I was sorry to see the death of cousin Gilly McKnight in the last Charlotte Journal   aunt Peggy has only one son left   that is the fourth one of our relations that has died there since I left   death makes its ravages everywhere   Times are very hard here   money is not only worthless and scarce but provisions are scarce and very high we have been without flour for nearly four months we and are now completely out of bacon, but I am in hopes [of getting some soon] . . .

I hope I shall see you all in the spring

I remain your
affectionate daughter
Isabella M Smith

It did not surprise Isabella that her father had not written about the death of Gilly McKnight. Aunt Peggy McKnight was one of the infamous Falls women, and James still kept his distance from them. Before Isabella folded and sealed the letter, Frank added a note of his own:

Dear Father

I suppose [you] think [that you are] forgotten from my not writing to you before this, but I can assure you it is not the case The reason was I expected to hear by every mail that you had left for Miss. and I thought it would not be received before you left. I have been greatly disappointed and grieved to hear that you have had so much sickness in your family. I hope when we hear again that you are all in good health. If I can be of some service to you in Tennessee let me know and I will attend to it with pleasure. It is not necessary for you to go all the way to Lauderdale Co. the balance due can be sent from here.   my love to all

Affectionately

Son Frank

Sickness caught up with James once again and kept him confined. Jane was also concerned and wrote from Salem on the eighth of November:

My Dear Father

Thinking that you have given up the idea of visiting me this fall, I will write to you and would have done so sooner but have been looking for you since I received your letter which was in September. I received a letter from Grandmother a few weeks ago and she said if you should come to see me, it was very uncertain whether she could come or not, but I hope you will try to persuade her to come for I am very anxious to see her. I am enjoying very good health as are also Dovey and Amanda. My piece in music is "Fly to the desert". If you do not come here before the middle of this month, please to have my clothes sent to me by the stage, or let me get them here. When you answer this letter let me know when you heard from sisters Isabella and Camilla and if they are well; I have not received a letter from either of them for a considerable length of time. I have been very uneasy thinking that you would write to me before this time if you were not prevented from doing so by sickness. Please to ask Margaret and Letitia if they have forgotten what they promised me when I left home. Tell brother I think he is very slow about answering my letter.

I heard that M^r. Williamson was very sick and not expected to live, when you write again tell if he is better, and give my best respects to him also M^rs. Williamson and Miss H. White. I expect Miss Chrisst will return from the North in about a week and take her place in the academy again. I will try to write to someone of you once a month and I hope to hear from you as often. Tell Ma I have been looking for a letter from her for some time and hope it will not be long before I receive one. Give my best respects to Uncle Robin and Aunt Peggy Davidson and tell them I would be glad to hear from them at any time. Do dear Father, write to me soon after you receive my letter, and tell me if you intend coming to see me or not. Dovey and Amanda join with me in love to you, all of their relations and friends. Give my love to Grandmother, Ma, brother and all of my dear relations and friends. Having nothing to write that would be interesting to you I will conclude my letter. May the blessings of Heaven attend is the prayer of your daughter

Jane

The weather had cooled and health returned to the neighborhood. Margaret gathered her energy and, with the help of some of the Negroes, washed, ironed, and packed Jane's clothes. She marveled at the convenience of sending them by stage; not long since, such a thing was unheard of. How thoughtless it had been to neglect the child's winter things, and here it was nearly mid-November. It had been several months since she had had any thought not related to her own illness or that of another. At least the cool weather was having the effect of clearing their brains of cobwebs and thickening the blood. Reverend Williamson had recovered and was back in his pulpit.

When James next wrote to his sons he told them of the death of their benefactor, Mr. John Campbell, and that he had received no communication from the estate about their loan. James had not seen one penny from his sons on the interest he paid last year and could not imagine how they would fare if pressed for the entire amount. On the fourteenth of November 1838, Frank wrote to his father:

Dear Father

I received a letter from you, a few days since & am surprised to hear that you have had so much sickness, and continue to have a goodeal. I thought that we had got into a sickly country, but I am convinced that this is a more healthy country than the one you live in. I have been living in the hopes that you will all be able to get through this spell, and that you never have such another attack I have been afraid that every mail would bring us sum bad news, but most happily we have received none, and may this letter find you and the family in as good health as it leaves us. I have nothing new to send you this time. Mr Mayhugh got home a few days since and says he left Grand Pa in better health than he has been for some time. he promised to call and see you and let you hear from us, but says he had not time.

We have been very bussy for sum time putting up a ginn house and getting ready to ginn. We will be able to commence in a few days. We received a letter from W. Latta a few days since and he says he will leave for Miss on the 10th or 15th of this month, an unexpected move to me, Isabella has concluded to stay this winter, and visit N Carolina in the spring or summer We have been expecting to hear from the administers of Campbell estate for sum time, but have heard nothing yet. if you should [hear] anny thing respecting the debt we owe them please let us know so that we may be prepared to meet the debt

Flour is worth 17$ per barrel & bacon 25 cts . . . corn is lower than it has been since we came in this country.

Our cotton crop will be high this year but is something better than the average crop.

nothing more for the present give my love to all the family while I remain your affectionate son

J F Torrance

Isabella was overjoyed at the prospect of seeing her sister again. Perhaps Camilla would bring them a barrel of flour or some other commonplace thing which had become a luxury. Their diet of fish, game, and cornbread had become tiresome. She could hardly recall a time when there was no grit of cornmeal between her teeth. She missed the groaning board of Cedar Grove, but they were not starving—not yet. Isabella's head swam with visions of Camilla and how she would show off their gin house, cleared fields, nearly chinked cabins, and her swiftly growing child. She prayed that William Latta would invite her and Jane along when they returned to Yorkville.

~ ~ ~

At Christmas time James again went to Charleston to sell his cotton. He regretted leaving Margaret at home, but her confinement was too near to safely travel. She had been enamored of the sweetmeats in that city and asked him to bring ingredients to replicate them at home. She also requested oranges for the Negroes. On Christmas Eve at Banks Simonton's grocers he bought barrels of sugar, several kinds of molasses, two boxes of raisins, a dozen pineapples, and two hundred oranges. For himself he bought five gallons each of rum and brandy and two dozen bottles of wine, half of them the Madeira that was so popular in Charleston. Pepper, cheese, and coffee were added to the order, and for 50¢, a box for the oranges. The groceries cost $165.50.[42]

The next morning he paid $5.82 for meals and lodging which included $2.50 for his two Negro drivers.

10   Troubles Deepen 1839~1840

As 1838 bled into 1839, letters became less frequent. It was during this time that Camilla wrote to her sister with deep apologies that she and William would not be able to visit the west after all. She was expecting another child and was afraid to travel, her health being fragile under the best of circumstances. Isabella was devastated by the news. She agreed that a journey over rock and rut was not advisable for one in Camilla's condition, but William could afford the most comfortable cabin in a steamship all the way from Charleston. Isabella crushed the letter in a tight fist. Between its lines was the bitter fact that Camilla would never shed her fear of the unknown. If she were to ever see her sister again, it would be in Carolina— and she had no concept of how to get there. It seemed hopeless. On the second of March 1839, she wrote:

Dear Father

We have been looking for a letter from you for some time, and we have determined to take it by turns and write to you oftener Brothers have both written to you since I did last but the mails are so irregular that there is a great uncertainty about the letters. We are all well at present, have had two or three cases of what is called the winter fever   it generally proves fatal   we were so unfortunate as to lose Patsey with it, she died in four days after she was taken sick. The winter has been very mild   we had a snow and freeze at Christmas and that is the only one,   vegetation is putting out very fast   the grass begins to look green and some few scattering flowers are in bloom, it has been quite warm enough to be without fire in the day until a few evenings ago   we had a thunder storm and since that it has been cooler   I am in hopes that this spring will not be quite so wet as the two last.

I received a letter from sister the other day saying they had declined coming   I was very much disappointed indeed I had fully calculated on their being here in a short time but I suppose they could not get off. I do not expect to be in Carolina this summer   times are so hard that it is just as much as we can possibly do to meet our contracts and I have determined to live as economical as possible. We sold our cotton at twelve and a half at home which is better I believe than taking it down the river   the expense is so very great and we are needing the money, we are waiding through our difficulties pretty well here, in a few [years] if we live and nothing happens we shall be entirely out of debt. Brother Hugh received a letter from Mr Reid he mentioned that you had a son   how I wish I could see him and all the rest but here I am a long distance from them and when they grow up I will be nothing more than a common stranger.

When you write me let me know how the children improve   I should be so glad to receive a letter (or a line or two) from Letta, and William   he has never written a word to any of us since here we have been

My little girl grows very fast I wish you could see her   if I ask her who she loves she says grandfather.

Brothers join me in love to you Ma and all the children and a kiss to them all for Jane and me   write me what you intend to call little brother

I remain your ever
affectionate daughter
Isabella M Smith

From the window she could see that wildflowers had inserted them-selves among the struggling early peas and greens. She would have to pull them like weeds when the time came for summer vegetables. She yearned for the luxury of a real flower garden, fat with fragrance and color. Ma would soon have roses, then blood-red hollyhocks as tall as a man. She added a note:

I have enclosed you a few tomato seed   some of them are large yellow ones I have heard speak of them and I thought I would send you a few seed.
I M S

The birth had been hard on Margaret. James had not written his chil-dren about it for fear that such a letter might be followed closely by another one announcing a death or perhaps two. John Andrew Torrance had been born on the twenty-eighth of January; mother and child remained ill through most of February. Dr. Johnston visited several times, occasionally remaining all night. The doctor advised Margaret that this should be her last child; another birth could be fatal. This information was not welcomed by

James; although his family was quite large enough, he was not yet ready to give up his pleasures. His wife's pale complexion and limp hands gave him the necessary resolve. He would do what was required to keep his dear wife with him. Margaret's sister, Jane, had been with them since the confinement. Her tender touch and ability to find smidgens of joy in mounds of despair eased James's anguish. By now there were enough Negroes on the plantation to provide a wet nurse at any time should one be needed.

By the middle of March, Margaret had regained her health and the infant had been pronounced out of danger. Jane was in her final session at Salem. She was excitedly preparing for her public examination which would take place in May. On the nineteenth of March, she wrote her father:

Again my dear Father, I have the pleasure of answering another of your much esteemed and kind letters; I was quite happy to hear that you were all well. I wrote to you two or three weeks ago but it seems that you did not receive my letter, as you did not say anything about it. It gave me great pleasure to hear that sister Camilla and Mr. Latta had been to see you, and also that sister Isabella would be in shortly; I hope we will all be together this spring, for it has been a long time since we were all at home at the same time. You said the dress for which I wrote was not to be had in Charlotte, perhaps you will see some thing that you think would do as well; I leave it to Ma and aunt Jane, as I think their choice would please me: as to my cap I will ask my teacher to have it made for me. I received the bundle you sent me and thank you very much for it; and tell aunt Jane I am much obliged to her for her letter, but cannot say when I will answer it. I think brother is a very lazy boy, for he promised to pay me a visit during his vacancy; it was a poor excuse that he could get no person to come with him, if he had tried I think he could. I was agreeably surprised by a visit from uncle Rufus, a few weeks ago, and spent my time very pleasantly during his stay, which was one or two days. One of our teachers Miss Ruede, was married on the 28th of the present month to Mr Vogler, a missionary; they are gone to Arkansas on a missionary station: she was much esteemed by the girls in the school. When I think I will be <u>home</u> in three months my heart throbs with joy. Tell me, when you answer this letter, if the children are going to school to Mrs. Williamson or not, as I heard she was going to Florida. Grandmother said she would try to come at the examination, please persuade her to come, for I am very anxious to see her. We had a musical entertainment on the night of the 13th of this month; several of the girls performed pieces on the piano and recited resitations. I expect brother thinks I have almost forgotten to answer his letter, but I received yours and I thought it best to answer it first; tell him I will write to him in a week or two. I told Amanda what you said, and it seemed to please her very much indeed. Dovey says tell her Mother, to answer her letter, and says she must be sure to come at the examination, and bring her little brother. I heard that aunt Jane was going to get married, tell her I hope that her wedding will not take place before I go home. Give my best love to Grandmother, and tell her I would be happy to see her here at the examination. We enjoy very good health excepting bad colds. It seems that sister Isabella has entirely forgotten me; when you write to her give my love to her, and tell her I have been waiting very patiently to receive a letter. Remember us kindly to M^{r}. and M^{rs}. Williamson and tell them we would be very sorry if they were to go away before we go home. Please dear Pa answer this letter soon after you receive it and be so kind as to send me some pocket-money, for I have spent nearly all of that you gave me when you were here. Give my love to Ma, aunt Jane, brother, and all of my relations and acquaintances. Kiss all my sisters and brothers and tell them it will not be long before they see Sisy Jane. I must bring my letter to a close, as I have nothing more to write at this time. Dovey and Amanda join with me in love to you and all of their relations.

　　Your affectionate Daughter
　　　Jane E Torrence

James would extend an invitation, or perhaps a command, to Mrs. Latta to join them when they went for Jane's examination. In the past few months the combined Latta and Reid clan had made a peaceful adjustment to their situation. Rufus Reid could certainly handle his assortment of children for a few days, and Jane seemed adamant to have her grandmother attend. James was amused at Jane's disappointment in William's failure to visit during his recess. Surely she was old enough to know that a sixteen-year-old college lad had more interesting pursuits than visiting younger sisters. Apparently William wasn't old enough to realize his college companions would be delighted to go with him to a place so dense with young women.

James would inform his daughter that Isabella would not be home this spring after all. Shortage of money in Mississippi had made it impossible. Jane would insist that he send her stage fare. He could afford to—had he not just ordered a whole roomful of furniture from Charleston? James would have some difficulty explaining why he could not do that. In fact he was beginning to have some difficulty explaining it to himself. He wanted his adult children to be independent of him, yet he had paid the interest on that foolish Campbell debt. He had made the second payment just last month. Did he owe Isabella as much? Or had her egregious sin absolved him of it? He had extended forgiveness, need he also extend money? It was a matter deserving much prayer and consideration.

He, too, had been gratified by Camilla's visit, and it would probably be some time before he had another. Her child was due soon; she would probably remain prostrate for a long while.

～　　　～　　　～

In the west the Torrance plantation had grown, as plots adjoining their land were gobbled up whenever money was available. Land was about the only thing that could be bought with the devalued currency. The three of them jointly held the property which now contained about fifteen hundred acres. They were land rich and cash poor.

It was difficult to find time for letter writing between the farming chores, or so it seemed to Frank. At least he kept telling himself that was the case. In reality he was torn between love and duty to his father which required letters and the unpleasant task of writing about failure. After much procrastination, he took up his pen on the nineteenth of July 1839: [43]

Dear Father

Some time has elapsed since I wrote to you last and I will now write such news as I have. We have been expecting a letter from you for some time, but attribute our not getting one to the irregularity of the mails. We sometimes get no letter nor paper for two or three weeks at a time.

Our prospect for a good crop is very promising, and if the season continues good, I have little doubt but we will make 150 baggs of cotton, and plenty of corn wheat and oats to supply our family. We had cotton blooms on the 14th of June, and in sum parts of the county they had blooms as early as the 6th June. their is plenty of cotton in this valley 4 & 5 feet high, our cotton will average about waste high. We have had little or no sickness this season, (no fever)

I think our country is healthier than Mecklenburg   I wish you could see our crop, you would be pleased   I feel anxious to visit N°Ca and hope I may be able to do so ere another year roals round. Isabella is quite anxious to see you and the family, and if we can make any arrangement suitable we will try and get to see you this winter, but it is very uncertain, in fact it is so much so that we cannot promise ourselves to go. We have [been] disappointed so often that we think it best to wate patiently and see what we can do.

The debt we owe the estate of John Campbell has [caused] us a great deal of uneasiness, and anxiety, and it is impossible for us to get the money here before we gather our crop of cotton. the best of our money is 15 per ct below par. a most retched state of affairs, but it is to be hoped it will not continue so much longer. The prescient cotton crop will relieve the state very much. We thought of shipping our cotton to Charleston to meet the Campbell debt if any arrangement could be made until that time, Hugh wrote to you some time ago on the subject, and we are expecting daily to hear from you.

We have been able to meet our contracts punctually so far, and if we can arrange that debt, we will have little difficulty hear after. Last year we mad something like five thousand dollars, and our cotton crop this year will be about double as much as last years crop.

We have kept clear of all speculations and have been endeavoring to pay what we owe   and if we are spared and can do as well as we have been doing we will not be in this situation. I never knew what it was to be in debt, and shall try and keep out here after. When a man is out of debt he is out of danger, — but few can say that in this state, the credit of Mississippians is at a low eb abroad, but the fault is their own. Land has been selling in this state, at Sheriff sale, from one to two dollars, that sold three years ago for fifteen and upwards, negros have not fallen so much. I believe I have nothing more to write to you at this time. Their is a report in N°Ca that Hugh is to be married, — there is nothing of it. All the family is in good health and I hope you and the family Enjoy the same   my love to all

Your affectionate son

James F Torrance

P.S. If you can assist us in settling the Campbell debt for the present,

you will confer a favor, and one that I will ever be gratefull for, I do not wish M^r. Reid and uncle Frank to have it to pay
             your aff— son

He hoped this letter would convince their father that they were being responsible, even under difficult circumstances. He knew James would grasp the part about being out of debt and out of danger. This Campbell situation caused Frank many sleepless nights. Hugh was equally concerned about settling it, but Hugh, in his business-like fashion, kept calm about it. Frank maintained a constant state of agitation.

Camilla gave birth to a daughter and named her Ada. The process took its usual toll on her health. On the twenty-seventh of July 1839, she wrote from Yorkville:

Dear Father
    I received your affectionate letter about a week since   I was glad to hear that you were all well. I should have been to see you in June but my situation was such that I could not with prudence have left home — you must excuse me for writing only a few lines at this time as my health is still not good — I hope however it will be better before long — William and the children are in pretty good health and join me in love to you all
             Affectionately
                 Your daughter
                     Camilla

Finally there had been word on the settling of the Campbell estate. Early in July, James received word that a Mr. Chambers was executor and had requested the loan be paid in full as soon as possible. He wrote to his sons of this news and reminded them that he had paid the two interest payments, a total of six hundred dollars. He told them that Mr. Reid's and Uncle Frank's signatures might be required on any documents concerning the settlement, but they were not to request any money from them, as they were innocent bystanders to this folly. He understood the paltry state of money in Mississippi, but times were hard in many places. There was less shame in being financially broken than being dishonorable. He reported that Camilla and William Latta had visited in the spring prior to her confinement, and he asked after the health of Isabella and her child. He made no offer to come for them. Isabella took this to mean they were still unwelcome at Cedar Grove. Hugh replied to this letter on the twenty-ninth of July:

Dear Father

I have just received your letter of July 8 In regard to the payment of our debt to Chambers   I shall be compelled to rely on the kindness of my friends to arrange it   at present it will be entirely out of my power to go to Carolina by the first of September — our currency is so bad that I should have to incur a loss of about 1500 dollars in getting such funds as will be required in the payment of that debt a loss that would be rather heavy on us. It would be greatly to our advantage if the money could be raised until spring by which time I can [get] cotton enough shipped to Charleston or New York to meet it or if our money should improve sell it in New Orleans and send you a check.

You will do us a great favor if you will assist in making arrangements to settle with Chambers. I pledge myself to comply with any you may make and to meet it promptly. Our money is in a wretched condition — it answers our purposes here but will pay no debt out of the state. I am in hopes we will have a better state of things before the Spring.

Our crops are fine indeed better than I have ever seen. We had cotton blooms the 8th June. the bolls are now full grown some open . . . We will make a fine crop without an accident. We must make over a hundred bales of cotton. More than half of the reports that

reach Carolina about this country are incorrect if we had good
currency we would get along well enough — The state of society is
not half as bad as it is represented. — I was rejoiced to hear that W.
Latta & Camilla paid you a visit. Give my love to all the family
Your Affct Son
H Torrance

James had grown weary of empty promises. He could no more get
money from his sons than blood from a stone. He met with Rufus Reid and
Franklin Davidson. They decided James should apply for a bank loan to pay
the Campbell estate with a due date in midwinter; by that time the crop in
Mississippi should be sold. Mr. Chambers had agreed to a payment of
$5225. That amount would repay the principle and the interest for the past
nine months. The bank complied with their request. On the twenty-first of
August they met with Mr. Blackwood at the bank in Charlotte and struck a
deal. Mr. Blackwood agreed to their terms; the bank would charge $150 in
interest. Franklin and Rufus agreed to act as securities; all three of them
signed the note:

$5375
Six Months after the 21st day of August A.D. 1839   we James G.
Torrance Principal and Rufus Reid & G.F. Davidson Securities,
promise to pay I. J. Blackwood Agent, &c, or order, five thousand
three hundred & seventy five dollars, for value received, negotiable
and payable at the Agency of the Bank of the State of North
Carolina at Charlotte.

J. G. Torrance
Geo F. Davidson
Rufus Reid

If his sons failed once again, he would lift the note in February and
subtract the debt from their share of his estate. He was weary of the whole
matter and wanted to hear no more of it. He hoped the guilt expressed by
his sons was sincere.

On the twenty-fourth of September, Frank wrote:

Dear Father
I received your letter on the 22nd inst. and am glad to hear that
you have had no sickness this season, and hope that you may not

have as much as you had last season, the health of our family has been unusually healthy this season — only had one case of the [fever] this summer, and a verry little in the country — we have had little or no rain for the last six or seven weeks   the dust has been two or three inches deep of late, and has rendered the roads very unpleasant for travelling. The cropps of cotton will not be as heavy as was expected, the last drouth has injured late cropps very much, but early cotton that was planted in good land will make 12 & 1500 [lb] to the acre. We have been getting along better this season gathering cotton than usual, we have been picking four weeks with part of our hands and have got out near 50.000 lb. i think our crop will average about 1,000 lb per Acre.

I am glad you have arranged our debt with Chambers, but I had little thought that you would have to get it out of Bank, it has been almost impossible to get money in this country, and when we do get it we cannot use it at par, there is but one or two banks in the state that has been able to keep it[s] bills at par, and they do no business in the way of discounts, our crop of cotton is the only means we have of raising money and we will not be able to do any thing with it untill we can ship it to N. Orleans which will be as soon as we can get it out. If it was not for what we owe for our land we would be able to get along quite easily and hope to do so at any rate. I had little [idea of] the cost of settling a farm in the woods and I hope we will not or put to as much expense here after as we have been. We lost all the horses that we started from N⁰C with, but two and three that we bought since which has been about two thousand dollars top. — having to buy other at a high price.

There has been more property sold at sherriffs sale this summer than I ever new in the hole course of my life before, [and] it seams that they have not got [more] than half through. We have had no business in court yet and I hope will not. We have been able to sustain ourselves so far and I hope by using industry and economy we will pay what we owe without a great deal of tro[uble]   our installment on our land will be due January next which is the most that we will have to pay. if we had not bought as much land by half as we did, we would have had lit[tle] difficulty at worst. to show you how we have been getting along I will state that we paid 7,000 *dolls last year, and only made a tolerable crop of cotton, this year our crop will be much larger but — I am affraid it will not be worth as much. I think we may safely calculate on making 135 baggs.*

Hugh or myself will be in this time enough to arrange the business with the bank. Isabella is anxious to visit NC but we are not able to spare the money. it is better that we should pay our debts with what money we get than spend it riding about. as long as we show a disposition to pay our debts and attend to our business we will find plenty to assist us and our creditors will be more willing to indulge us

He had used up his page even though he kept his hand as tiny as possible. He turned the page sideways and draped cramped words around its margin:

Seeing you would afford me more pleasure at this time than anny thing that I can mention   you may think me ungrateful for leaving you contrary to your wish, but, — I new it would not soot me to live in N°Ca   I regret not being able to see you oftener. I hope it will not be so always

I have filled up my paper and have written little that would interest anny other than a father — and I hope he does feel interested. I have had more trouble than most men of my age, and I hope what has passed within my view has not passed unobserved and will be of sum value hereafter   my love to all
                    Your affectionate
                    Son
                    Frank

Sadness crept over James's heart as he read the letter. The words on the margin were hard to read, as pen strokes in one direction crossed those in another. For the first time Frank had nearly offered an apology for acting contrary to his fathers wishes, and he had signed the letter simply Frank, an intimate departure for him. He could see no teardrops on the page, but he knew that his emotional son had shed them. In spite of Frank's contrite nature, he had not seemed to understand that the entire amount was due in February, not just the interest. Perhaps James had not been clear; he would write one more letter on the matter and then let it drop. Unpleasant circumstances which brought Frank down whimpering sent Hugh on the path of avoidance. James had not heard from that son since July. Hugh seemed to have thrown up his hands because it was out of his power, and he would have to rely on the kindness of friends. What friends? James wondered. None had come forward. No one had offered a cent. As he folded the letter and tucked it away, his sadness was tempered by disappointment and anger. If only they had listened to him.

~ ~ ~

It was winter before he heard again from the west. Just after the turn of 1840, Frank wrote:

Dear Father

It is now the fifth of January and we have not had rain enough yet to raise the river moor than six inches, we have had sum bad weather notwithstanding; and if we were to judge from the present weather, we cannot expect the river to be up for sum time. and how we are to get the [money] that we owe in N Carolina is more that I can at present tell. We had but little doubt but we could by this time have shipped our cotton and have been in N Carolina in time to have met the note in Bank, but as it is I am afraid we shall be sadly dissapointed, Our cotton crop will be large to meet that debt, if we could only make sail. We have already gathered 170.000 ^{lb} of which 109 Bagg is pack averaging 450 ^{lb} and besides that we have 80 acres to pick, which is very good cotton, the cropp will be much better than we had any reason to expect We have 100 baggs at the river wating the first rise and will shipp as soon as we can safely. [44] If I should not be able to get their in time it might be that the Bank would renew for a month or two as to give me time to get in. I would rather sacrifice the cotton than disappoint you, we have already put you in a goodeal of trouble to settle our matters but I hope to bring them to a final settlement in a short time. It is allmoast impossible to get any money that will pay out of the state moast of our Bank paper is from ten to twenty percent below par, and continues to get worse. I [ought] to have written to you before this but I have kept putting it off from day to day until a month or more has elapsed, nothing of importance has transpired in the family to trouble you with all is well and continues to get along as usual If the money could be obtained for that land that was in Tenn. that you promised me a portion of, could be collected would be a great assistance to me *if it could get it, and I should be glad you would let me [know] what Jones has done and what I can expect from that sourse.*

I would be glad you would write to me as soon as you get this, we have not heard from you for some time, but I hope to get a letter soon, the mails are very irregular in this part of the country at this time, and it takes about twice as long to hear from Carolina as it ought to do

Your affectionate son
J F Torrance

A Mr. Charles Jones of South Carolina had expressed an interest in the Tennessee land, and James had decided to sell a portion of it if the price were right. Perhaps it would be wise to make some inquiries. He had heard that many people were suffering losses of unoccupied land in some of the western states. If someone were to live on his land and farm it for a number of years, the state of Tennessee might consider that man the rightful owner—squatter's rights it was called. He would inquire to satisfy Jones's interest; he had no intention of turning over a part of that property to Frank to settle the debt. That sounded to him like robbing Peter to pay Paul.

James waited as long as he dared, hoping for a miraculous rise in the river and soaring cotton prices in New Orleans. The due date passed and he had no more letters nor a dime from his sons. On the twenty-fourth of February, James went to the bank in Charlotte and quietly lifted the note with his own money. He was charged an extra $1.76 for being three days late. He made a note of it on the back of the paper, which he tucked away in his secretary with letters from the west. [45]

On the third of March, Frank wrote his father. News from the west never was good:

Dear Father
I received your letter of the 1ˢᵗ Feb. four days since (just one month on the way) which gave us much pleasure — to hear from any person in our native country gives us pleasure. — but when it is from our own family it gives us tribble the pleasure, — whear everything that takes place no matter how trifling in itself, — excites our [interest] or simpathy — more or less — distance and time may separate us, and we may forget many old acquaintance, but to forget the place of our nativity, and the scenes of our youth is impossible and would be ungratfull

Hugh left on the second for N Orleans with our cotton, but I am affraid we will not realize much from it,   the last accounts we had from N Orleans, cotton was selling from 6 to 8 1/2   our cotton or such as is is raised in in this section of the country will not bring more than 7 cts,   Money is very scarce here and little account when we git it;   our bank paper is from 20 to 40 per ct below par in N Orleans, our crop amounted to 180 bagg averaging 400 ^{lb},   I expect Hugh will be gon about three week. We shipped our cotton on a flat boat; from a landing within four miles of home, it is a great convenience to be able to ship so near home, but our rivers are very uncertain and, and it has happened so that we have had no tide in ten months, which was the case the last year

Mr Simons arrived hear on Wednesday last, and expects to return in a few days. You stated you thought you would be troubled with a law sute about the land in Tennessee, if you should be compelled to institute a sute, and I can attend to it, it will be a great deal more convenient for me to attend to it than you, — as it is only about four or five days ride from here

Isabella is as [eager as]she can be to get back but — I am not certain that we can [find a] thing to take her in. I hope we shall be able to get something that will answer.

We are about getting into a difficulty about our land, and in fact we have already got into it. The titles we thought were good, and the judge of one of our courts has passed on them as being good, but it does not all do. for the sherriff has lived on 320 acres and intends selling or try to sell   besides that there is about 160 acres that we will lose sertain   there is no alternative but to go to _law_, the worse business of all. The man that we bought of has failed and wound out to be a most infamous scoundrele, he has either swindled or tryed to swindle every person that he has had in his power. Three hundred and twenty acres is to be sold on the 13th of the month and the other 160 acres in a short time. We might save the land if we could arrange the debt in N^{o}Ca   I cannot say when I will start for N C — as soon as I can — all [well] — my love to all

your affection son
James F Torrance

Frank set the letter aside intending to mail it on his next trip to Coffeeville. Before the opportunity arose, Hugh walked in the door with a long face and said there was not enough water in the river to float their boat. Frank added a post script:

Mar 6   Brother Hugh returned last night, not being able to get the boats out of the Yalobusha. We will now have to wait another rise in the river

James was amused by the letter's rhapsodic opening. Was Frank sincere in his nostalgia, or was he washing their travail with rosewater? Probably both. In any event, it was March, their crop was not sold, and their land was in peril.

~   ~   ~

Isabella had kept silent. The necessary attention to money matters was distasteful. Her late husband's recklessness had left his affairs, and consequently hers, in a worse state than her brothers'. Yet it was her sin and her father's love that troubled her the most. He had offered forgiveness, but she was still in Mississippi doing penance. At least she supposed that was her purpose here in her father's eyes. She had never worked so hard nor lived so poorly in her life. She accepted that her father's trip to fetch her was scuttled because he was ill. She understood that Uncle Frank was reluctant to undertake a journey with a woman and child in tow, although she had not gotten over the rebuff. (Little did she know that he was planning to be in Alabama again within weeks.) And it had been folly to think that Camilla could get off, baby or no baby. But why had her father remained silent for so long? It had been a year since there had been any talk of her going home. Did he think she was happy here, or did he believe she deserved more punishment? Her brothers' letters mentioned her distress in little sentences buried within the money woes. The time had come to write a carefully composed letter of her own. She must convince her father that she had a mature acceptance of her situation but no comfort in it. She would tell him of her love for her homeland and family and especially her church. She would not beg or plead nor ask for anything. On the seventh of April 1840 she wrote:

Dear Father
*   I hope you will forgive my negligence in not writing to you in such a length of time I was scarcely aware of it myself until I came to reflect. We are all enjoying fine health but we have had so much*

rain, and the weather is so disagreeably warm that I am fearful that we shall have some sickness this season. the leaves on the trees are already half grown   the gardens are very forward and will soon have vegetables to eat.

Times are very <u>hard here indeed</u>   I don't know how we are going to get along   there are sales (public) almost every week property put up to be sold for specie or its equivalent and of course it goes for little or nothing,   good lands sell for a bitt and two bitts an acre sometimes you hear of a planter who works forty to fifty hands and is security for some of his friends for four or five thousand dollars and be worth nothing and the marshal seizes the security property sells it for specie and it will scarcely bring the amount due. There is not a bank in the state that is worth anything   I don't think that times can get much worse here in the way of money matters.

Our cotton will not bring as much as it did year before last and it was not half as much as we made last year   Brother Hugh did not go to N Orleans with it   he started but the boats could not get out of the river then and he could not go when they left   I am afraid that our cotton will not bring us more than four cents   if it does not I do not know how we are to get along   we have lived as economically as possible since we have been in the state and yet it seems as if it was all to no purpose. I had flattered myself that I should [see] you all this summer at least but it is out of the question that I should do so now while times are so hard   we have no conveyance and are not able to buy one and it will cost to much to go in the stage   I did think that if uncle Frank came to see us that I would go with him but I suppose he is in Carolina long ere this and thought so little of us that he would not deign to give us a call   I suppose that he was fearful that I would trouble him with my company to Carolina was the reason of his not coming. I don't know now when I shall be there if ever or not   if I had the wings of a dove how soon I should see you, how much pleasure it would give me just to be with you one sunday if no longer and accompany the family to church as I used to do, here we have no preaching scarcely and there is not a sabbath passes over my head but I think of the difference between my two homes one the family all going to church with an air of solemnity reigning over the whole place and hear we all stay at *home and as is often the case with a house full of company   there is no telling what it is to be deprived of the benefit of going to church until we are tried. I have not the faintest idea of being with you this summer*

Brothers join me in love to you   Ma and all our brothers and sisters   kiss the children for Jane and me.
                    I remain your
                            affectionate daughter
                                Isabella M Smith

She read over the letter and hoped it would soften her father's heart. Every word she had written was true, but there were other true words that not been said. Words that were bitter, complaining, and self-centered. Those words did not come to mind so often anymore, perhaps she was grown after all. She folded the letter, wrote the address on the front, and pressed sealing wax on the back where the edges overlapped. She prayed that her father would take pity on her and send for her even though she had not asked. He could never understand how much she hated this place and how sorry she was to have come here.

The letter did mellow James and everyone else in the household. Margaret was adamant that the exile should come to an end. "When will it be enough?" she had asked. "She had nothing to do with the debt or the sorry state of money in that place. If God wants to deal her more grief, I am sure it is his power. When the boys asked for more time to prove themselves, you gave it to them, although reluctantly. All you have offered Isabella is a modicum of forgiveness."

"And I have a little niece I barely remember," said Jane. "Papa why must you be so stubborn?"

Then the little girls clamored about wanting her home. "Why should anyone be mad with her?" asked Delia; she was too young to know the nature of Isabella's sin.

"And it appears to me," Margaret added in a voice barely above a whisper, "that our granddaughter is being raised in a land of infidels."

He winced at the thought and agreed to discuss the matter with Reverend Williamson and abide by his counsel. James was still the treasurer at Hopewell and would never offend the congregation. After his visit with the Reverend, James relented. "I have been convinced that you are right, Margaret," he said. "Although Isabella's wrongdoing was serious, it was of human frailty. She has repented and asked for forgiveness and shows no signs of an evil or malicious spirit. The session believes she has been censured long enough and will accept her back into the fold if she displays an air of piety." It was finally settled. James went to Charlotte to inquire about sending stage fare to Coffeeville, Mississippi.

～   ～   ～

Frank had truly hoped their fortunes would change and he could go to Carolina that spring with money in his hand. He hoped with such fervor that he came to believe it was possible. It was not to be. He put off writing as long as he dared wishing, for a better mood, but the dismal onus of failure would not leave him. On the twenty-eighth of May, he reluctantly took up his pen:

Dear Father

I know not how to commence this letter although I have plenty to write, yet I have never in my life been so unfit to write as I am at this time and have been so for a short time, but the longer I put it off the more difficult I find it to commence, and I am affraid that I have delayed too long already; but if I have I hope you will forgive my negligence. I have been putting it off from day to day until I find that three weeks has passed, and I have not yet written to you. I know that instead of a letter you will expect to see me in N^oCa — but the disappointment to you [cann]ot be half so great as it is to me. I had fully calculated on seeing you this spring, but we are all liable to disappointments, and my life so far seems to be nothing else, but who can I blame, — myself only. however if time and health will only permit I hope I shall be able to work out of my difficulty I have never had any thing to distress me so much, as not being able to pay that debt which you were kind enough to assume — and which among other things, I can never forget and you can never know the advantage it has been to us, for you to have assisted us so far that is the only debt that has distressed or caused us any uneasiness, it is certain we owe some debts here; but we can pay them off with such currency as we have here, if we could pay the debt in Carolina as easy as we can what we owe here it would be an easy matter compared with what it is. We have little or no money here that is worth more than fifty cents in the dollar and consequently it would take double the amount of money to pay the debt. I am affraid Pa you may think that we do not wish to pay the debt as long as we can [still] get you to pay it for us. but that is not the case. I would willingly pay it on time as on others as it has to be paid sometime if we are able. Our cotton has not been sold yet or I have not heard of it. Hugh left here on the 10th for N Orleans and has not returned yet, he will bring the returns of our cotton with him I hope, The last account that I had from N. Orleans, cotton was selling from 5 to 9 — cotton raised in this part of the country has been selling from 6 to 8 and we cannot expect to get more than 7 cents neat, if that. We have some few debts here that we have to pay and I am affraid after they are paid the proceeds of our crop will be exhausted.

I am affraid it will put you to sum trouble and inconvenience to raise the money at this time and it is that among other things which has troubled me so much, if the times were as as easy to get money now as they were three years ago their would be little difficulty attending it. Their is no money to be had in this county that is worth having or w[e] coul[d ge]t it. If you cannot get the money a[nd do with]out the use of it, we will be compelled to sell sum of our negros and raise it that w[ay]   negroes is the only property that will bring money in this country, and they bring but little. If you should be able to get the money for us, we would be very willing to secure you in any way you may wish — by a deed in trust or judgement — we have not been pushed for anything that we owe here, and will not be, so long as we shall be able to get along as we have been, I have suffered greatly with my head for some time, but that has been triffling compared with my mental sufferings since I found out that I would not be able to get to N^o Carolina. Isabella is as much disappointed as I have been, if not more, I think Hugh will be back in a few days. Our crop this spring is only tolerable, the season has been very wet, and with it a great deal of hail. Our family has been as well as usual,   we have been expecting Uncle Frank, but it is doubtful wheather he will get here   Give my love to all the family, your affectionate son   J. F. Torrence

Frank read over the letter and considered rewriting it. It was not neat; he had scratched through many tentative words until the proper ones could be summoned up. The last lines had been scrawled in a hand almost too tiny to read, as he had reached the end of his sheet before his heart had been emptied. Melancholia enveloped him the cruelest when Hugh was away; he could no more improve the letter than any other part of his life. He turned the page sideways and wrote an apology in the margin:

> *You must excuse the blunders that I have committed in this, I ought not to send it as it is, but I am affraid I would not better it much, if I would try.*

By the time James received this letter the stagecoach fare for Isabella and Jane had been sent to Mississippi, and he assumed she was preparing for her journey or perhaps was on her way. This should relieve Frank of some of his gloom. Hugh was certainly back from New Orleans with some money from their crop, which would also improve his outlook. But as James reread the letter, he saw that Frank's black choler was more profound than he had ever known it to be. The time had come, he concluded, to inform his sons that he had lifted their note in February. He had saved this information believing his sons would be more motivated by a debt to the bank than one to their father, which was true. But he had never intended to drive them to despond. Hugh's letters had become rare, and Frank's were filled with anguish. With Isabella on her way home, it was time to make peace with his sons.

11 A Relative Peace 1840~1842

In June of 1840, Isabella received the letter from her father offering to take her into his home and the precious gift of stage fare. She had not been so overjoyed since that cold December day when she had embarked on this adventure. And now, thank the Lord, it would soon be over. It took only a week or so to make all her preparations for leaving. When all was done, Frank took her small party to Coffeeville to meet the stagecoach.

They arrived early enough to pay a last visit to the cemetery on the hill. With closed eyes Isabella knelt at Franklin's grave and tried to conjure up his image in her mind. Their marriage had been so brief and seemed so long ago. He had been gone for three toil-filled years in which grieving had gotten short shrift. She would keep forever fresh the memories of the steamboat and the gallop through swamp land, and in little Jane she would always have a part of him. She looked up and filled her eyes with the town to the east and the green hills to the south and west, willing the image burned into her memory. She would miss her brothers and the ponderous beauty of this place but nothing else. "I'll tell your mother," she whispered, "that you lie in the most beautiful spot in all of Mississippi." She ran her hand over the stone. She was glad she had been so extravagant. She doubted anyone here would remember the man, but they would not forget he had died here.

Isabella, Jane, and three Negroes composed the group waiting for the stagecoach. Isabella had selected an older woman and her two nearly grown daughters; the rest were left behind to work her brothers' plantation. She hugged Frank close. "Don't worry," she said, "I know you will do fine. I aim to tell Pa how the plantation improves, and in no time at all you shall be visiting us at Cedar Grove." She brushed a tear from his cheek, then one from her own.[46]

The trip was swift compared to the arduous one over three years ago. The primary mission of the stage was to carry mail; passenger service was a courtesy. They traveled long hours, and nighttime accommodations were often sparse. Some nights only a few hours of sleep were permitted, unless one was willing to await the next stage. Since horses were changed frequently, such a pace could be kept. In less than four weeks the weary party arrived in Charlotte to be met by James.

She half expected to see the dark-circled, stony-eyed visage of her father she had carried in her mind the past several years and was pleasantly surprised to be met with a broad smile. His embrace was strong and she shed her uneasiness. She knew her repentance was genuine, and she could see he accepted it. It need never be mentioned again.

The welcome at Cedar Grove was equally warm. How everyone had grown! Jane had been home from Salem for a year now and had become a lovely young woman of seventeen. William, at eighteen, was a worldly college man. It would take some time to catch up on all their doings. Twelve-year-old Lettitia and eleven-year-old Mary had become proper young girls. They had spent the previous winter with their Uncle Thomas Allison in Statesville attending a log school where they were taught by an elderly Frenchman named Mr. Ney. They bantered back and forth like a pair of giddy magpies. "He's very large person," said Lettitia, "and he has the most delightful accent."

"He carries himself like a soldier," added Mary, "although with a bit of a limp."

"You should see the scar over his eye," continued Lettitia. "It gives him the most frightening appearance, even when he smiles."

"But when he's angered, it turns red as a beet!" Mary giggled.

"And he writes acrostics on our names."

"Acrostics? Whatever is that?" asked Isabella.

"It's a poem," replied Lettitia. "It's composed using all the letters of your name, taken in order, for the initial letter of each line. He has done one for each of us."

"Very flowery poems they are," said Mary, "but they make precious little sense."

"He wears French perfume," said Lettitia. "Have you ever heard of such a thing?!"

After a few days of settling in she wrote to her brothers. Her letters overflowed with family news. James wrote mostly of business matters; she wanted her brothers to know how the children improved and about the mysterious Mr. Ney. She included the acrostic on Jane's name. She hoped her brothers would enjoy the new amusement:

J oyless my life must pass away
A nd restless 'till my nuptial day
N ew pleasures in my bosom move
E mbracing all the fruits of love

E ncouraged by fair prospects, I
L ook forward with an anxious sigh,
I nto my future fate — But no
Z any shall ever be my Beau!
A llured by Virtue I'll persue
B enevolence, and keep in view
E xalted merit, honor, worth,
T he true nobility of Earth!
H igh heads and haughty hearts, Be gone!
— O! give me modest worth alone.

T ruth may be told — why should it not
O f <u>Him</u>, who ne'er shall be forgot?
R emembrance and repeated sight
R enew for <u>him</u> what sweet delight,
E ngendered in the Cognate mind
N ature implanted in our Kind
C ome, gentle Swain, I long to be
E mbarked on Hymen's voyage with thee.

Isabella was anxious to meet the interesting Mr. Ney, but first she needed to become reacquainted with her family. Nine-year-old Delia and seven-year-old Dick had lessons with Mrs. Williamson who still taught at Hopewell. Sarah Jane was four-and-a-half, the same age as her own daughter. They took to one another right away. Then there was little John, the brother she had never seen. He had had his first birthday last January and was beginning to toddle about and say a few words. Isabella scooped him up in her arms; it felt good to hold a baby again. Best of all was to see Ma. The tendrils that escaped her cap were flecked with silver, and she seemed to accept the luxuries life gave her with an easier grace. Otherwise she was the same Ma, and Isabella vowed to never again be so far from this dear woman.

From the window she could see her Negroes rejoining their families. They whooped with joy and tousled the youngsters in the swept yard. A dozen had been born while Isabella was gone. She was eager to speak with Peggy after chores were done. Peggy was Flora's child, the one who had been taken from the breast when Isabella's mother had died; Isabella had always harbored a kinship toward her. Peggy's Harry was the same age as her own little Jane, and Ma had written that she had another child since. Isabella had wanted to take Peggy to Mississippi, but James would not hear of it. One infant on that foolish journey was enough.

The mood in the west had brightened, although it was still far from blissful. On the third of September 1840, Frank wrote:

Dear Father

I received a letter from you a short time since, and will now answer it, since receiving yours, Hugh received one from Isabella. I am glad she was able to get to N Ca without accident. Since she left here we have had a goodeal of sickness and have several cases of fever at present, but had none yet that was dangerous, the country is generally sickly — more than has been for several years, and but few deaths in comparison to the number sick, we have had to send for a doctor but once and I hope will not have to send again. The weather has been remarcably hot and very dry in this neighborhood for the last eight week. the cotton of this state will fall short of the last years crop one third if not more. the heavy rains in the spring and the dry weather immediately afterward was very injurious. Hugh has concluded to make you a deed in trust of his property, and that will save Isabella the trouble of sining it which would be a considerable trouble, if she was to sign it, it would be necessary to have it acknowledged and recorded there, and thin sent back and get our signature and acknowledged, and recorded here. Hugh is security here, for one of our neighbors to a considerable amount and a short time since he had a sale and disposed of all his property and if he should be so disposed he can make Hugh pay the debts. Their has been a great deal of swindling in this country of late and I am affraid it is not yet over. Politicks is the all absorbing topick at this time. we entertain strong hopes that this state will go for Harrison, the changes throughout the country are very numerous, some of the most prominent men in the state have come over to Harrison.

Since the last day of August the weather has been quite cool and before that it was very hot, if it was not for the dust we would have pleasant weather, if it should continue cool we may expect an early frost — which will be very injurious to cotton. our cotton has been dying very fast with the wurm of late, and I believe it has been the case through out the county. We commenced picking cotton on the last day of August. give my love to ma and the family

> your affectionate
> son Frank

To Isabella

I will scratch you a few lines now for fear I should not do it son, Hugh will answer your letter soon — I suppose. We have had little to do but phisic the negros for the last three weeks and how much longer I cannot till. Since you left the little mule that I was in the habit of riding took the liberty to through me off and break my shoulder, which has not yet got will. I have been sick a few days but am now as well as usual. Hugh has not been unwell since you left. D^r. Malone returned a few days after you left and since that his child has died. M^{rs}. Edmons has been very low for some time with the fever and little hopes was entertained of her recovery until a few days since. M^{rs}. Hairston has a fine son, and Mr Hairston left for Virginia last week. M^{rs}. Wynic has been down with the fever I believe. M^r. Topp has moved to Columbus. James Muter is married to miss Jones. M^r. Bird is down with the fever. All Mister Hairston family has been sick white and black. last week I had the pleasure of seeing Mises Lugh Powile and the Crawleys, what do you think of that, for a man that has not seen any ladies in a year to see so many *in one week,   tell Jane she must not forget me,   M^r. Hairston and old Billy Kerr has disolved copartnership.*

Your affectionate

Brother Frank

B Williams has had a sale and disposed of all his property. old Mrs. Williams bought it and gave it to Mrs Bn Williams   I do not know how it will stand, a gooddeal has been said about it and some hard things.

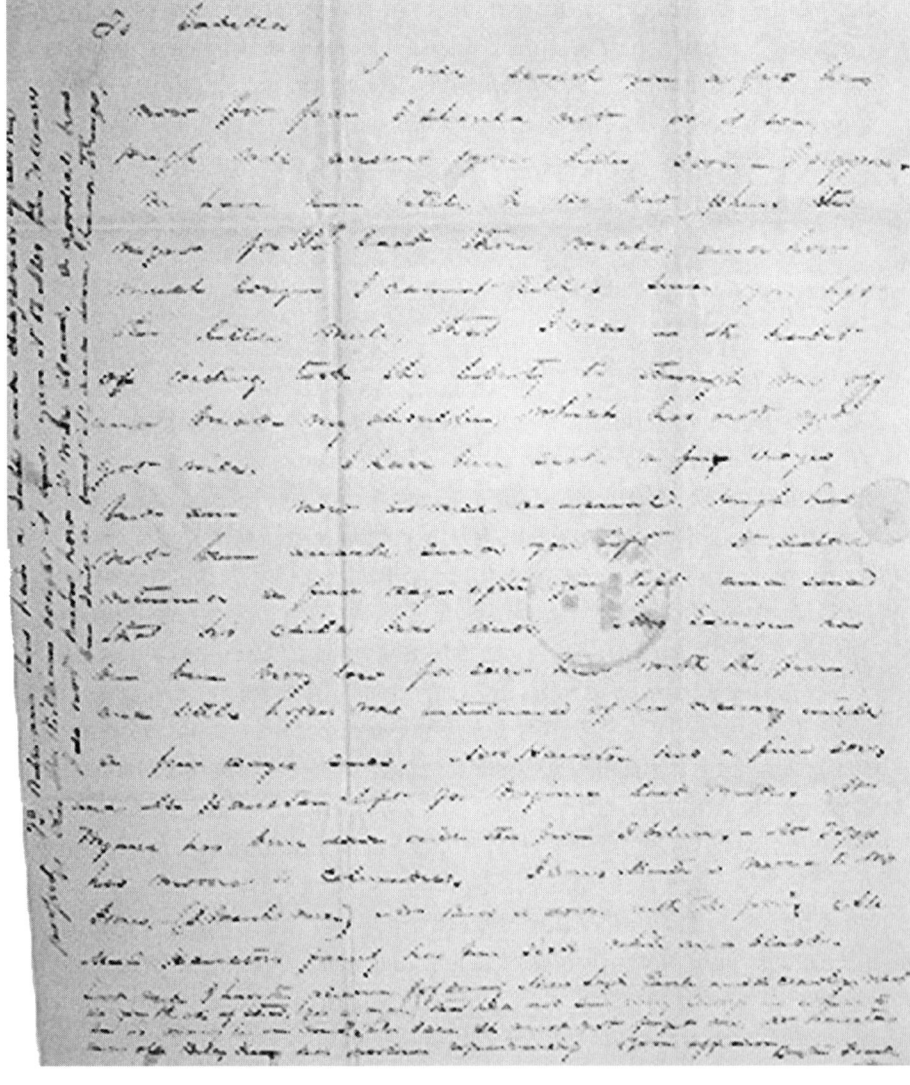

Isabella sat at her father's desk and read the letter. She was glad that hers had been a newsy one; perhaps that had spurred Frank to report the neighborhood gossip. She had nearly lost interest in how a drought or freshet or worm had spoiled their crop. She could imagine the two Mrs. Williamses cackling together over their deed. How clever of the old woman to buy her son's property and deposit it at her daughter-in-law's door. Ben was something of a scoundrel anyway; he must be fuming. She hoped the tonic given to the Negroes was preventative; Frank had not mentioned illness, so that must be the case.

As she folded the letter her eye was caught by a slim copybook. It was covered in marbled paper, red and orange swirled with cream and flecks of blue, and on it was written "Ages of Negroes." Perhaps the census taken that year had prompted James to compile it; it was dated 1840. There were nine pages of names, and each page listed a family group. Most of the names were followed by that person's age. Some of the little ones had birth dates instead.

Isabella read the names calling the familiar faces to mind. The first page began with "Flora, Sam, John, Sollomon, Melisa, and Peggy": the objects of that malicious lawsuit dealt by the Falls heirs. Had Mindy died? Her eyes scanned the page. No, there she was, near the bottom with her husband Joe and her children, John and Ann. She read through the pages noting the numbers besides the ancient ones. Ned was sixty and Nelly sixty-two. They had always been simply old to her; she had never thought how old. Barney and Bristo were both sixty-five. They had been storytellers to the little ones for as long as she could remember. She was sad to see Jim had died. She had not seen him around, and now she knew why.

There were ninety-two names in the book, a population grown through the generations. It had begun with the five Negroes her grandmother had brought into her marriage and a handful acquired by her grandfather Hugh. A few had come as dowry from James's marriages, and six were given by James Latta to his grandchildren. Most of the rest were born on the plantation. The book noted that Peter had been bought in 1823; the receipt was tucked between its pages:

State of North Carolina
Mecklenburg County ——————— All men by these presents that I
Joseph F Gillaspie have this day bargained and sold to James G.
Torrance in the county aforesaid one negro boy named Peter aged 19
or 20 years for the some of five hundred and eighty Seven Dollars &
fifty cents to me in hand paid the receipt where of I do hereby
acknowledge and which said boy I do hereby warrent to be sound
and I also warrent the said boy from the quit claims of any other

person or persons given under my hand and seal this the 14th day of May 1823

Joseph F Gillaspie

In the fall James took Lettitia and Mary to Statesville for another school session. Since he would be in the area doing business for a while, he took Dick along. He would let the boy sit in on the lessons as a sort of trial. Dick proved not to be ready for the flamboyant Mr. Ney. He was found more than once curled up and asleep on a school bench. Had James forgotten that seven was too young for a child to board?

In December, when James went to retrieve the girls, he brought Thomas's daughter, Selina, home with him to spend the holidays at Cedar Grove. Isabella was delighted. Selina was nearly her own age and one of her favorite cousins. What fun they would have at holiday festivities. Ma gathered up the girls and took them to Charlotte to shop for the occasion. They bought yards of bright plaids and ginghams and shiny black silk. The girls also needed shawls and ribbons and hose and gloves. Two of them bought dresses. Isabella was amazed. She had never before seen dresses all made up and ready to be worn sold in a store. Times had changed while she was away. Selina requested a package of snuff. Times had indeed changed. Altogether it was the best Christmas Isabella could remember, at least since the one spent in Yorkville.

~   ~   ~

Hugh had not been heard from since he declared the debt to be out of his power. James had made a peace offering and assumed that Hugh had not accepted it. On the twenty-sixth of December 1840, Hugh reached out for the olive branch but took no responsibility for its necessity:

Dear Father

It has been a long time since a letter passed between us. You I have no doubt have forgotten to answer mine for I wrote the last yes the two last and I have been waiting for one from you until nearly twelve months have roaled around   I know you think it strange that you have not received a letter from me in that time — but I think I am in some degree excusable when we take into consideration that mine have remained unanswered — I feel satisfied that you have forgotten to do so — and that it could not have been from any feeling of displeasure on your part and I hope you will not ascribe my silence to any thing of the kind.

I was glad to hear by a letter from Isabella a few days since that your family had been remarkably healthy during the last summer and fall. We have had excellent health here. I have not taken a dose of medicine in two years which you know is unusual for me. this climate suits me. I have had better health here than I had for a number of years before I came here. We have made a short crop this year not exceeding ninety bales but corn and pork enough to do us the next. The claim you hold against us we are willing to secure at any time. to have it done by deed in trust it will have to be executed according to the laws of this State   it will be necessary for you to come here or appoint an agent or trustee and have the trust placed upon record. If you can do so come out in the spring or fall. You need have no uneasiness about the debt for if there is no deed in trust or other security given the money shall be paid. I would sell everything I have if necessary for that purpose   I always look upon it as one that must be settled at all events and at any sacrifice.

Isabella seems to have some uneasiness on account of a suit brought by the Danville Bank against the heirs Wm Smith and that they may come against her property here. there is no danger in the world of that for there can be no property made liable for the contracts of Wm Smith than the property held by him at his death. [47]   they can only follow up that property and sell it when found. there is none of it here and none of it was brought here. The property here is liable for the debts of F.L. Smith dec^d. there is enough of this to take all the property here both his and Isabellas if the claim were pushed. but the creditors being mostly of his relations they have indulged. He left his affairs in great embarrassment. it will take some time to pay off the debts. I wish to get them settled without selling Isabellas property if possible. You have heard before this that our state voted for Harrison for president   we gave him a majority of over 2500 which is a large vote considering that the other party had the state before by a majority of about 3000. Every Whig is rejoiced and confidently look forward to better times. The people need a change everywhere but more particularly in this state. They have felt the presure more than any other part of the union. Cotton is advancing in price in New Orleans   That is cheering to the planter. I feel confident that if the planters of this state can realize a fair price for their crop that the state will be nearly if not entirely relieved from her embarrassments — they have had a stormy time of it for the last four years

Give my love to Ma and the children

Your affectionate son
Hugh Torrance

James hoped Hugh's confidence would be proven. He was correct in his assessment of the past four years. Martin Van Buren had been the most damaging president James could remember. He was a New York aristocrat who was opposed to slavery, westward expansion, and mending the banking crisis he had caused in 1837. His governance was unpopular in North Carolina; in Mississippi it had been devastating. Although William Henry Harrison was the product of an affluent Virginia plantation, he was more readily identified as a humble leader against Indian uprisings. He understood the plantation economy and was a hero to those engaged in westward expansion. Whether he could rescue the failed banking system remained to be seen.

James understood Hugh's reluctance to sell Isabella's property. Since they owned the land jointly, his motives were not entirely altruistic. James wasted little time answering Hugh's letter. He loved this son in spite of his somewhat irascible nature. Margaret had reminded him that Hugh's stubborn streak had come to him naturally—from father to son.

~   ~   ~

Isabella and her daughter had settled into their living arrangements at Cedar Grove. The four upstairs bedchambers were generous, and even this large family was not crowded. The two littlest Torrances still occupied a trundle in their parents' room. William and Dick shared a room, although William boarded at Davidson most of the year. Mary, Lettitia, and Delia had the room adjoining their parents. Delia could not wait until Sarah Jane was old enough to move in with them; the older girls were in Statesville so much of the time, and she was lonely. Jane gladly welcomed Isabella and her daughter into her room. They had begun to call the child "Jane Camilla"— two Janes in one household brought confusion.

Jane had developed a pattern of visiting Grandma Latta at Mount Mourne, and now Isabella and Jane Camilla joined her whenever possible. Horseback riding was good exercise for young ladies and much speedier than a lumbering wagon. As soon as they finished their breakfasts they made out for the stable where one of the Negroes would have their horses ready. When the ladies were mounted, he would hand up Jane Camilla to her mother. Sarah Jane sometimes went along, sharing Jane's steed. They galloped away as fast as the terrain would allow and covered the twelve miles in about two hours' time.

They usually arrived to find Mrs. Latta instructing her granddaughters. By now all of Betsy's sons had left Mount Mourne. The oldest boy had settled in Alabama, little Ben was still with his Uncle Robin, and the rest were at Oak Lawn. Isabella and Jane sorted through their grandmother's sewing basket and found some quiet work to keep them occupied. Sallie,

Flax, and Nannie recited their lessons until Grandma was pleased. Rufus had pinned the pet name of "Flax" on Mary Jane, for her hair was so pale a yellow it was nearly white—only Grandma Latta called her by her given name. Sallie had poor eyesight and was a special challenge; fortunately Mrs. Latta was a woman of unending patience. Bettie was too young for lessons, so she joined Jane Camilla and Sarah Jane in play, outside if the weather was fine. At the proper time the books were closed and dinner was served.

When business permitted, Mr. Reid joined them for dinner. Isabella was pleased to see that he was still a handsome man. His temples bore a tinge of gray, but his square jaw was still firm and his dark eyes as piercing as ever. Age had added only dignity to his features. He had expected to find the old Isabella at his table, the self-centered girl with the pouty lips intent on bringing misery to her father. Instead he found that her raw vivaciousness had ripened into tangy fruit. He was surprised to find himself so intrigued by this creature some twenty years his junior. He made careful note of Mrs. Latta's attentions toward Isabella and saw that her manner was more than cordial, it was clearly affectionate. Christian forgiveness was part of her powerful faith. These visits continued over the winter and spring, and Isabella became well acquainted with Rufus Reid and his little daughters.

The Mount Mourne excursions often included a visit with Grandpa Davidson who lived not two miles away. He had reached his seventy-ninth year and his health was frail. Uncle Frank was often away, and the General's daughters and many grandchildren kept an eye on him. On fine days chairs would be brought outside and placed under a shade tree. Jane Camilla nestled in the old man's lap, and his eyes crinkled with pleasure at having the child in his company. Other days the visits had to be conducted in his bedchamber. The curtains were drawn against bad air, and no amount of cleansing could remove the stench of illness from his chamber pot.

~   ~   ~

Although Hugh had not become a frequent correspondent, he seemed anxious to keep the rift mended, and on the twelfth of April 1841, wrote James:

Dear Father

I have received your letter of Feb. 19ᵗʰ We have had the most tremendous rains since the 25ᵗʰ of March I ever saw fall the water courses have been higher than they have ever been since this country was settled by the whites. The Yalobusha river has been to high to cross for the last two weeks. Frank left on the 18th March for Orleans with our cotton and has not yet returned he will be home

*in a few days. I have been entirely alone since he left. I am tired
enough but I have as much as I can attend to about the plantation
which makes it more bearable than it would be if I had nothing to
employ me. I have been busily engaged in planting cotton for some
days past. I shall finish in about three days more (good weather) our
corn is up prettily. I commenced planting the 18th March. The trees
are green and the weather warm. We had our cotton taken off this
spring on a keel boat from within a mile and a half of the house
which saved us a great deal of hauling. there has been two boats up
this spring   one carried 209 bales and the other upwards of 300. I
think we will have no difficulty hereafter in getting off cotton.
the stream is a good one for keel boating. We made last year 98 bales
of cotton averaging 400 not much over half the number we made the
year before and the price not much better*

*I am unable to say when we will be able to pay you the money on
the Camble debt   I think it would be best for you to come here and
take a deed in trust on property enough to secure yourself. I shall feel
better satisfied when you are entirely secured. It takes all we make
to keep us along here. I hope times will change for the better soon
I find it hard getting along without Isabella   I miss her and Jane
very much. I hope you will not object to her coming back. You have
a large family about you & will not miss her so much. I will do all I
can for her*

> *Give my love to all the family*
> *affectionately your son*
> *H Torrance*

A keel boat, thought James, what a grand and simple way to tame their
unpredictable waterway—if only the Catawba could be so easily conquered.
A reliable canal system had never materialized, and the prospect of a railroad still seemed remote. James supposed Hugh kept bringing up the ubiq-
uitous deed-in-trust to assuage his guilt and could not fathom how it would
benefit him. Should those faraway lands revert to him, it would be a responsibility, not a windfall. He smiled as he read Hugh's stoic laments of loneliness. This often distant son did love and miss his family, especially Isabella.

Camilla's letters continued to be filled with plagues and fears of plagues,
dwelling on perils in spite of her husband's boundless prosperity. The
Torrance family had learned to dismiss her claims that every fever had
proved to be entirely fatal and were stunned when she wrote that little

Willie had died on the twelfth of July, drawing his last breath at nine o'clock that Monday evening. It was a crowded carriage of Torrances that arrived at Yorkville's Rose Hill Cemetery to bury the six-year-old child. Camilla was truly distraught and could find little comfort in her newborn child, Annie. That would come later.

On the first of August, Frank wrote to his Father:

Dear Father

I have intended writing to you every day for the last two weeks but have not done so as you will see from this. I write so little that I find it almost impossible to get at it. Since you heard from us we have been getting along about as well as usual. the health of our family has been very good, although there has been a great deal of sickness in the country, and still continues to be, — I have heard of but few deaths yet.

We have had a very severe drought in this country this summer, which continues without any remission   the corn cropps will be shorter in this country this fall than they have been since I have been in the country. the cropp last year was short, and corn has been worth $1.00 per bush all spring and summer, and it is thought by sum that it will be worth 1$ per bush at the heap this fall.

Thoˢ S Cowan of S[a]lisbury spent two nights and days with us a short time since, he has been engaged in speculating in lands in this state, and is out trying to get the company which he has been engaged with to assist him in paying the debts of the company in Nº Ca   he is very much distressed and is afraid he will be broken up. the other members of the company have done very little or nothing, and seam to care as little about his troubles as if they were not the cause.

I new very little about him before I left NC, but I had heard you speak of him in the highest terms, which always led me to respect him. I find him a very different sort of man from his brother, James Cowan of Tenn. he is the right sort of a man. he spoke of you very frequently while he was with us, and expressed a great desire to visit you, but said his business had been such, that he had not been able to. I hope he will be able to get through with his difficulties without much sacrifice, the lands the company own in this state are very valuable

Notwithstanding the drouht our crop is tolerably fair, the stand of cotton is not good, but is growing very finely and I think we will make a fair crop. the corn is better than any in the neighborhood, or country. We planned a large crop of corn, more than usual and more than is necessary in an average crop year, and by that means we shall be able to make enough to do us. our wheat crop is good for this country   about 15 bush per acre, and the oat crop is also fine. We make a little of almost everything for sale, which is not usual in this country among cotton planters.

I received a letter from Isabella on yesterday which I will answer in a few days

Give my love to all the family while
I remain your affectionate
son J F Torrance

Frank was determined to write cheerful letters and show his father how their lot had improved. The brothers continued to buy land and raise more of their crops for sale. This was the demarcation between prosperous planters and mere farmers. James would understand; still no money was sent.

Late in the summer William was at home between college sessions. A frequent visitor was his classmate William Davidson. William had known the Davidson boy all his life, after all he was a cousin to Aunt Betsy's sons, which meant the boys were also cousins of a sort. The Davidson plantation, Rural Hill, was the grandest in the county and was the beacon by which James measured his progress; according to his reckoning, Cedar Grove was not far behind. The two Williams had not been close companions as children, as the Davidson boy was four years older, but now the age difference was moot. They were classmates from similar families with an abiding interest in becoming doctors. Each boy hoped *that* profession was honorable enough to elicit paternal support in abandoning agriculture.

An added attraction at Cedar Grove was Jane. William Davidson remembered her vaguely from the Sundays at Hopewell, when an eleven-year-old girl was of little interest to a lad of sixteen. Her four years at Salem had overlapped his tenure at Davidson, and their paths had not crossed for some time. William immediately noticed her metamorphosis, and Jane was not oblivious to his attentions. In fact she decided that her presence was needed at home and perhaps Isabella and Jane Camilla should visit Mount Mourne without her. "Mr. Reid seems to direct all of his conversation to you, Isabella," she had said. "He must be seriously fond of you; after all he already has Grandma to care for his girls."

"And I suppose you are needed here to help Ma set a place at the table for William's friend? Poor Ma, she could not possibly lift an extra plate by herself!" They both laughed; it had become a delectable summer.

Mr. Reid was frequently away for weeks at a time. In addition to operating his plantation and tending to the farms he rented out, he was often in New York, Philadelphia, or Charleston buying goods for his mercantile business. And when requested by his neighbors, he sometimes bought and sold Negroes.[48] Isabella enjoyed his company when he was available, especially when dinner was followed by a long walk.

"Have you always lived at Mount Mourne?" she asked. Although she had known him nearly all her life, she knew little about him.

"No. I bought this property just before my first marriage. I was raised at Catawba Springs; you've heard of the spa there? My parents were the proprietors and catered to a very fashionable crowd. Some came to take the waters for their health, but most came for frivolity. My childhood was spent amid horse races, balls, and card games. The rice barons and others of their sort came every year from the low country to escape coastal fevers. They seemed to have no limit to their pocketbooks or their yen for pleasure."

"It must have been exhilarating. I love to ride, but I've never competed. Were you permitted to race?"

"Sometimes, but I was also required to groom the horses. We lived beside the privileged class, not within it. It was a grand life, but you can imagine Mrs. Latta did not find it suitable for her daughter."

"I can see that she would not," replied Isabella.

"Understand that we had a fine home, and my father fought bravely in the War for Independence. Mrs. Latta fully approved of my family, but she did not want her grandchildren immersed in such worldliness. Nancy and I did live there for a short while until I could build a house here."

"The house you live in now?"

"No, the small one Mrs. Latta occupies across the road. I built this house when I married Betsy. I had saved some money by then and thought it would be a great disservice to remove her from Oak Lawn to a tiny cottage."

As their friendship deepened, Isabella knew there was a delicate question she would have to broach. "Grandpa once mentioned that he rarely sees you at Centre Church; is there another one that you prefer?"

"No," he replied, "I sometimes go with my children, but generally they go with their grandmother. I'm afraid I am not a bona fide member of any congregation." This was the answer that Isabella did not want to hear.

"Oh, I am so sorry," she blurted. "I mean, I'm sorry to have pried. Grandma never said a word. Does she approve of this arrangement?"

"Not entirely, we have made an amicable truce over matters of faith. I respect her convictions but I cannot embrace them. She has my permission to pray for my soul as often as she likes, as long as she does so privately. And she is free to see that her grandchildren are churched. I respect the right of anyone to believe as they wish, and she respects, although reluctantly, my deism. Should I have a change of heart, she will be the first to know." Isabella would give this some thought. If someone as devout as Grandma could accept his lack of conviction, then surely she could.

It was quickly becoming obvious that she and Rufus were well suited. Neither of them had any use for the mundane, yet they took their responsibilities seriously. He possessed the same impetuous spirit that had been so enticing in Franklin Smith but none of Smith's reckless flaws. Mr. Reid displayed a gentleness that would have seemed unmanly in a meeker person. Isabella watched him with his girls and saw that their good manners were bred from a desire to please this kindly bear of a man. They were indeed two of a kind. Near the end of the year Rufus proposed marriage to Isabella. He had discreetly asked for Mrs. Latta's approval, and she had given it. She was confident that Isabella would be a fine mother to her grandchildren.

The new year was a time of new beginnings, and once again James launched into a project. Hopewell Church and Davidson College were thriving without his supervision, although his money was still welcome. "I think we should open a school for young ladies," he said to Margaret. "A half dozen girls in addition to our own should make for a fine school." A dark cloud had begun to swirl around the fanciful Mr. Ney. James still admired the man's erudite manner, but rumors about his personal life invited caution. Ney's love of wine was no secret, and there was a persistent tale about a dangerous past in France. His scars and limping gait supported the wild talk. He might be a suitable tutor for boys, but girls were much too fragile to be under his care.

The idea evolved into a plan. Mrs. Williamson did not offer the higher branches of study, and his girls were not yet prepared for Salem. By opening his own school he could decline Ney's services without embarrassment, an ideal solution to his predicament. He inquired of Mrs. Williamson, and anyone else who would listen, about proper teachers for young ladies, especially those ready for the higher branches. Finally a woman was retained who met all of his requirements. Margaret agreed with his concept but was wary of the details. "Where shall we put six girls and a teacher?" she asked, "and where do you plan to hold classes?"

"There is plenty of room in this house for the students; we managed before with eleven children under this roof. Isabella will be gone soon and William is rarely at home. I believe the log house will make a fine school. The tutoress can use the living quarters, and she can take her meals with us and have as much privacy as she desires." The log house had been resurrected one more time for yet another use.

Days later James placed a notice in the *Charlotte Journal*:

> Having obtained a Lady of fine accomplishments as a Tutoress in my family, I propose to take in 5 or 6 young ladies as borders and pupils. Boarding will be provided at $7½ per month.
>
> | | |
> |---|---|
> | Tuition in the common branches of English Education, per session of 5 months | $8 |
> | Higher Branches | 10 |
> | Music | 20 |
> | French | 10 |
> | Drawing and Painting | 6 |
> | Needle Work | 5 |
>
> Session to commence the 1st of March

It was not long before girls began to arrive. Beds were shifted about to form small dormitories, and doors connecting the parlors were folded back. Drop leaf tables were opened up and pushed together for a dining hall. Rufus Reid had planned a business trip in the north, and James requested that he buy books. In Philadelphia Rufus spent over seventy dollars for a dozen copies each of twelve textbooks, many boxes of paints, pencils, drawing papers, and other requirements for a school. He read over the titles as he placed the books neatly in their packing crate: *Colburn Arithmetic, Watts Mind, Mitchell Primary Geography, Burrows Primer, Smith Grammar, Mitchell and Atlas*, and several levels of the *Emerson Reader*. The terrestrial globe came with its own handsome box. It was going to be a fine school. [49]

~ ~ ~

On the twenty-sixth of February, one of Ephraim Davidson's Negro boys appeared at Cedar Grove. "The young Mr. Davidson sent me to get you," he said to James. "The old General has died in the night, and Mr. Davidson says he needs you to come." James rode with the boy to Mount Mourne. In the darkened parlor he found neighbor women and Ephraim's two daughters laying out the body. Their hands dashed through the air like butterflies lighting briefly on pails of water, washing rags, and cakes of soap. They moved deftly as if to a well-known dance, lining the box with a soft cloth, dressing the washed body in his silk suit, and arranging the parlor for the occasion. It was an ancient ritual orchestrated by women to high-pitched whispers. Frank Davidson looked lost in his own home. James led the man into the study and poured them both a glass of brandy.

"Isabella told me your father was weak when she was here last, but we had no idea his time was so near," said James.

"Sunday last he became quite ill, and I sent for Dr. Houston," said Frank. "He told me Pa had pneumonia and left behind some medicine. Pa seemed to rally for a bit, then day before yesterday went into a decline. I had the doctor fetched again, and he spent the night at Pa's bedside. Yesterday he remained for a while, then left us with another vial of medicine stating there was nothing more he knew to do. Last night Pa lost his struggle for breath. His lungs gurgled as if he had drowned."

"He will be greatly missed," said James.

Frank buried his face in his hands, and was silent for a while, then raised his head to sip his brandy and spoke at last, "I am thankful you relented and sent for Isabella; her presence and her little girl have been the brightness for Pa this past year. I can see that I was selfish not to have brought them home from Mississippi, and I apologize to you, sir."

"There is no need to apologize. I was probably not yet ready to take her in, or I would have gone for her myself. It took me a very long while to understand that to forgive is not to condone. But that aside, you must know what a great comfort your father and mother have always been to me. I was nearly helpless after my Nancy died. It was your parents I have to thank for keeping my family knit together."

Ephraim willed his home, his Negroes, and most of his land to Frank. He had invested heavily in bank stock during his lifetime and left hundreds of shares to Frank, his daughters, and his many grandchildren. Thirty-five shares, worth a hundred dollars each, were divided between Hugh, Frank, Camilla, and Isabella. He also left five hundred dollars to care for his daughter's insane child. [50]

~   ~   ~

In the Carolina piedmont spring begins to unfold itself in March and by mid-April reaches its most splendorous peak. The flowering trees of the woods are in high adornment, and the orchards are in full blossom, promising bounty. Isabella and Rufus were married on the nineteenth of April 1842, in the midst of nature's most unabashed display. Isabella was radiant. She truly loved Rufus Reid, and at last she had pleased her father. At Mount Mourne she began assuming her duties as mother to her new children. She was careful to take her cue from Grandma Latta; it was not her desire to upset a smoothly run household.

James wrote to his sons in the west and encouraged them to come home for a visit. The houseful of girls would leave in July; that would be the perfect time. Hugh declined, being otherwise occupied; but Frank scraped together money for the stage and made his first trip home in nearly six years. It was a joyous visit lasting well over a month. Frank took delight in becoming reacquainted with his large family—that is, all except Dick who had been sent to Statesville to study. Mr. Ney was still considered an acceptable tutor for boys. Frank was in Mecklenburg on the unfortunate occasion of the death of Reverend Williamson. He had been Hopewell's preacher for nearly twenty-five years and left a cavernous void. Frank regretted that he could not stay for Jane and William Davidson's wedding scheduled for December, but he was needed in Mississippi to help complete the harvest and arrange for its sale. As usual, he spent too much time in the sun, and his skin began to erupt with boils. When he returned to the west, he wrote on the twenty-eighth of November 1842:

Dear Father

I have been home near a week — had a pleasant trip and was fortunate enough to have company from Lincolnton N^o Ca to Columbus Missi. I have been verry much affected with biles since I left N^o Ca. I had a second one on my neck, and since my arrival I have had a verry severe one on my left arm, near the elbow, which has prevented me from doing any kind of business. I have been quite well in other respects. I found brother Hugh well, but has not been so all summer   the country has been remarkably healthy this summer, no sickness of any kind. The crops of cotton and corn are verry fine, our crop is as good as the crop of 1839. — the fall has been favorable for gathering. we have at this time 80 Bagg packed and several more to Ginn. I think we will make about 120 Bagg of 450^{lb} Each. we will also make plenty of pork to do us, and have a plenty of everything else. We have nothing to buy but shoes and hats this year and will have nothing more the next. Bagging & rope (Kentucky) is selling very low, Bagging from 12 1/2 to 18. Rope 6 to 8. Corn is selling at 25 cents per Bush. Cotton from 5 to 7 1/2 cts.

Since I arrived we have had a very cold spell   have had ice 3/4 inch thick, the weather is quite cold at this time,   the day I got home it sleeted very hard. if the weather continues cold any length of time the planters will lose near one forth of their cotton crop. a great deal has already wasted

Give my love to all the family

Your affectionate son
James F Torrance

Excuse the shortness of this
Tell William I will write to him soon

12 Plantation Life 1843~1844

The marriage of Jane to William Davidson extended the Torrance family to yet another plantation. Letters and visits meandered between Rural Hill, Mount Mourne, Yorkville, Mississippi, and Cedar Grove. Farm life was similar from one place to another, nevertheless everyone was interested in keeping up with their relations.

On the third of January, William Latta wrote to his father-in-law from Yorkville:

Mr Torrance

Dear Sir — I rec^d about an hour since yours of yesterday morning in relation to the condition of my jacks foot — The jack happened to be here and I got two gentlemen to look at his foot, their opinion is that the jack is not worth more than half price — that is very doubtful whether he will stand well enough on that foot to cover a man this season — both consider it an old sore and that it procedes from the scratches. I think the jack stands and moves rather better on that foot than when I got him probably from his being rested — but the sore is certainly getting larger — trusting to Mr. Halls statement that it was a recent hurt and that rest and clenliness would relieve him. I did not venture to do anything for him, more than to wash   guess I tore the sore —

He has improved in appearance since I got him   is very much admired, and I should be very much grieved should his foot seriously injure him. My fears on that seem as such now that did I know how to return him to Hall, I should certainly insist upon it. I would advise that nobody would be safe in trading for the note — as further time on my part will be necessary to ascertain the injury the foot may do the jack — I would write to Hall on the subject but I do not know where he is to be found —

Mr. Jacobs has rented Pa's house for a female school   it is convenient to our house. Camilla would be pleased to have Letitia and Mary for company   If you and cousin Margaret can consent sending them here. I think you will be pleased with the result. The session commenses the first of January — I feel so confident in the superiority of the institution over any that I have ever known that I

165

feel no hesitation in saying that Letitia and Mary at their ages would derive great benefit from going to it — If it suits your views let us hear from you soon on the subject. Camilla and children join me in rememberance to yourself mother and family — children send kisses to all

affectionately

your son

W A Latta

Please write soon [51]

James well understood his concern for the jack. Jacks and mules were the most useful of plantation work animals, but mules could not reproduce. It took a jack and a mare to get a mule. Horses were speedy—good for transportation and sport but fragile and much less efficient at the plow. A good jack could bring four times the price of a mule, and sometime ten times that of a horse. It was nearly a year later that William Latta wrote to say: "My Jack's foot has improved considerably but I do not think it will ever be sound." James was surprised to see that Robert and Eliza's house was to become a school. It was certainly large enough to house a number of young ladies and had been empty since Robert moved his family to Columbia, but James and Margaret were satisfied with their own little school. They would continue it for one more year until their girls were ready for Salem.

At Mount Mourne, Isabella's new daughters were a charming and challenging lot. Their raising so far had been accomplished by an indulgent father and a pious grandmother, and the results were surprisingly pleasing. Sallie was thirteen and nearly blind. Isabella aimed to be as helpful as possible, yet teach the child independence. It was a task like none she had ever encountered. Flax, at twelve, had become her sister's eyes. Their lessons were always done together; Flax read and Sallie memorized. Nannie was ten, and Bettie and Jane Camilla were both seven. It was a lively household.

On the eleventh of February, Isabella gave birth to Emma. It was such a pleasure to have a baby in her arms again. She nestled the fragrant infant against her turgid breast, and prayed that peaceful thoughts would help eclipse the pain. She was determined to nurture her own infant and not look for a wet nurse among the Negroes.

On the eleventh of April 1843, Camilla wrote her father from Yorkville:

Dear Father

I received Janes letter and was pleased to hear that you were all well, we also had a letter from Mr. Reid the same day we were sorry to hear that Isabella had suffered so much with her breast, I know it must be very painful, we had not heard of it until Jane wrote. I was thinking that she would soon be able to pay us a visit.

I expect your words will come true with regards to Jane and William Davidson, you will be down to see us before them, we have been looking for Jane ever since we left your house in the winter, I feel sometimes as if we were forgotten by all of you — we seldom have a visit from you   I cannot immagine what is the matter, I am sure that no one could be more pleased to see you than we would be at any time, I do hope dear Father that you will come down soon and bring ma with you —

Mary Ann and Mr. Osbourne were down this week   he said that he had seen you in Charlotte and that all were well — I was much pleased to see Mary Ann   she is very lively and looks quite as well as ever, the same old Mary Ann and has changed as little as anyone in my knowledge. The[y] made a very short visit only one day Mary Ann told us that Sarah Williamson had become a citizen of Charlotte and that James Johnston was married. We had before heard that John Davidson had taken unto himself a wife quite young I think, but doing very well I believe.

We have no news in our little village. our school is flourishing and I hope Mr. Jacobs will succeed well

We have had several fires lately which have kept the village busy in endeavoring to find out who the perpetrator was, we have had four barns burnt down during the winter. Jane says nothing about what they intend doing.

We have had a very backward spring and I think farmers are very much behind hand. We have not heard from brothers Hugh and Frank   William and the children join with me in love to you Ma and all

Give our love to Jane and William Davidson   Say to Jane that she must come down soon

Your affectionate Daughter
Camilla

We heard that Uncle Frank was to be married and I hope it may be true as we would be glad to attend another wedding, they seem to have gotten into the spirit lately.

It was a cheerful letter for Camilla. Perhaps losing Willie had taught her to dwell on what was, not what was feared. Jane had whispered that she was expecting a child. The prospect had pleased her until she visited Isabella and saw her sister's silent tears flow more freely than her milk. She knew that she would also suffer for Eve's sin. In time Isabella's swelling subsided and feeding the child became a pleasure to them both. When she was fully recovered, she and Jane planned a visit to John Davidson's new wife. They giggled at the idea of it; it had been many years since a woman had lived at Oaklawn. The rumor of Uncle Frank's marrying was simply that. His bachelor home, being brim full of books, would be even more difficult to tame. As much as she loved her uncle, Isabella could not imagine the woman who could fit his establishment.

James received a long-awaited letter from Mississippi written by Frank on the twenty-ninth of May:

Dear Father

I have been much longer writen to you than I intended when I wrote last, but nothing has occured since of any importance and I am in hopes you will not be uneasy

I received a letter from William a day or two since which [has been the] only one that I have received [since I] wrote I did not receive [yours] until the court was over in [Tennessee] and consequently did not [attend]

I have been [in better] health since my return than [I have] for several years I have been [very] closely confined at attending [to our] business. We have been building better [houses] than we have lived in since we came [to this] country and both Hugh and myself have been more busily engaged than usual

I am generally so worried by night that I am not in a mood to write and in day time I cannot find time to stay in the house long enough to do so.

I know that you have had experience enough to know how a man feels after walking all day from one part of a farm to another and particularly in the spring when we ought to be on the foot from day untill dark and very often an hour or two after. Brother Hugh was in N. Orleans several weeks in the early part of the spring which made it a little harder on myself. [We have] an unusual fine prospect for [crops] corn is very fine and wheat [is too. We have an] exelent stand of cotton such as [we have never] had before. our corn is from

*[waist] high which is very fine [despite] the lateness of the spring
we [endured the] severest weather in March that [has been]
experienced in this country since it was first settled   we had [many
snows] in that month, the weather [has] been fine since the first of
April and every thing has grown very rapidly*

    *I have not heard from Isabella for some time and I don't think I
have received a letter from Camilla since I got home. William does
not mention William Latta family in his letter and I am in hopes
from that, they are well. William writes me that your crop of cotton
has turned out very fine. I expect you will think you have as good a
cotton country as ours if the seasons should be as good as the last.*

    *I am better pleased with our country since I visited N⁰ Ca than
I was [before] and I think there is a few of [circums]tances in N⁰ Ca
that could not [be helped] by coming to this country   [living] is
cheap hear. Corn 37 1/2 cts [bacon] 2 1/2 to 5 cts. and every thing
else in [plentiful]*

    *I will with [pleasure] give my love to Ma and [to yourself and]
to all the family — tell Letti[tia and] Mary to write me a few lines
[We] think sum of the girls might write to us two or three times in a
month and I hope you will get them to do so*

Your affectionate son
James F Torrence [52]

The summer was an uneventful one at Cedar Grove except for a persistent illness first suffered in June by Sarah Jane. The doctor was called for her
several times, then sporadically throughout the summer as the malady leapt
from one Negro cabin to another. Isabella kept close to home at Mount
Mourne. The children in her charge had increased from one to six at near
blinding speed. All of her energies were absorbed.

Rufus continued to tend to his various rented farms and other business
in the neighborhood. In September he left on an extended buying trip in the
north. In Philadelphia he made a purchase for James—Margaret was again
in need of china. He bought two sets of white ironstone ware, each consisting of seven dozen plates of assorted sizes and nineteen serving pieces
including nine meat dishes. Two tea sets, several dozen wine glasses and
tumblers, and a handful of ewers, basins, and chamber pots completed the
order.

On the fifteenth of October 1843, Frank wrote from the west; the edges
of his melancholia were beginning to encroach once again:

Dear Father

I received yours of the 28th August three weeks ago at which time I was very sick and continued so until about the time the court came on in Tenn. consequently I was unable to attend. My health has been good with that exception since I left NºCa, and am in hopes that I will be well again in a short time

The health of our family has been good, with the exception of myself, this summer, not having to call in a physician this year. I think we are blessed with as healthy a country as any in the U States. we have great reason to be thankful for the good health which our family has enjoyed and the abundance of our crops.

I think we are truly fortunate in having settled in so healthy a country. we have been unfortunate in sum respects, but in others we have been more than as fortunate   Experience is said to be the best knowledge, and surely it ought to be, for we generally pay dear enough for it. The lessons which I have had since coming to this country has taught me at least to believe so, and I am in hopes the sad lessons which we have had will not be without their influence upon us in future. Although such lessons are useful, yet they will not extricate us from difficulties which our evil judgement and folly may have brought upon us, but with the kind assistance which you have given us, and our own exertions I am in hopes we will be able soon to get through with difficulties. Our crop notwithstanding the dryness of season is fair, we have not gathered much cotton yet, in consequence of the rain which has lately fallen. At this time the weather is fair and quite cool, for the last three mornings, we have had frost.

Brother Hugh will be married shortly. (perhaps this month.)   the time I believe is not yet fixed upon   Miss Powell is the name of the young lady, her mother is a widow lady, and lives in about six miles of us. she is an amiable young lady and is beloved by all that know her. I am indeed glad that he is going to marry, and that so soon. Isabella I think had a slight acquaintance with the young lady

If there should not be a decision of the sale in Tennessee I will try and git to attend the next court if you think it necessary. Write to me as soon as you hear. Give my love to Mother and the family

   Your affectionate Son
   James F Torrance

To Sister Mary

  As I was not able to write you a few lines when I wrote to Letty I will do so now. I am at a loss what to write but must acknowledge the few lines I received from you. I was very glad to find you had not forgotten me, and that you complyed with your promise to write to me I hope you will not let it be the last, if you only write three lines some times they will always be acceptable. I have been very sick, but have gotten mostly well again. I have a very lonesome time when I am sick, no one to keep me company, — brother Hugh having to be out all day in the plantation, each day appears long enough for two or three. our house is lonesome enough when I am well, but to be sick is awfull. Give my love to sisters Jane and Letty Delia and Sara

    Affectionately
     Your brother Frank

To Brother Dick, dear Dick, I was very sorry that I did not see you when I was at Pa, and I think after my long ride from Mississippi to see you all, you might have rode thirty miles to see me. I am affraid I will not get to see you soon. I was glad you thought enough of me to write to me. I hope you will learn fast and get through your studys and come out and see us,

     Your affectionate Brother Frank

Isabella did remember Hugh's young woman. They had not been close, but her unusual family was not easily forgotten: Miss Jane Powell had twin brothers and twin sisters. Her widowed mother was admired far and wide for keeping such a household on the frontier.

At Rural Hill, Jane gave birth to a little boy on the twenty-first of October. They named him James Torrance Davidson after her father. James was pleased to finally have a grandson bearing his name. With good humor William Davidson conceded to this name for his son. The Davidson names had been so often used as to be nearly worn out, he had said. In fact he carried two middle names to avoid confusion.

James planned to take Margaret to admire the new grandchild, but the painful labored breathing of asthma threatened to hobble him again. He increased his dose of quinine and soon felt well enough to make the short trip. He wrote to Camilla and reported the vigor of the infant and how he had averted trouble and been able to see the babe. On the fifth of November 1843, she replied:

Dear Father

I received your letter and was pleased to hear that you were all better, I was glad to hear Jane was doing well, hope she will soon be up.

I have not had a letter from brother Hugh or Frank since I saw you. We have all had a slight attack of chill and fever since our return, we attribute it to our trip to N Carolina, we were all sick at once   one was not able to wait on another. I do not know what we should have done if it had not been for kind friends. I have been looking for Isabella and M Reid down ever since Mr Reids return. We have nothing in the way of news in our little village. We expect to have an agricultural meeting on Tuesday next   on Wednesday Mr Jacobs examination. We expect to go to the plantation on tomorrow to make a short stay. William finds that they do a great deal better when he is out there. We talk of going there to live, we expect to stay there the greater part of the winter. We would be pleased to see you soon. William and the children join in love to you Ma and the children.

> *Your affectionate daughter*
> *Camilla C. Latta*

Camilla's old habits had begun to return, James thought; at least the entire letter was not about illness and death. Mr. Jacobs's school must have been successful enough to hold examinations. And William had come to terms with the difficulties of being an absentee planter. They might some-day find themselves permanent residents of Bullock Creek.

When Rufus was in Philadelphia, James had requested that he select a piano for Isabella. He had given one to Camilla some years before, and he knew how much Isabella desired one. Music was as important as any branch of learning. Early in November, the letter arrived:

Mr R Reed
Mt Mourne NC
> *Dr Sir*

> *I hereby take the liberty addressing you in order to inform you that I yesterday shipped . . . to the address of McGee & Shannon Charleston S.C., E. Waterman   Georgetown SC & Felix Long Cheraw SC   Three Boxes contg the Piano Forte, Legs, Stool, etc of*

Mr. James G Torrance   Mecklenburg Cy NC, & all marked with the above directions

Hoping that above said goods safely may come to hand and after opening meet with entire satisfaction   I remain

Very Respectfully

Your Most obedient servant

E. N. Scherr [53]

Isabella beamed as she read the note. She had long desired a piano, but that was only part of her satisfaction. The implicit approval of her father gave her the most pleasure. She had heard that the blind often excelled at the piano. Was there someone nearby who could instruct Sallie? She wondered if the boat from Philadelphia took longer than the post. She would insist that she accompany Rufus to Cheraw to fetch the precious cargo.

Meanwhile, William Davidson achieved his dream and became a student at the medical college in Charleston. It was difficult for him to leave his wife and child, but he could not afford to pass up the opportunity. In spite of his choice of profession, he was completely ignorant about infant care. He did not know that merely eating and sleeping could devour entire days and weeks for both mother and newborn. He had much to learn at medical school. On the tenth of December, he wrote to James burying panic beneath duty and excitement:

Dear Father

I have set apart this evening to fulfil a promise which I made you when I left & that was to write you as soon as I arrived in Charleston. Owing to my being very busy reading since I came some of the lectures which was over before I came here   I have not wrote you as soon as I intended & have not fulfiled my promise. I hope that you will not think it the cause of neglect on my part. Since I came to Charleston I have written two letters to Jane and have received no word from her yet. I have anxiously expected a letter by every mail for the last week: but have been disappointed every time I go to the office. What can be the cause I know not. You will please write me as soon as you can & let me know for I am very anxious to hear. It is two weeks today since I came here. Had a very pleasant trip here the weather was fine. Detained one day in Camden longer than I expected to be   Had the company of Mʳ Chambers of Salisbury from Charlotte to Branchville.

Business I found quite brisk here   Merchants from various parts laying in goods this last week. . . . The cotton market seems to be on the mend   I seen Mr Chambers last evening & he says that it is bringing from 7.25 to 8 1/3 ct. Some lots of upland has sold for as high as 9 — He says that he thinks it will still be better. I send you a paper which contains the current prices at the market.

The medical college is in a very flourishing state . . . Some are still comming in. So I find that [I] was not the last one coming or the only one <u>married</u>. There are twelve or fourteen (married) I believe that are in the class — A number of the students rarely attend the lecture rooms

The faculty of the college I have made the acquaintance with some of them & think them talented men, well calculated to fill the post which they fill. I have seen several very important surgical operations performed since I came. This morning I visited the <u>Marine Hospital</u> with the attending physicians. They were between 3 & 4 — the hospital afflicted with various diseases — some incurable

The general health of Charleston is very good with little sickness. My acquaintance with it is very limited   Know but three or 4 of the students & they are boarding at the same house. I get private boarding on King Street with a widow lady at $3.50 per week. It is getting late. My eyes seams somewhat disposed to close & my fire has nearly gone out except one or two coals   So I will bid you good night & close

Your affectionate Son
W S M Davidson

Tell William to write me & let me hear what he intends doing

Jane was fine, merely caught up in baby care and regaining her strength. James would reassure the young man and give Jane a stern talk about distressing her husband. He passed the letter along to William who was at home after completing his studies. It had taken him several years longer than William Davidson to finish the course, being younger and less prepared. James agreed with his son-in-law's assessment of the cotton market. Cotton farmers all over the south were seeing a turnabout in cotton prices. For forty years the price had dropped nearly every year as more and more acres were put under the plow. As long as demand was high, few people suffered. Over the past five years demand had waned but production had not. Now the market seemed to be righting itself. James was relieved to hear that the men in South Carolina had reached the same conclusion. In a few weeks he would make his annual trip to Charleston to sell his crop.

The trend was the same in Mississippi. For the first time since his sons had gone to that place, prices were creeping up. On the nineteenth of February 1844, Frank wrote an almost cheerful letter:

Dear Father

After a long silence I again have the pleasure of writing to you. I have not heard from any of the family for sum time, a few days ago we received a letter from Isabella which is the only one that we have had for several months. The mails in this part of the country have been very irregular for nearly four months during which time we have had scarcely any weather that was fit for business. We only finished gathering our cotton on the 16th of this month, and our corn crop about two weeks before. the watter courses have been very high, but at this time are [below] boating order. We have shipped a portion of our crop which brought from 8 1/4 to 10 cts. — the extreme prices in N Orleans at this time is 7 1/2 to 12 1/2 and going up a little, the cotton will no doubt be a short on[e] compared with the crop of '42. We have not got quite through ginning, but will make about 120 Bales (400 each) our corn crop was good, and we made a plenty of Pork to do us,   We are getting along as well, in every respect as we have reason to expect, and I hope, since cotton has got to bringing a good price we will soon be able to get out of debt.

We commenced this morning to ploughing and hope soon to be able to plant another crop, the weather for two weeks past has been good, and the prospects good for a continuance. I am in tolerably good health and in better spirits than I have been for several years in fact I might say since I left you, for my troubles commenced soon after and continued to increase until lately. I am troubled greatly with a pain in my rite side, which at times is very severe.

Our home is much more pleasant than it was before Hugh got married, and I may say, I think he will never regret his choice. his wife is an excellent woman, one of the best I ever knew. The more I see of her the better I am pleased at her. I think he has done better than he would have done to have married M.A. and I have no doubt he is convinced of it.

I wish you could find time to visit us, and bring Ma and girls we would be most happy to see you. Hugh will leave for N Orleans in a short time, to attend to our cotton, the trip is a short one taking not more than 18 or 20 days and not expensive. The cost of getting our cotton to N Orleans has been but little this season, 787 1/2 & $2.00 from within a mile and a half of our gin house. Give my love to Ma and all the family.

   Your affectionate son
   J F Torrance

Tell William I have been expecting to hear from him for a great while, but in vain, — he must be full of business. I have not had a line from Jane since I was in N C   I hope she will find time enough to send me a few lines.

   J F T

And on the eleventh of March, Hugh wrote:

Dear Father

 I received your welcome letter of January 23ᵈ a week ago. I am truly sorry to hear of your ill health and the sickness of the family — Your letter came too late for Frank to go to Tennessee to attend to your land suit. We will endeavor to find out something about it   and if it is not decided go up and attend to it at the next term of the court.

 You think I might go to N Carolina and spend a summer with you — It would give me a great deal of pleasure to do so but it is entirely out of my power   I am so situated that I cannot leave home for any length of time. I hope to be able to visit you in a year or too and make acquaintance with the family for I have been absent so long that I should not know any [one but] yourself and Ma   they have all grown up since I left. You mention a trip you had intended to take to this country   We will be rejoiced to see you. I hope you will not give it up entirely. the trip may be of service to your health. My wife would like to make acquaintance with you. She says she wishes very much to see you   She sends her love and a kiss to you and the family

 We have had a very rainy winter — but a warm one and of course have been backward in gathering our crops. We finished

picking our cotton on the 16ᵗʰ of Feb — and made in all 150058 ˡᵇ
seed cotton — it is not all baled yet.[54] *We had 58 bales of our first*
picking sold in N Orleans in January for 8 1/4 & 10 cents   It is
uncertain when the remainder can be got off — the river is too low
for boats to run — Since the rains ceased which was about the first
of February — we have had delightful weather — nearly as warm
as May — We are about half done planting corn — vegetation is
very forward. We had peas up more than a week ago.

I shall not visit you until I can go prepared to settle up
everything — and now that cotton has got to bring a better price I
hope it will not be long
Give my love to Ma an[d all] the family
your affectionate Son
Hugh Torrance

The ordinary course of winter ills afflicted Sarah Jane the most that year, although James's bouts of asthma and fevers seemed to come with more frequency. He had entirely given up the prospect of going west. He would enjoy a visit with his sons and seeing their land, but he was nearly sixty years old and did not feel up to such an endeavor.

〜　　　〜　　　〜

Mr. Ney had relocated his school to Mr. Lytle's farm just across the Catawba River, a much more convenient site. James's doubts about the man were tempered by the admiration Ney gleaned from scholarly minds at Davidson College. He was a frequent patron of the library there; and his knowledge of the classics, languages, and especially French history was widely admired.

On Monday mornings Dick and Isaac, a black boy of his same age, would climb on a pony and ride to a ford on the river some four miles from home. Dick would be met by Mr. Lytle or one of his neighbors on horseback and taken across the rocky shoals. He waved quickly to Isaac, then grabbed onto the horse's mane with all his might. His escort usually rode bareback, and the shaded side of river rocks bore slippery moss. Isaac returned to Cedar Grove to be assigned his tasks, and Dick began a week of learning.

Dick opened his copybook with the blue and brown marbled cover and penned the phrase dictated by his tutor: "*Rich men should be kind to poor men.*" Over and over he wrote the words until Ney was satisfied they had been mastered by the hand and the mind. Elsewhere on the page Mr. Ney had written, "Richard A Torrence commenced with Mr Ney 2d time on 26th March, 1844." The old gentleman was well into his seventies but still an authoritative figure. His shoulders were broad, and his back was ramrod straight, attributed to his skill at fencing. A few fiery strands remained in the wild fringe of gray curls below his bald pate. His presence would have been menacing, if not accompanied by finesse and utter charm.

Dick slept in a shed room adjoining that of his teacher. It was in the night that Ney's nether persona emerged. Dick could hear the clank of bottle against tumbler and anthems sung in French. One evening he was called into Ney's chamber and asked to untie his tutor's neck stock. The stock was composed of several lengths of silk wound around and around the man's neck with the various ends tucked under to hold the whole thing in place. Dick pulled and tugged but could find none of the ends, and Ney's numbed digits were useless. Dick stood on a chair to get closer to the problem since Ney was a tall man, then Ney suddenly lurched away from him. He turned to the child, "My little son in the army in France used to do this for me less awkwardly." There seemed to be a tear on his cheek. "I had to leave him behind. I left everyone behind. I had, after all, been executed. But I did not commit treason. Napoleon assigned me the impossible. No man could have carried out his order. The Russians could not be vanquished!" He picked up a brandy bottle, saw that it was empty, and dropped it on the bed. He reached for the small perfume vial on his dressing table, pressed its fragrant lip to his, and drank with satisfaction. Dick understood not a word of the man's ramblings and could put no meaning to the strange scene. He slipped quietly back to his room.

The next morning, as instructed, Dick poured cologne into the small bottle from a larger one, and at week's end he carried a packet of Ney's letters to be mailed. Isaac was waiting at the ford. Dick hopped on the pony with the black boy and they headed for Cedar Grove.

"Isaac," he asked, "have you finished your chores today?"

"Yes sir," replied the boy, "all but carrying you home."

"Is this not a fine day for fishing? I think a stop by the mill pond is what I need to rest my mind; it has been a very odd week."

There was always a stash of fishing poles at the mill, and worms could be dug in a minute. The Negroes were permitted to fish when their work was done. It refreshed their souls and supplemented their dinner pails. Dick and Isaac had fished together since they could bait a hook and found peace straddling a log, bare feet dangling in the water. They were as close to equal here as they could ever be. Dick told Isaac about the incident with the neck stock but left out the part about the perfume. Isaac agreed it was odd, but to him anything about schooling was foreign. Before mounting the pony and heading for home, Dick peeked into the packet of letters. They were all addressed in an elegant hand to places in France. Dick wondered if one of them was to the little son left behind.

Dick did not repeat this tale to his father, and notes from the tutor gave no hint of trouble. On the fifth of April, Ney wrote:

Mr Torrance, Madam, of the list of books which Richard brought on Monday last he need bring only "Davies' Arithmetic and Porter's R Reader" — at present — thank you for sending Richard — I will take care that his time shall not be misemployed. Hoping you, Mrs Torrance, and family enjoy good health I am with high respect, yrs
P S Ney

James had heard the rumors. Tongues wagged that Ney had been a marshal of France during the Napoleonic Wars. But at war's end Napoleon blamed Ney for his own failure to destroy Russia and his defeat at Waterloo—an ominous burden for one man. In 1815, Ney was ordered executed for high treason. The deed was carried out in secret, and some wondered if the shrouded body, so quickly buried, was Ney at all. Several years later a French visitor to South Carolina spotted the tutor and shouted to all who would listen, "It's Marshal Ney. I would recognize him anywhere!" In an instant the tutor packed his belongings and retreated to the backcountry. If the marshal were alive and discovered, his family and compatriots would be slain.

Ney professed to be a simple tutor but could not hide his excellent swordsmanship, military bearing, and obsession with Napoleon. His fondness for drink often loosened his tongue which fueled the rumor mill. At the Davidson College library, he read histories of the French Revolution and Napoleon and became enraged at inaccuracies and romantic renderings of war. He took up his pen and scribbled the true story in the margins of the books. He took umbrage at a drawing of Napoleon's marshal which looked nothing like himself. "This is not a true semblance" he wrote in French. Elsewhere on the page he drew a self-portrait and under it he wrote, "Ney, By him Self."

Some thought the tales outrageous, and Ney, when sober, denied them—but most believed. The evidence seemed unshakable, and it was tantalizing to have such a figure in their midst. James was merely amused.[55]

James continued to encourage Frank to look into the situation in Tennessee. On the second of June 1844, Frank wrote:

Dear Father

I have as usual put off writing to you much longer than I ought, and longer than I intended. I am attending to the farm this year, and have been closely confined to business. We have a very heavy crop (about 17 acres to the hand) which has kept me constantly going without a single moment to spare. Our prospect in the early part of the spring was very flatering, but since that time the cut worm has destroyed more than half our cotton crop, we replanted and got only a tolerable stand. The crop through this country has been injured greatly. The farmers generally have planted over, but cannot promise themselves a full crop unless we have a late fall. The cotton that was not injured by the worms is very fine, a great deal of it will measure 18 & 20 inches in height.

Your letter was not received until it was too late for me to Tenn it was received only a few days before court. I will attend the next court if it is necessary, please let me know soon. If you would instruct Mr Jones to write to me it would save much time and it would enable me to get their by court. if I knew Mr Jones address I would write to him.

The health of our family is, and has been good, excepting myself. I have suffered a great deal this spring and am afraid I will not be better soon. My health is gradually getting worse. I am attending to business but the Dr. advise me to keep out of the sun as much as possible. I have not seen a well day for months. I hope as soon as I can get the crop a little more advanced, I will visit some mineral springs. I am advised to do so by the Physician.

Our home is much more pleasant since Hugh got married. his wife is such a woman as would be esteemed as soon as known, and improves on acquaintance. We would be glad to see you and Ma, and hope you will try and visit us sometime soon, a trip might be of service to you bouth. I have been expecting a letter from William, but cannot get one. I hope he will try and find time to write a few lines soon. We have not had a letter from Nº Ca for sum time

Give my love to Ma and all the family

Your affectionate Son

James F Torrance

Some months before, Mr. Jones of the Union District of South Carolina had made an offer to buy James's Tennessee land. James's father had recorded the deed in 1801, and Frank had assumed the paper he had so carefully carried to Mississippi proved ownership. The court was not convinced. General Loving, a Tennessee lawyer, was engaged by Jones to prove James's title to the land. Confusion ensued. Court calendars were changed, cases continued, and letters between James, Mr. Jones, General Loving, and Frank traveled slowly. And it appeared that there were indeed squatters on the land. Dreaded lawsuits were in the making. Finally by fall there was a hint at resolution.

On the twenty-sixth of October, Frank wrote:

Dear Father

I received your letter informing me of the time of the court in Ripley Tenn in due time. I went as far as Brownsville whear I met your Lawyer, Gen W^m H Loving who informed me the time of holding court in that county had been altered and that it would not come on for two weeks later than you wrote. Gen Loving is a lawyer of fine standing and you may rest assured that he will attend to your suit faithfully. He has received the appointment of judge of the district south of the one he lives in and it may prevent his attending to your sute at the next court as the[y] boath come on about the same time, if that should be the case your case will ly over until the next time of the court, as he is unwilling to leave it to another lawyer. He informed me there would have been no difficulty about your case had your deed not been so defective   he is affraid it is so much so that he will not be allowed to read it in court, if this should be the case he will have some difficulty, but thinks he will be able to overcome.

Thus in a great measure, he also informed me, that under the laws of Tenn Porter would be able to hold all the land he had had in cultivation of seven years on peacable possession for that length of time. I think Porter has about 40 acres he will be able to hold in that way. Gen Loving thought it was unnecessary for me to remain until court, and I was convinced I could do nothing, if I did remain, and I returned immediately. he told me he would not let the case come on unless he was fully prepared. He was glad that I went up, and requested me to say to you that you might be assured, that he would neglect nothing that might injure your case in the least. he has had a good deal of experience in business of that kind, and I think Mr

Jones could not have made a better choice. Gen William H Loving, Brownsville — is his address if you should wish to write.

I inquired what his fee would be, he explained it would not be much, and not to give yourself any trouble about it, until the case was determined

Our country has been unusually sickly, and is not entirely free from disease at this time. Our family has been quite unwell, but at this time all is well. Our white family has been healthy, my health has been better than it has been for several summers. I have more hopes of recovering now than I have since I was first taken.

Our cotton crop is very fine (for as dry a summer as we have had.) I think it will average over one thousand to the acre, or fully that much. The season was too dry for corn or anything else but cotton. We had not rain enough for nearly five months to weat the ground more than two inches. We have had a fine season for gathering our crop, and would have been more than half done had our family been healthy — not withstanding, we have more cotton out than we have ever had at the same time of year.

The political contest is going on warmly in this state. The Whigg party is doing everything that can be done to carry the state for H Clay. The Whiggs think the contest will be very close, but the democrats think or say they will carry the state by three thousand. let it be as it may be we will fight to the last.

Give my love to Ma and all the family & to sister Jane. (I believe she is out of the family at this time)   I received a letter from brother William a short time since and will answer it soon.

> *Your affectionate son*
> *J F Torrance*

James hoped that General Loving would live up to his reputation. He had never seen his Tennessee land and had no need for its income, but a perfect stranger had set himself up there and would probably hold on to a portion of it. James was furious—the land was his, and it should not matter how long the man had farmed it. What audacity could convince a man to occupy land he did not own? James was glad that his sons' black family had recovered their health and that the harvest was progressing. Next to bad weather, ailing Negroes were a farmer's worst bane.

In November, Clay lost the election. James K. Polk, a relative unknown from the state of Tennessee was elected president. Mr. Polk was a native of

Mecklenburg and had spent his childhood there. He was also the absentee landlord of a Mississippi plantation a few miles from the Torrance land. None of the Torrances were aware of this odd coincidence.

Early in the winter a malicious epidemic settled in on Mecklenburg County. The disease was erysipelas, and the county's doctors believed the first casualty was a hog drover from Kentucky. When he fell ill in the home of a man who had given him lodging, his host called for a doctor. The drover's death was soon followed by that of the doctor, and the epidemic was on. Victims first suffered chills, followed by a blistering fever. The throat and head swelled to extremes which hindered swallowing and breathing. Some heads were said to be the girth of a half-bushel basket. Finally the victims emitted a putrid odor, as if the body had first rotted, then died. Throughout the winter the deaths continued at an alarming rate. Churches often had several funerals per day. They were poorly attended, as those who were well were frightened. Many of the ill were neglected. It took great strength to face the fear of contagion and the overwhelming stench. The doctor was summoned several times to Cedar Grove to treat both the white and black families. Fortunately their fevers passed without fatality. Perhaps they only suffered ordinary seasonal fevers. Rampant fear clouded judgment.

At Rural Hill they were less fortunate. Jane became ill and died on the third of December. Her husband was helpless at her bedside; nothing he had learned at the medical college in Charleston was of any use. Little Jimmie Davidson was barely a year old. [56]

13 Full Circle 1845~1847

James wrote to his sons and told them of the epidemic and Jane's death. The sad news summoned Frank's demons, dragging along guilt and regret over the debt. On the sixth of January, he wrote:

Dear Father

I received your letter of the 7th Decemb containing the melancholy and distressing news of the death of my sister. I was wholly unprepared for it and have been greatly distressed, — but their is consolation in the depth of distress, and I will console myself with the hope that she has gone to happier world where I hope and pray we may all meet.

If bad health was any indication of speedy disolution, I think I have had as much reason to suppose that my life will not be a long one as any person would wish, for the last four or five years I have scarcely had a well day, and it may be that I shall never be well, as bad as my health is, I am thankful that it is no worse, and I hope in future to be better able to bear with my afflictions.

Dear Father I have had many things to distress and harass me since I came to this country and I am affraid there is yet more to be met with and over come, but I do hope I may not have as many at any one time as at the present. I will not give you a catalog of my troubles and distresses, but there is one which presses so heavily upon me, that I am compelled to mention it, and I hope if I am wrong you will forgive me — which I hope and trust is the case; — it is the thought that you have lost confidence in me — I trust Pa I am mistaken, for I feel that I have done nothing to forfit your confidence, — that I am in debt is true; but not disgraced and I hope you will not suppose for a moment that we have thoughts of letting you suffer by us. As a son I am ever grateful, a[nd] shall be; you have given me what I have, and by your kindness saved that from being taken away from me. and I hope you will not at this time withdraw your kind assistance, when we so much need it. We have no debts here that can injure us and I do assure you that we are in no danger of breaking, and if there was any you should be the first secured. In your letter you seemed to be of the impression that we expected you to give us the debt, you paid for us, but so far as I am concerned I can say that such a thought has never entered my head, I have always been satisfied, and I am fully satisfied with what you have done, and have promised to for me, and I do hope you will never suppose I have been dissapointed.

When in N⁰ Ca Dʳ. Johnson told me off a message that Mrs Black had sent to you by <u>him</u> which I am affraid you have supposed I had some agency in, but I do assure you I had nothing to do with the message, as Dʳ Johnson can testify and as son as I saw Mrs Black, which was in company of Dʳ. J., I told her I was more than satisfied and was sorry such a thing had been mentioned. I regretted it then and I regret [it] yet.

We are willing to secure you in any way you may wish, if you think a note is not sufficient. In order to secure you by mortgage or deed in trust it is necessary that the trustee shoud live in this state, and that the instruments should be recorded in the county which we live in, and in order that the instrument should be binding, it would be necessary for you or your agent to be present at the taking. If you should feel satisfied with a note we will send you one as soon as we can hear from you. You can send the amount of interest you have paid and at what time you paid it, or the amount we owe you, and if you are willing you can give me credit for what you intended giving me out of the sale of the Tenn land. I hope Pa you will not give yourself any uneasiness about our paying you   We have offered our land at a reduced price to raise the money, but have not been able to [get a buyer.]   We will sell as soon as we can at sum [price.]

He turned his page sideways and wrote in the margins:

I have filled my paper but not finished my letter   Give my love to Ma and all the family, your affectionate son
J F Torrance
We finished gathering our cotton crop last month, and made an average crop — 120 bales. Our corn was light but I think we have enough to do us

At Mount Mourne they had escaped the dreaded disease. Isabella had wisely kept close to home and protected her family from infected people and strangers. The previous December, barely a week after Jane's death, she had borne Rufus his first son, and she would let no hint of danger enter their sphere. James Rufus was his name, but no one ever used it. "Little brother Rufus," Isabella had said, introducing the newborn to Emma. The toddler's eyes grew wide with amazement and she repeated, "Little bud Rufus," and Bud Rufus he became. Isabella's only regret was that Rufus was absent during much of his son's first months. He had been elected to the state legislature the year before and was often at the state capital. She was proud to have him so honored but wished Raleigh were closer to home. [57]

Isabella maintained a structured household for the girls. Structure and education were important, especially for Sallie. There were now three Torrance girls at Salem. Delia had joined Lettitia and Mary last summer. The Reid girls pleaded to go. Sallie was fifteen, and Flax and Nannie were not far behind. But Isabella was adamant that it was too soon. Sallie's age did not negate her blindness, and Isabella knew full well that Salem's riches were wasted on the ill-prepared. They would be instructed at home for a while longer. Grandma Latta taught them her rock-hard faith. She read from the Bible bound with gilded calfskin, a gift from Wilson Davidson many years before. The cover had become supple as her hands grew leathery. The constant contact of book and hands had nearly bound them as one. She heard catechism from the black and white children alike. Some of the black ones had picked up the skill of reading. The law against it was largely ignored where the soul was involved.

～　　　～　　　～

Hugh and his father were growing distant; letters became rare. Hugh thought his affection for his family should be obvious, and he displayed no remorse or responsibility about the debt. On March 1, 1845, he wrote:

Dear Father

I have no letter from you to answer   The last one I received was dated the 23 January 1844 which is now more than twelve months. I must acknowledge that I am a good deal remiss in writing to my relations. I never was much of a letter writer. But I shall be truly sorry if they should ascribe my want of promptness in that particular to anything like want of regard or affection for them. If such was the fact I know I could not feel the pleasure that I do when I receive a letter from them — and I feel confident that if they could witness the pleasure it gives me to hear from them they never would think of charging me with want of feeling.

Our crop of cotton for last year was all picked and packed by Christmas and has been all shipped to New Orleans out of our river one mile and a half from our house at one dollar & fifty cents per bale I have not yet heard if it is sold   in fact the price is so small that I can make but small calculation upon it. the price is ranging from 3 1/2 to 7 cents.

You have before this heard, I suppose of the melancholy accident that befell one of the Steam Boats running the Yazoo river by which we lost some of our citizens and among the number Saml Calwill who you will recollect lived in Charlotte. also a W. Huggins a neighbor of ours and from the Eastern part of N Carolina — The boat (Path Finder) loaded with cotton about 50 miles below this at Greenwood on the 3ʳᵈ Feb and left for New Orleans. on the night of the fifth she was discovered to be on fire about three o'clock. the fire had made such rapid progress that there was no chance of saving her. She was immediately abandoned by the officers and crew who got possession of the yawl and made off to Shore   Some of the passengers amid the alarm and confusion jumped into the river and were drowned. One is supposed to have been burned others got onto cotton bales and were saved. The greater portion of the cotton lost was owned by citizens of this county & mostly <u>*insured*</u>*.*

We have planted 60 acres of corn — and will plant the remainder next week. Our oats are up finely   vegitation is coming on rapidly. We have had peach blooms here since the middle of January

> *My wife sends her love to you. give my love to the family*
> > *your affectionate son*
> > *H Torrance*

p.s. I hope to get to see you some time. When it will be I am not able to say.   H T

James was gratified to receive Hugh's account of the accident. He had known Samuel Caldwell and knew many of his kin. The newspaper reports had been sketchy and possibly inaccurate; a firsthand account was always welcome. James took offense at his son's arrogance. He still had not mentioned the debt nor offered apology. It had long ago become clear that James might never see his generosity repaid. He stewed for months, then decided the time had come to make a new will. After much deliberation he drafted the document, then had it witnessed and duly recorded. At least Frank was properly remorseful about his failure. Hugh was in for a surprise. That done, he wrote a scathing letter to Hugh filled with admonitions about familial duty and respect for one's elders. He loved this oldest son but did not understand him.

Hugh's emotional distance was bolstered by time and place. The debt did not worry him because it rarely crossed his mind. His growing plantation, wife, and now a child kept him well occupied. Only with effort could he dredge up a clear memory of his father's face or voice; and when they came to mind, they were harsh with disapproval. At first James's letter enraged him, but prayerful thought and his wife's counsel subdued him. He promptly wrote on the eighteenth of August a letter as devoid of blame as he could muster:

Dear Father

I received your letter of July 18th. I cannot account for the irregularity of the mails between this and N. Carolina. the letters from there generally reach this place in the course of one month — when they shoud come to hand in half the time — from this they are generally longer and sometimes never get to hand at all — at least I so conclude for I wrote to M Reid and Jane Camilla both sometime in February or March and have had no answer from either The first and only time since January that I have heard from them was by your letter. I have had no letter from Isabella or Camilla this year.

I am glad to hear that Camilla's health is better for we heard some time ago that it was very bad. I am sorry to hear that you have had so severe a drought it has been bad enough here but nothing to compare with the one you have been suffering under. we will make corn enough to serve us and a tolerably good crop of cotton. It is not a general thing however there are portions of this county where the drought is as sore as it is with you — then there are other portions where the crops are very fine. We have one advantage that you are deprived of in the way of getting supplies when the crops are short — that is navigation. there is a good deal of produce brought here every year by the river from the North Western States. but when the crop proves a short one every man has it in his power to get a supply from the river before the spring closes Last year the corn crop was short but the supply on the river was sufficient to prevent anyone from suffering. The people in this country can never suffer whilst there is Corn Wheat & Pork made in the upper states for they are compelled to bring them South to find a market.

There has been but little sickness in this country My wife has suffered and is still suffering a good deal with her breast — the child is healthy and fine looking. She had the thrush badly sometime back but has recovered. I call her Isabella — My wife Jane, sends her love to you & family — give mine also

your affectionate son
Hugh Torrance

The arrogance had abated, but responsibility and intimacy had not emerged. James took some consolation in Hugh's businesslike letter but not enough to amend his will. This report on wheat and corn and a bare mention of the grandchild was the last letter he would receive from his distant son.

∼   ∼   ∼

Isabella did not enjoy the company of Camilla nearly as often as she wished. Mount Mourne was some forty miles from Yorkville, and travel by horseback was impractical when droves of children were involved. Camilla's frail health had not precluded fertility; she had given birth to her sixth child. Isabella gathered up her two youngest, a nursemaid, and a driver and went by carriage to spend a few days with her sister. William was at Bullock Creek, and when Camilla regained her strength she planned to join him. Meanwhile, she welcomed the company of her sister, Emma, and Bud Rufus.

Isabella gathered her new niece in her arms, "Camilla, she is a lovely child; I know William is pleased."

"He is. He would never admit to it, but I know he prayed for a boy. He doted so on little Willie. He used to perch the child before him on his horse and ride all over the plantation. Willie was displayed far and wide, as if no one had seen a boy before. Of course the Negroes were full of admiration, or at least they acted the role for their master. I miss Willie as much as his father does, but I know that another son would not replace him."

"What have you called this little one?" asked Isabella.

"Jane Elizabeth," replied Camilla, "in memory of our sister." [58]

"How perfect. I know she would have been pleased, and Pa will be delighted."

Isabella could see that her sister was in good care. Margaret, Ada, Annie, and Adeline hovered around their little sister determined to be as helpful as tots could be. There were also Negroes and neighbors, and William always spent the Sabbath in Yorkville. After a satisfying visit Isabella returned home. It was time to relieve Grandma Latta of child care and tell her about Camilla's infant, especially its name.

By September, James had had his fill of Mr. Ney. The rumors of his dual life had escalated. Most believed them to be true, but some thought the man was deluded or demented. Several children had been withdrawn from his classes. James considered the man's behavior more troubling than his history. For years it had been customary to invite Ney to an occasional dinner at Cedar Grove. The man had always enjoyed his wine and brandy, as did James, but after dinner he had been sober enough to engage in sprightly conversation and compose his idyllic acrostics. Lately he seemed to have lost all control, and his glass could not be kept filled.

One fine September afternoon Dick borrowed a horse to ride alongside his tutor to Cedar Grove for a midweek dinner. The story he told his father when he came home the following Friday was the most disturbing of all. On their return to the school, Ney had ridden with his customary straight back but leaned first one way then another and gave the horse no direction. The road and the trails through the woods were clear enough for the horse to follow, but the ford across the river was not. Ney made no effort to keep to the protected shallows and rode dangerously close to rapids where the current became deep and swift. Dick had laughed at the man spiraling on his horse through the woods, but when they reached the river he became terrified that Ney might topple in. He tried to herd the indifferent tutor toward the ford but was hindered by the blackness of the night. The scent of fear arose from both horses, and Dick was unsure if he had been splashed by the rapids, or was simply drenched in his own sweat. At last the western shore was reached much to his relief; he knew he could not have dragged such a ponderous figure from the water. At twelve Dick knew the effects of spirits but not the perils. In innocence he told his father this story and other anecdotes of outlandish behavior.

James concluded it was time to remove his sons from Ney's influence. John had been with him for only a few weeks. If the man was not dangerous, he was surely a bad example. Ney's advanced age was reason enough to give for withdrawing his sons. The next Monday morning he sent with Dick a note addressed to Ney and told the boys to gather all their belongings. Isaac would meet them that afternoon with a wagon. Ney replied:

29 Sept 1845
Dear Sir
Richard acquaints me this morning that he must leave me. This gives me some pain; for I do not wish to part with him so soon. But

no doubt your reasons for taking him and John away, are quite satisfactory to yourself. Best respects to you and Mrs Torrance
                                              P S Ney

The enigmatic tutor died one year later at the age of seventy-seven.

~   ~   ~

James continued to write to Frank who was determined to maintain the family connection. On the seventh of December 1845, Frank wrote to his father:

Dear Father

I received your kind letter a short time since which gave us boath pleasure and regret, it is ever a great pleasure to us to hear from you, and to know that you enjoy good health, I hope you may be fortunate enough to keep from being attacked with the caughf which has troubled you so much. I think you and Ma ought to be very careful off yourselves during the winter months, and avoid taking could. I hope Mas health is better than it was when I saw her

We regret very much to hear of your short crop, it has given me more trouble than anything that has happened for some time. I am greatly in hopes when I hear from you again, to hear that your crop has turned out better than you had expected. I wish you would let me know when you write again, how much you will fall short, of having enough to do you, and what prospect you have of getting it. When you wrote you said you were affraid your bottom corn would be ruined by a fresh[et] that you had about that time, please write concerning it. — I would be glad to hear anything from you, that may interest or effect you in any digree. Hugh and myself both feel the greatest anxiety to hear more from you respecting your crop and hope you will write to us soon.

The crops in this country is not good, but much better than in many others that I have heard from, the corn crop is quite light, so much so that but few persons have made enough to do them,   the cotton is something better, and upon the whole it is thought that an average crop will be made, our crop will average about 900 lb per acre. We finished about two weeks since, our corn crop is much better than an average one, we will make more than enough to do us.

In this section of the state we do not labor under the same disadvantage that you do in relation to provisions. Were there an entire fail[ure] to make provisions we could be supplied from the Northern States as cheap as it could be had with you in a plentiful year. Corn can [be had] from the river near us at any season of the year at from 50 to 75 per Bush.

I received a letter from William a short time ago which I will answer soon. I also received one of Lettitas which is the first I have received from her since you sent her to Salem, I was pleased to see the improvement she has made, boath as to penmanship and composition, I am in hopes Mary and Delia are doing as well.

We have not heard from Camilla or William for some time.

Our family at present enjoys the greatest of blessings; health. We have had no sickness of any kind for sum time. My health has been better for the last six months, than it has been for several years, and is improving. Hughs daughter is doing well, and is quite a sprightly child.

Tell William John Sample has been with us and is at present in Grenada; he has been trying to get a school, and I heard yesterday that he had succeded, his health is not good, and I am affraid he will injure it by hard studdy.

Give my love to Ma and all the family
Your affectionate son
J F Torrance

The spring of 1846 was quiet at Cedar Grove; of James's large brood only William and the three youngest were at home. William's college education had widened his view of the world, and farming looked to be a dull trade. He envied and admired his brother-in-law, William Davidson, and begged his father to send him to medical school. James was disappointed that yet another of his sons wished to abandon his plantation. He knew he had struck the first blow driving a wedge between him and his older sons when he opposed their move to the west. He had no interest in repeating the process with William. Medicine was an honorable profession; he had been delighted when his son-in-law had chosen it. He must make every effort to look toward William's choice in the same light. He covered over his disappointment and gave William his blessing. They would ask the new Dr. Davidson to recommend an institution, and they would also ask Dr. Johnston who had cared for the family for many years.

As he walked the plantation directing the Negroes in their tasks, he thought of Dick and John. At eleven and eight they were still children. There was time to cultivate in them a love for the land. He would teach them gently and patiently to appreciate the soil and the magic of its bounty. He prayed he would live long enough to accomplish this goal. The attacks of asthma and rheumatism were more frequent and more bothersome with each passing year.

In March, the illness began. On the seventeenth of that month Dr. Johnston spent the entire day and night at Sarah Jane's bedside spooning a syrup between her parched lips to break her fever. Two days later he kept vigil over her and Dick. Only the direst of circumstances would keep a physician at one farm for such a length of time. Gradually the children began to recover; Margaret and her Negro woman Dilcy took over the nursing. It was on the twenty-seventh that Dilcy came running into the dining room where James was eating his breakfast. As Margaret's personal servant, Dilcy was usually in the house, but she had been trained to be gracefully unobtrusive. The fright in her eyes excused her rash behavior. He put down his fork and went with her to her cabin.

She leapt across the yard like a hare, her arms flailing about her; James was close behind. His eyes adjusted to the darkness as he entered the tiny room, and he saw her four children lying on pallets on the floor. The room stank of illness and wood smoke. Eight-year-old Stephen was the only one who slept peacefully. His brown work shirt was drenched in sweat, and his black curls glistened. His fever had broken. Three-year-old Echo was whimpering and restless but not deathly ill. It was the middle children, Nancy and Pheby, who shook until their teeth chattered between violent spells of croup. Dilcy knelt beside them and bathed their brows. She was two years older than Isabella, and it seemed only yesterday that James had watched them together in childhood games. Dilcy was now a strong woman who had done her duty at breeding. James knelt over the girls and heard their short raspy breaths. He had genuine compassion for Dilcy and her children—he also knew the need to protect his investment. He took her fluttering hands in his own and held them firmly until she began to calm.

"I will send Mrs. Torrance with some extra blankets and quinine and one of the boys for Dr. Johnston. Try not to worry. My little ones looked nearly as bad not many days since and are now almost fully recovered. I shall ask one of the older women to help you." Dilcy thanked him. The terror had left her eyes but not the tears. James left the cabin to attend to the details. Ten-year-old Dave was sent to fetch the doctor. Black boys of this age made excellent messengers. They were old enough to ride well and bear the responsibility of it but too young to think of running away.

By the time the doctor arrived Nancy's fever had broken; only Pheby lay limp and glassy-eyed. Dr. Johnston administered hive syrup to ease her cough and rubbed her body with a paste made from the pulverized bodies of Spanish flies to raise blisters which would draw the poison from deep inside her to be expelled through her skin. When the blisters burst the noxious fluids would be released, and the child's humors would be in balance. Recovery should quickly follow. He returned two days later as promised. Stephen, Nancy, and Echo were well enough to sit in the yard and watch the other children at play but too weak to join in. Pheby had not improved. More blisters were administered but to no avail. He made his third visit to Dilcy's cabin on the second of April and treated Pheby once more. Yet while he stood watch, the child took her last breath and died in Dilcy's arms. She was buried in the Negro cemetery among her people. Dilcy found a large fieldstone to mark her place. Stones for the Negro cemetery were simply gathered and placed, neither sculpted nor engraved. Very few of the Negroes could read even their own names. What purpose would be served by words on their gravestones? [59]

Late in the spring there was a frenzy of activity at Cedar Grove. Three commencement dresses would be needed at one time. A seamstress was engaged to do most of the work. Margaret did the fancy work and finishing touches herself. Sarah Jane sat at her mother's knee and helped with the sewing. Plans had already been made for her to enroll at Salem in the fall; she would be prepared for ornamental needlework.

The entire Torrance and Reid clan gathered at Salem for the public examinations on the thirty-first of May. Lettitia, Mary, and Delia performed their recitations and musical pieces. Near perfection was expected of them, and it was delivered. Such expectations were held in common by the Moravians and the Presbyterians. Mrs. Latta had lost count of how many of these events she had attended in her seventy-one years. The first had been for Betsy, thirty-five years ago.

Isabella and Rufus took advantage of the visit to Salem to consult with the Sisters about Sallie. She was seventeen and had absorbed everything that could be learned at Mount Mourne. The Sisters were very sympathetic and eager to help but admitted their experience was limited in teaching the sightless. The Inspector might have a suggestion. Academies for girls had increased enormously since Isabella was a child. There might be a number of suitable places. The Inspector recommended the Edgeworth Seminary in Greensboro. "It is a fine institution," he had said, "with an excellent reputation. It acquires its instructors from a variety of places; they are perhaps a more worldly lot than our Sisters." It was excellent advice. As soon as they returned to Mount Mourne Rufus began corresponding with the seminary and found that they indeed had someone with the special knowledge to teach Sallie. Of course Flax would go with her. Sallie would need a reader, and who better than her inseparable sister? For Rufus there was an added advantage. Greensboro was about halfway between Mount Mourne and Raleigh. He could visit his girls when traveling to his post at the legislature. [60]

Cedar Grove seemed nearly deserted that fall. William had left for medical school in Philadelphia, Dick was at Mr. Wharton's school, and Sarah Jane was at Salem. Whenever possible Lettitia and Mary spent time in Yorkville with Camilla. The social season was much more interesting in that place. Now they were inquiring about schools in Charleston. They felt they needed some polish. James wondered what kind of ideas Camilla was putting in their heads.

Once again Frank had the pleasure of spending part of the fall in Mecklenburg. Family closeness had an urgency for him, and he had tried to convince Hugh to visit the east. Hugh was disinterested: it was too complicated to travel with a wife and child, business was pressing, and he had promised his father that when he returned home he would bring money. He could no more round up five thousand dollars than pluck stars from the sky. In truth he had lost interest in North Carolina. James and Hugh were not possessed of a bitter estrangement, simply an uncomfortable distancing bred by James's disappointment and Hugh's neglect.

For several delightful weeks Frank traveled amongst his relations at Cedar Grove, Mount Mourne, and Yorkville. He also took the opportunity to visit Dr. William Davidson at Rural Hill. Frank still felt Jane's loss and wished to know her son. Little Jimmie had just turned three, and he had his mother's eyes. Back at Cedar Grove Frank's pleasure was interrupted briefly by a recurrence of his fever. James provided him with quinine; it was not serious enough to send for the doctor. Upon recovery he took Lettitia and Mary to Salem. He wanted to visit Sarah Jane, she needed her winter clothes, and the older girls could not get their fill of Salem or traveling. It was a satisfying journey. Late in the fall he boarded the stage for Mississippi. He wished to stay longer but knew the folly of stage travel during harsh winter weather.

William had selected the University of Pennsylvania Medical School which met all of his expectations. He plunged himself into its erudite aura. On the twentieth of December 1846, he wrote his father:

My Dear Father
    I have been very anxious to hear from you & all of my friends as I have written several letters one to you, Dr Davidson Uncle Rufus Reid Cousin Sallie Reid & have not as yet received a single Epistle

being hear one round month I am determined not to dispair but wait with patience. I have been studing very closely   I hope on my return to be able to do honor to my profession & not abuse by Quackery the Science which is here so much honored & esteemed by the great & wise. My dear Father I have concluded to be Dr. Horners private student next summer   I have given him my name. He is one of the greatest Anatomist & Surgeons in the United States. He is the Professor of the University in which I attend. I will not be able to come forward before next February coming a year and after this winter I will be free of all expenses with the exception of Horners private ticket & boarding & have access to all the Lectures during next summer & winter. The house in which I Board is very agreeable. My roome mate is North Carolinian Mr. Simonton of Salisbury. Mr Johnston & Gibbons & also Mr Smith all North Carolinians Boarding in the same house. We have had some very cold weather here. Some snow though the climate not as great in the way of change as I anticipated though we have ice here thick enough to bear a man's weight. I am very anxious to know if Brother Frank has recovered of his illness and wether he has left for Mississippi or not. I have understood he & sister Letitia & Mary made there trip to Salem from which I would conclud he had recovered his general health. I have seen some very important operations performed by Dr Gibson professor of Surgery & Dr Horner Professor Anatomy. I deposited my money in the hands of Dr Horner and not in the bank as I expected to do, finding that they would be some difficulty in getting when I stood most in need; the bank opening at nine & closing at two in the evening which would have interfered with my attention to Lectures during my course. I feel perfectly safe in depositing it with Dr Horner. He is a man of great firmness whose name sounds at home & abroad as being one of the men in his Profession. Give my love to Ma & say to Letitia & Mary I will write to them soone. Pa please write to me soon & direct your letters to the University of Penn. The number of the students at the University I would suppose were three or four hundred.

Kiss little Jane for me I hope the Little Boy is well. Sarah & Delia I hope is doing well. Give my love to sister Isabella & Grandmother; to Wm S Davidson and Miss Polly   My love to all of the family &

inquiring friends   Except a greater share for yourself. I remain your
most umble & obt Sun

W L Torrance

Frank had been alarmed at his father's appearance when in North
Carolina. He seemed to have aged twenty years in the past five and looked
much older than his sixty-two years. His rheumy cough could be heard
throughout the day and deep into the night. The acrid odor of the balm to
soothe his swollen joints permeated every crevice of the house. The old
brandy bottle on his night table contained a mixture of a raw egg, a half-pint
of vinegar, an ounce of spirits of turpentine, a quarter ounce of spirits of wine,
and a quarter ounce of camphor. Its aroma preceded James's every step.

Frank made a pact with Isabella: she would keep a closer watch on their
father, and he would write more frequently keeping his gloom to himself.
On the twenty-eighth of February 1847, he wrote:

Dear Father

*I have been in receipt of your kind letter for sum time. I expected
to have answered it sooner, but had nothing of importance to
communicate. I regret to hear that you are still suffering from your
old complaint. I hope you will try the syrup of wild cherry tree if you
have not already done so. it is highly recommended, for diseases of the
character of the one you are suffering with.*

*Since writing to you my health has improved greatly. I have had
a severe attack of scarlet fever since my return, I am now in as good
health as I usually enjoy.*

*I was most fortunate in leaving N°Ca when I did. about two
weeks after return, the weather changed from fair & dry to weat &
cold, which has continued with but little variation up to this time,
so much rain has fallen that the farmers are unusually backward, for
the last two weeks we have had a little fair weather, but scarsely
enough to enable us to plough.*

*I received two letters from Letty on yesterday   she appears to
be well pleased   I was afraid they would not be so well satisfied
being entirely with strangers. I have not heard from William since I
left N°Ca. I have written to him, but received no answer as yet.*

*We are very busily engaged preparing for another crop; the
advance in the price of cotton acts as a powerful stimulant in this
county. it is astonishing the effect it has already had on the trade of*

our country, it effects alike the great and the small. Every effort is now making in the cotton growing region to get a large crop in, and if the coming season should prove to be a good season for cotton, we may expect the largest that has ever been made.

Our crop is unsold. I regret now that we did not sell before the decline. — the last two arrivals from Liverpool has brought unfavorable news. We have just received the news of a further decline of 3/8 of a penny. — the last accounts from N Orleans cottons now selling from 9 to 15 cents. We will, now hold our crop until May, unless the market recovers what it has lost sooner than that time.

Our family has been quite healthy, we have had a great many cases of Hooping cough but no deaths. The Scarlet Fever has been prevailing through out the country, "but as yet" we have had but one case. (myself)   a number of deaths have occured from it among the children. in some families as many as three or four deaths have taken place.

Give my love to Ma, & Dick & John   remember me to William Davidson, I have been expecting a letter from him, if he has not written I hope he will do so soon

Your Affectionate son
J F Torrance

With the rains over and the planting behind schedule, it was difficult for Frank to keep his promise. From morning to night he was on the land. On the sixteenth of May, he wrote again:

D   Father

I received a letter from you two or three weeks ago, which I ought to have answered sooner, but concluded not to do so, as I was writing to William Davidson, & Letitia, about the time I ought to have written to you.

Since I wrote to you last we have enjoyed uninterupted good health, our family has recovered entirely from the hoping cough without any deaths. we have been more fortunate than many families, sum have lost as many as eight children, and others not as many. At this time the measels are prevailing to a considerable extent. We have had them within a mile of us, we are using every precaution to keep our family from having it. Should we be so unfortunate as to have it at this season, I am afraid we will not be able to cultivate our crop & consequently make another short crop.

Our crop of cotton is not so promising as I have seen it at the same season of the year, but more so than could be expected from the very unfavorable nature of the spring. our corn crop looks well, we have finished working it the second time, except sum planted late, & now working our cotton the second time.

Our last crop of cotton was sold, the last of March for 11 3/8, a good sale; cottons are now selling in New Orleans from 10 to 15 cts. Had we have held ours up until this time, we would have been able to have gotten only a fraction more, than it was sold for. We have been greatly disappointed in not being able to send you some money, as I promised to do. I hope it will not be as great a disappointment to you not to receive it, as it has been to us not to send it. Our expenses last year, or for the present, was much more than usual, for the last year or two, our hogs have been dying until we were left nearly without stock hogs. consequently we were under the necessity of buying all our meat. from present prospects, I think we will not be compelled to buy for the next year.

I received a letter a few days ago from Mr. Reid dated New York. I suppose he is at home by this time. I have not had a word from Letty or Mary since about the first of March. Mr. Reid wrote they have got home. I have wrote three letters to Letty, one to Charleston & two to Cowan's ford since I heard from her. I have not heard from Camilla and William since I left until a few days ago when I met with two acquaintances from Yorkville Mrs Steel & More, they were traveling in the stage & I had only a moments conversation with them.

Hughs little daughter grows finely, and enjoys good health. Jane sends her love to you and Ma & the family. Give my love to Ma, Letty & Mary & the boys. If Letty does not write to me soon or before you receive this, I shall be very much disposed to scold her

Your affectionate Son
J F Torrance

The Mecklenburg Torrances were now receiving their mail at the post office at Cowan's Ford which had opened some two years before. It was more convenient than Mr. Springs's office at his Hickory Grove plantation. It was little wonder that Lettitia's mail did not find her at Cowan's Ford or Charleston. She and Mary had become social gadflies flitting from one place to another as the notion took them. Lately she could be found in Yorkville. While visiting with Camilla she had been introduced to the very large and interesting Bratton family. The Bratton plantation was about ten miles from both Yorkville and Bullock Creek, the three places forming a triangle with one another. In addition to farming, the Brattons operated a school for girls, and physicians in every generation tended to the sick. Young Dr. Samuel Bratton had swept up Lettitia's heart, and she was thoroughly smitten. Frank and Lettitia had grown close during his last visit. If she were not so completely occupied she would have written him the news of it.

James's illnesses continued to plague him. He rarely sent for Dr. Johnston. The man's pukes and blisters left him weak, and the morphine first dulled his senses, then conjured up tormenting monsters. Instead he treated himself with the newest tonics from the apothecary. Frank's suggestion of syrup from the wild cherry tree was as satisfactory as anything else. He wrote to his son telling him how little time he spent on his land and how grateful he was to have well-trained Negroes. He was better now and felt in a way to recover. Frank, again alarmed, replied on the fifth of July 1847:

Dear Father

Your kind favour of the 18 Ultimo was received by the last mail. We had heard of your illness, but was not aware that you had suffered so much & as long as you have. We are much gratified to hear that you are able to be out again., & hope you will be careful of yourself & not have a relapse. Your health has become so delicate of late that you ought to use more caution, & expose yourself less than you have done in bad weather. I sincerely regret that I do not live near enough to assist you in your business. — it would be a great pleasure to me, & particularly when you are so unfit to attend to business. I have never regretted leaving you so much as I do now, & should your health grow worse, or continue as bad as it is, my regret [will] be greater.

When I left [you] last fall or winter, I was affraid my health was gone [but] thanks to a kind providence, I am in better health now than I have been for several years. I am at this time able to walk all day, over the plantation. I have not attended to any business since my return untill, within a week or two ago. Hugh[s] health is not good, nor has been for some time, he is quite unwell at present, but not confined to the house. he has another "daughter", Jane gave birth to it on the 23 Ultimo, she is doing as well as could be expected, they have not given a name to it yet, — it is quite a large child. Since writing to you last, our cotton crop has improved very much, at that time it was quite unpromising, it is now promising. — our corn is very fine, — we finished ploughing it ten days ago. We have had a great deal of rain of late, & still no appearance of fair weather, Sum of the rivers have been very full. — our oates have suffered a little, but I am in hopes we will not lose any.

I am sorry Hugh & myself have disappointed you, in not being able to send you some funds. — our disappointment has been great, but I am in hopes we will not be so again. You spoke of taking a large amount of stock in the Rail Road. I think you will be able at any time, so buy the stock after the road is in operation, and perhaps before. I am disposed to think, it will not pay well. — as the fewest number of Rail Roads do, — I discover from the returns of the various roads, that none pay well unless whear there is a great deal of travelling which would not be the case on that road. The only thing in favor [of] that road, is that it will cost but little, in comparison to what roads of that kind generally cost. — Their is no mountains & but few streams to cross. — I think it would be well for the citizens, generally to encourage the enterprise, but for now to go into it too largely — so if it should not be successful the loss will fall light on all.

I have been expecting a letter from Letitia for the last two weeks but cannot get one. William wrote to me a short time ago. he spoke of taking a walk to the falls of Niagra. I think he will be tired of it.

Give my love to Ma, and all the family. tell the girls to write to me. I am always anxious to hear from home. Let me know how your wheat crop turns out. I heard a few days ago that the crop was a failyure. I hope it is not the case

Adieu
Your Affectionate Son
J F Torrance

Tell Letty I will write to her as soon as I hear from her. I have three letters unanswered.

Frank had gone to great lengths to console his father and conceal his own mood, but it was obvious, even to James, that Frank's recurrent mental sufferings had returned. This letter contradicted previous reports of his good health, and the advice about the railroad stock was ambiguous and confusing. The proclamation that Niagara Falls might be tiresome was the most telling statement of all. Frank had expressed regret about the debt and leaving North Carolina, but his words were couched to hide his soul-consuming guilt.

James was enthusiastic about the prospect of railroads. For years planters in Mecklenburg had suffered a disadvantage, first to those who farmed near a navigable river, then to those near cities connected by rail. The cost of transportation ate deeply into the profit of piedmont farmers. In April, the Charlotte and South Carolina line had been proposed to run all the way to Columbia. However, it would not be built unless local investors could be found. James bought stock at the first opportunity. It had been his lifelong habit to invest for the future of his community: first a church, then a college, and now a railroad. Of course he hoped to see a profit, but that was not his primary motive. Studying news accounts and investing his money were among the few pleasures left to an old man in poor health. He relished visits from Rufus, Frank Davidson, and Robert and William Latta. They sat in his study with their brandy and discussed at great length the brilliant future of railroads.

Isabella regretted that she had been unable to give greater attention to her father during his illness. Addie had been born last March. Although Sallie and Flax were at school in Greensboro, six youngsters were still in her care. She, too, had been distressed by Frank's letters and hoped that Hugh's new daughter and her father's improving health would be cheering to him.

On the seventh of September, the wedding of Lettitia to Dr. Samuel Bratton was held at Cedar Grove. Samuel, the middle of five sons, had taken up the profession of his late father, as did most of the Bratton men. The Torrance family was becoming populated by an abundance of doctors. Although the Brattons owned a good deal of land, it was rumored that they were not very good at farming. Fortunately they succeeded at healing. The Bratton boys had been followed in birth by five sisters. Mrs. Bratton and all the rest who could break away from business or schooling came to celebrate the marriage. Samuel's youngest brother, Robert, had taken a shine to Mary and made a point to attend.

Camilla, William, and their five little girls took the opportunity to spend time with her family. A good portion of the Yorkville District seemed to be at Cedar Grove—some stayed for days.

The latest fashion was to have one's portrait done by daguerreotype, a process much simpler than hiring an artist. A gentleman was employed to make a likeness of Lettitia and Samuel dressed in their wedding clothes. Lettitia's fancy white bonnet framed her dark hair and round face that was so typical of the Torrance women. Her demure smile belied the excitement in her dark eyes. Samuel was dashing in his tall silk hat and cutaway coat. His square jaw lent a serious look to the portrait. They were indeed a handsome couple. [61]

When the last of the guests had left Cedar Grove, James hoped that a period of rest would replenish his energy. On fine days he sat on a porch and observed the harvest. Some days from the south porch and some from the north, he watched the wagons bringing in corn, then wheat, and finally cotton. When the days turned crisp he watched the hog slaughter at the far end of the barnyard. The hot bloody carcasses were strung from trees, and smudgy fires were lit in the smokehouse. More than five thousand pounds of meat were preserved to feed his white and black families over the winter. On foul days or when his joints complained too vividly, he remained in his bed most of the day. Gradually the days in bed began to outnumber those on the porch. His inflamed joints throbbed, and his asthmatic cough shook him inside out. Margaret begged to send for Dr. Johnston, but James declined. He doped himself with laudanum and quinine and the syrup from the wild cherry tree and bathed his gnarly joints with the malodorous camphor balm. As fall slipped into winter, James drew his last raspy breath. He died on the twelfth of December 1847, one month into his sixty-third year. [62]

Reverend Cunningham performed the funeral service. He had been at Hopewell for five years but was still a newcomer in Margaret's eyes. She longed for the familiar voice and comfort of Reverend Williamson. The sermon was a signal to her that life would be forever changed; she was now in charge of Cedar Grove and its vast domain. They buried James next to his mother. On her other side were his father, then Polly and Nancy, his wives of long ago.

14 Mount Mourne 1848~1855

After a somber Christmas season in which all of the visits were of condolence, the family gathered at Cedar Grove to hear the reading of James's last will. He had named Rufus Reid and his longtime friend and physician, Dr. Sidney Johnston, as executors. They had surveyed James's possessions and determined that his Mecklenburg estate consisted of 109 Negroes and 3,244 acres of land. [63]

The family gathered in the parlor to hear the particulars. Margaret's brother, Dr. John Allison, had stayed with her throughout the holiday season, and it appeared his stay might be indefinite. Margaret was distraught and would need someone to oversee the planting season. Dr. Allison was a bachelor in his mid-forties and had attended enough suffering for one lifetime. Perhaps it was time to give up his practice in Statesville and become a gentleman farmer. Isabella sat close to Margaret and held her hand; Camilla and William had also come to offer their comfort. None of the children living at Cedar Grove had reached their majority and were excluded from the reading.

As was the custom, James had directed most of his wealth be given to his widow and minor children. It would be folly to endow self-sufficient adults when there were still children to be educated. Rufus began to read:

To my son Hugh Torrance all the negroes which I have already given him up to this time and their increase before and up to this time, also a waggon and team of horses, household and kitchen furniture all of which articles have already been into his possession.

That was all for Hugh. This disappointing son was allowed to keep his Negroes. The horses were all dead, and the furniture, mostly cast-offs hauled across the country ten years before, had long since been replaced.

Frank, Camilla, and Isabella were also willed the Negroes and their increase, furniture, et cetera, already in their possession. In addition they were to divide the proceeds from the sale of the Tennessee land less five thousand dollars, and six hundred in interest. Then Rufus read the stinging words: "which note was paid to Campbells Executors by and with my money." In addition Frank was given $150 to purchase a wagon and household furniture to make him equal with the others. A piano was included in the household furniture for each of the girls.

Rufus continued reading:

I will and bequeath to my beloved wife Margaret Torrance Negro men Jim & Jo, a negro woman July and her children & their increase which negroes were hers at our marriage also negro boy Tom, Mitchell, Dilcey & her children & their children & their increase, Sam & Solomon all which negroes are for her use and at her disposal provided she does not marry again in which case they are to be divided equally between our six children namely Letitia, Mary, Delia, Richard, Sarah Jane & John also I will and bequeath unto my wife M. Torrance all necessary household and kitchen furniture the Piano the carriage and harness also a waggon and gear horses, hogs, cattle, & Sheep & complete farming utensils all of which articles are to be apportioned to her according to judgment of my executors . . . I will and bequeath unto my grand daughter Jane Camilla Smith a negro woman Matilda and her three children and her and their increase.

Matilda had already increased; her children now numbered four. Little Jimmie Davidson was willed the Negroes, livestock, and furniture which included a piano that had been given to Jane during her lifetime. The remaining Negroes and the land were to be divided among the seven youngest children, although Margaret was to remain in residence. All other property was to be sold, and the proceeds, along with the shares of bank and railroad stock, were to be divided between Margaret and the same children except the gold watch which was willed to Dick. The executors were given leniency to sell property of the minor children and invest the money safely.[64]

Rufus and Dr. Johnston announced that the sale of James's estate would be held on the first of February, and they would place a notice in the *Charlotte Journal*. A copy of the notice was passed around the room:

Very Important Sale

The executors of James G. Torrance, Esq. dec'd. will sell at his late residence, on Tuesday, the first day of February next, a great variety of valuable property, viz: Horses, Mules, Cattle, Sheep, 1 fine Jack Ass, 1 Jack Colt, One Jennet, unusually fine, 1 Carriage, 1 Buggy and waggons, a large quantity of corn, wheat, oats, fodder, hay, farming utensils in great variety, black smith tools, household and kitchen furniture. And a great variety of other property not here mentioned: Terms will be made known at the sale.

Another notice was placed in the same paper requesting those indebted to James to make payment and those who were owed money to present their claims.[65]

The first of February dawned cold, but it was a perfect day for a sale. There were few farm chores in the depth of winter, and people were free to come from miles around. Some came to buy, some out of curiosity, and some to socialize. All during the previous week Rufus and Sidney Johnston had gathered the items to be sold and arranged them in categories and lots. The children were directed to place the merchandise about the yard keeping like items together in an orderly fashion. Lists were made of the livestock, farm gear, and the fruits of the field.

As people arrived they walked about looking over the goods. Some leafed through the thirty-two lots of books stacked in neat piles around the porch, some examined boxes of bottles, tools, and other sundries. Several men peered through James's three pairs of spectacles to see if they would suit. Dick was in charge at the barn where the horses, mules, wagons, and highly prized jacks could be seen. Rufus and Sidney circulated among the crowd with a ledger book and carefully recorded the sale each time a deal was struck.

The bulk of the estate was purchased by Dr. Allison on Margaret's behalf; she wanted to keep the farm intact. He bought four horses, fifty sheep, sixty cows and calves, and twenty-five thousand bundles of fodder to feed them. He also bought three thousand bushels of corn, five thousand pounds of bacon, and eight hundred bushels each of cotton seed and wheat. The list went on to include thirty-eight plows, five wagons, a carriage, all sorts of farming tools, several thousand pounds of iron and metal, and blacksmith tools. Hundreds of feet of planks, eight thousand shingles, two millstones, and a windmill would keep the mill in operation producing both lumber and flour. Four spinning wheels, six pairs of cards, and one hundred thirty pounds of wool would provide industry for the older black women. For her personal use he bought a bathtub, a bird cage, a backgammon board, a dozen candle stands, four lots of books, a globe and gazetteer, an encyclopedia, and a cane. It had been James's favorite cane, the one he had bought in Philadelphia more than forty years before.

All of this was in addition to the widow's share allotted by the executors according to the terms of the will. Margaret was entitled to all the household furniture she wished to keep which included two mahogany bedsteads and eight common ones, numerous tables, dozens of chairs, chests, carpets, washstands, dishes, lamps, gilt candlesticks, kitchen ware, a clock, a secretary, and her precious piano. She retained possession of the lumber room, milk house, cotton rooms, and all their contents. In the barnyard she was allotted nine horses, thirty-five or forty hogs being all on hand, fifty sheep, and twenty-one cattle, but no mules.

Being newlyweds, Lettitia and Samuel Bratton had use for many things. Samuel bought all sorts of farm gear, two lots of books, various boxes of sundries, some cotton seed, five mules, and the young jack. He paid $205 for the jack; it was a fine animal. Margaret wondered at her brother's wisdom in not buying mules. The man was a doctor and perhaps did not understand the value of such homely creatures to a farm. She would buy mules later if need be, maybe from her new son-in-law.

William Davidson bought two mules and the jennet, a table, three pictures, and a rifle. He also bought a child's crib; since his little Jimmy was already four, he must be having wishful thoughts about starting a new family. [66] William Torrance, now proudly putting "Dr." before his name, was preparing to return to Philadelphia as Dr. Horner's private student. He had need for only a few items: a gun, a pen knife, a box of razors, and some axes. At the other extreme, Rufus had a well-established household and also needed nothing. He bought a few tools, a plow, one lot of books, fifty-two pounds of iron, and five pictures. Altogether the sale brought over five thousand dollars; the dearest item was the jack bought by Elias Springs for four hundred fifty dollars.

Dr. Allison became the legal guardian of the Torrance children and thereby owner of their Negroes. William was no longer a minor, and his share had been determined by Rufus and Sidney Johnston as executors. The point was moot for Lettitia. She had been given her share as dowry when she married Samuel Bratton. In April, Dr. Allison made a list assigning future ownership of the Negroes to the minor children. He endeavored to keep family groups together, apportion the old ones among them equally, and make the total value of each group the same. He changed the list several times before he was satisfied. In the end he assigned twelve people each to Dick and John, eleven to Sarah Jane, ten to Mary, and nine to Delia. It was only a list. As the Torrance children grew into their majority, Negroes would die and others would be born; at least they had a guideline.

~   ~   ~

Isabella mourned quietly for her father. She thanked God for giving them reconciliation and for removing his suffering. At the same time she deeply missed his presence. Her family duties kept her well occupied. She occasionally went with Rufus on short trips but could not leave nearly as often as she wished. The care of her children and Grandma Latta sculpted her life into one of domestic tranquillity. Yet she was satisfied. It surprised her to find that a lifestyle that she had once considered mundane and trivial had become so deeply satisfying.

In the early spring Isabella allowed Jane Camilla to visit her grandmother Smith. Isabella had maintained a minimum of contact with the woman who now lived at the Charleston Hotel at the mercy of her son. She was still a disagreeable and self-pitying sort who had alienated several of her children to the point that some of her grandchildren were not permitted to visit her. Isabella felt sorry for the old woman, even though she had invited the alienation at every turn. But most of all, she remembered how precious Grandma Davidson had been in her life, giving her some embodied sense of her own mother—Jane Camilla deserved as much. Franklin Smith had been her father, and his family should be privy to her company and she to theirs. Rufus would deposit her in Charleston, make his business rounds of the coastal cities, and retrieve her several weeks later. Isabella hoped the experience would not be too unpleasant for the child. [67]

Mrs. Latta continued her habit of teaching the children at Mount Mourne. The older girls were politely cooperative, although they considered themselves far too mature for such lessons, and five-year-old Emma understood little of them. "Cassie, Cassie!" Mrs. Latta would call as she entered the house, "where are the children? Go gather them up; it's time for their lessons." Cassie was a bright Negress in her late teens who had earned Isabella's respect and become her nursemaid. She had seen Mrs. Latta cross the yard and had already begun gathering the little ones, black and white. On raw days Mrs. Latta sat in the parlor; when the weather was fair she preferred a rocking chair on the porch. She brought her own Bible, for she had marked the passages she intended to teach with strips of paper. The children gathered around her for reading, reciting, and learning. Later dinner was served, and when they had eaten, Mrs. Latta made herself useful to Isabella. She took on tasks suitable for a woman of seventy-some years: rocking colicky babies, shelling peas, sewing, or mending. Idleness was wicked and she was not, but in sultry weather she did permit herself a nap on the daybed. In the evening after a light supper, she recrossed the road to her small home. She still preferred her own quarters. Isabella enjoyed her company and the calm that always surrounded her.

With Mrs. Latta and Cassie attending to much of the child care, Isabella could do her work in an orderly fashion. Rufus owned about eighty Negroes. He directed the field chores; it was Isabella's responsibility to task the women and see that everyone had food, clothing, and attention when ill. She made lists of the edibles on hand and which ones were subject to spoilage. She then decided how they could best be used to impart health and energy with little or no waste. She assigned chores to the women unsuited for farm work. The stronger ones cooked, made soap and candles, hauled water, and sometimes wove cloth. Most cloth was bought, but some was still woven by the Negroes for their own use. The older women and those near confinement sewed, spun, and tended to children. Each day Isabella inquired as to the health of the Negroes. It was desirable to stem illness before it became dangerous or spread, but it was not always possible. Measles, in particular, visited plantations every few years and spread until all the little ones were afflicted. One could only hope that it would be swift and there would be few deaths.

On the twenty-first of April 1849, Isabella gave birth to another boy, John Hugh, whom she called Johnny. On the twenty-third of May, Mary Torrance was married to Dr. Robert Bratton. Once again large numbers of Brattons descended on Cedar Grove for a wedding. It was fitting that the sisters, a year apart in age and as close as twins, would marry brothers who were both doctors. Later that year Sallie and Flax graduated from Edgeworth Seminary. Rufus and Isabella beamed with pride at their daughters' accomplishments. In spite of her poor vision, Sallie had been named a valedictorian and delivered an address at the commencement. Their hard work in preparing her for a life among the sighted had been rewarded.

In 1850, a baby boy was born to Camilla. William at last had the son he had longed for. They named the boy Robert James after both of their fathers. It had been five years since Camilla had given birth, and she was thirty-six years old. Her recovery from childbirth was slow. In July, sixteen-year-old Nannie Reid was at last sent to Salem. Edgeworth had done wonders for Sallie, but Isabella was still partial to Salem. Nannie agreed Salem was the place for her.

With Nannie dispatched to Salem, Rufus decided the time was right for his older girls to see some of the world. He had business to conduct in Philadelphia and New York, and he proposed to take Sallie and Flax with him. After a brief stop in Raleigh where he still had many friends in state government, he would treat them to a tour of Washington and introduce them to a variety of important people—Rufus Reid was well-connected. Arrangements were made, and in mid-August they set off. On the twenty-fifth of August Flax wrote to Isabella from Philadelphia:

> *My dear Mother*
> *It is my intention to inform you of our whereabouts, and how we are getting along. I will give you an outline of our trip and fill up when I get home. The evening we left home it Rained a good deal on us and when we got to the creek this side of Harts we could not cross it and were until twelve oclock getting to Salisbury, as uncle Dick has no doubt told you. We left Salisbury next morning at 8 oclock. The stage was full all the way down. always nine passengers and sometimes ten. Two or three would sometimes ride outside and we would have a little more room, but it was awful in there sometimes. I thought I would melt about the time we got to Chapel Hill. A company of engineers got in with us at Salisbury and we liked them mightily. They were so merry and so good to us. We left them in Raleigh. We reached there about one oclock at night and*

stayed until eleven next day. Govr Manly called on us in the morning and went with us to the State house. He tried to make father promise to leave us with him when we returned. I believe father did half way promise to write to him and let know when we would be in Raleigh on our way home. We sent for Bessie Lacy. She seemed mighty glad to see us. We reached Washington Thursday evening and Staid until Saturday morning. We found it mighty pleasant   Mr Jas Caldwell was mighty clever to us. He took us to the presidents house, where we had the pleasure of seeing Mr Philmore. he is very fine looking and mighty pleasant. We called on Ex governor Graham and found him very pleasant of course. We then went to the patent office and saw a little of everything. I wish I could spend about a month there and then I would'nt see half — from there we went to the Capital and Saw some of the big men of the day. We were very sorry we could not see Clay . . . Mr Clay was absent and we heard this evening of his arrival here so we may see him tomorrow. We saw Ned Wilkes in Washington. he is the same queer fellow. he is going to college next week at Cambridge. Mary Martha Caldwell called to see us with Miss Margaret Blake and her father. Mary was very pleasant, and has none of that stiffness about her that she had the last time I saw her. She says she is going home — October. Mr Henry Williams arrived in Washington Friday evening. Miss McClary is with him. I dont know how to spell her name. They got here this morning about four oclock. We met with Myra and Albert Bamsour between Raleigh and Washington and they have been with us ever since. We got here yesterday evening about three oclock, we had'nt been here long before Mrs Brevard and Mrs McDowell called   they are here on their way home. We went to see them last night and spent the time we were with them very pleasantly   Aleck came home with us. I do like him so much. he staid with us until eleven oclock. There were several southern gentlemen here last night Mr Michael Mr Zimmerman Mr Seagle and some others   A Mr Bogh from Alabama came all the way with us from Salisbury. he is a mighty clever fellow. he is here now, also Mr Myers the Jew from Salisbury. We are staying at the United States Hotel a very good house. I spect we will go on to N York Tuesday or Wednesday. Jim Latta and his lady are there so Mrs McDowell told us. I want to see them. Mrs McDowell *says Mrs Latta is fussy in her manner I recon Jim has [been] so used to a fuss all his life he could'nt do without it. They say every hotel in New York is crowded. I spect we will have to stay at some private boarding house. . . . This is Sunday and it rained so hard we could not go to church, it looks like clearing off now though and we may go this evening. I hope it wont rain tomorrow. There was a small fire in the city last night but it was so far off we could'nt see anything but the smoke. they soon put it out. In Washington we staid at the United States Hotel and I never saw a hotel cut up as funny as it is. We got lost two or three times. I believe father and Mr Bamsour did too. We saw a Mr Redick in Washington that staid at our house all night on his way to Mexico with that company of volunteers. He was very gallant, almost too much so, he was mighty clever though and we liked him mightily. We did'nt see the Misses Wilkes they are in New York. Mr Joe Caldwell wants us to stay in Washington when we return until he goes home — he is such a tease I like him mightily. We did'nt see Fannie in Raleigh. She was so far away from where we stopped we had'nt time to see her. . . . it rained on us both nights that we were in the stage but we did'nt get wet. Well Mother I must stop. this letter is written mighty badly but I will do better next time. Give my love to Grandma and all the children and all Dr Gibbons family. We have not seen Dr Gibbon or Mr Lardner either. they are in New York. Sister and Myra send love. Father wrote to you I think today.*

 With much love your daughter

  Flax [68]

Isabella read the letter several times, vicariously exploring the great northern cities. It seemed as if half the population of Mecklenburg was gadding about the countryside visiting one another in Philadelphia hotels more often than they did at home. She wished Flax had written more about Millard Fillmore. The man had ascended to the presidency after the recent death of Zachary Taylor and remained an enigma. The ancient rift between north and south over the ownership of Negroes had begun to widen. She hoped Mr. Fillmore would be content to leave the southerners alone.

She laughed about Jim Latta's fussy young wife. Jim was William Latta's much younger half-brother, son of Robert's Quaker wife. Robert was well known for being humorless, orderly, and completely devoted to business. Jim had indeed grown up amid a lot of fuss. Isabella wondered what Robert thought of Jim's marriage at the youthful age of twenty-three. If the young lady's manner was as Flax described, perhaps it was satisfactory. She would ask next time she wrote Camilla.

Before she could compose a letter to her sister, bad news came from the Yorkville District. Robert Bratton was dead. Poor Mary. At twenty-one she was a widow, having been married only a year and a summer. Isabella had not had the opportunity to know Dr. Bratton well, but she knew intimately the brutal pain of losing a husband in the first blush of marriage. At least Mary had the large Bratton family and Lettitia and Camilla close at hand.

In the spring of 1851, Dick rode up to Mount Mourne to share his good news. He had been accepted as a student at the state university in Chapel Hill. "Well," said Isabella, "I can see you are pleased with yourself. Is Davidson not good enough for the Torrance men any more?"

"Of course it is," he replied, "but I prefer Chapel Hill. Most of the great men of North Carolina were taught there. Uncle John approves. He said Pa's will stated that his younger children were to have an education equal to the older ones. Since you went to Salem, shouldn't it be required that I attend Chapel Hill?"

Isabella laughed, delighted at his glee. As fine as Salem was, there were no Chapel Hills for women. Although she shared his joy, she was disappointed that he had not chosen Davidson. The college was less than three miles from their plantation. She often shopped there, and its talented men frequented their table. She had looked forward to bringing Dick into the heady intellectual mix. "Stay for dinner," she said to Dick. "Rufus and Grandma will want to hear your news."

He did stay. He had not visited Mount Mourne as often as he wished, for life had been hectic at home since Pa died. Uncle John seem possessed of the naive notion that a gentleman farmer need not work. It was all he and Ma could do to dispel him of it. Dick entertained them with the goings-on at Cedar Grove. "Ma has been driven nearly wild by critters," he said. "Minks have got into the hen house and destroyed a great many of her best hatching hens with all their chickens. Then the hogs began to eat the turkeys. I suppose Uncle John had not fed them properly. So Ma gathered up all the young turkeys and put them in the front yard where she could keep a close watch on them. She has assigned John and some of the little black children to be guardians of the turkeys. None of them can keep a straight face about it. All day John and his little companions march round and round the yard with long sticks chasing turkeys inside and hogs out."[69] They were all amused by his tale, especially Bettie. "I suppose I shall spend the summer training a doctor to farm, which seems a backwards thing,"

Dick continued. "I will be at school by harvest, and I pray Uncle John will have learned how to gather crops."

After Dick had gone, Bettie approached her grandmother. "Just how is it Uncle Dick and I are related?" she asked.

"In several ways that are rather round about," the old woman leaned back in her rocker and gathered her thoughts. "He is an uncle being brother to your Ma."

"But Ma and I are not blood-related, are we?"

"No you are not, so I suppose he is an uncle by marriage. You are also cousins of a sort. Dick's brother William is a nephew of your own mother; since Dick and William had different mothers, that makes you cousins by marriage."

Bettie was a bit confused, but she thought she had gotten the only part that was important to her. "Then Uncle Dick and I are not blood-related at all."

"Why all these questions? Surely you are not setting your cap for a young man at your age?"

"No, just considering the possibilities." Bettie had not remembered Dick as being so handsome. Perhaps his elation over Chapel Hill had enhanced his appeal.

Frank's letters from the west were cheerful ones telling of prosperity. Money was more stable, and Mississippi had at long last become a land of opportunity. Isabella had nearly forgotten that she was part owner in this newfound bounty. All those years ago she, Hugh, and Frank had bought their tracts jointly, and she supposed one third of their plantation belonged to her. She decided to take a bold step and try to accomplish what her father had been unable to—get money out of Hugh. She wrote to him of her proposal and was surprised at his answer. He agreed to pay $3800 for her share of the land, mules, horses, cattle, sheep, hogs, wagons, farming tools, gin stands, mill corn, fodder, oats, and every kind and description of property.[70] He also reported that his Jane and their daughters were in good health (they had named the little one Mary), and that his wife seemed to be in the family way again. Isabella was bitterly pleased that Hugh could come up with nearly four thousand dollars now that their father and that wretched debt were dead.

On the twenty-third of June 1851, Isabella gave birth to another girl, and they named her Lucy. Camilla also had a little girl that year. The child came too soon on the heels of the last one, and Camilla was not up to the strain. This sickly woman who had spent a fair portion of her life recovering from childbirth passed away on the twenty-ninth of November. Among the Torrance kin, November was indeed a time for dying. Camilla was thirty-seven years old and left William with seven children to raise.

Early in 1852, Isabella received a letter from Frank full of more joy than she thought him capable of knowing. First Frank explained that he was selling his interest in the plantation to Hugh. Isabella was a bit puzzled by this news. Was Frank planning to establish himself elsewhere? Loneliness always invited his demons; she read quickly, hoping a rift had not developed between her brothers. Then he announced that he planned to buy his own farm. Hugh had bought Frank's interest in the jointly held property and agreed to sell him back the parcel on the west side of Turkey Creek; he also had his eye on an adjacent plot.[71] He would have his own place next to Hugh's.

Frank saved his best piece of news for last—he was going to be married. He was absolutely buoyant that such a lovely young lady would have an old bachelor of thirty-six. He wrote about his dear Margaret at some length, stating that his only regret was that she had not met Pa. Since he had become fond of her he had not had a single boil, taken a dose of medicine, nor experienced any mental torture. As soon as his new place was established he would visit and bring his new wife; he knew she would be highly esteemed. And, by the way, he had one more bit of news: Hugh's wife had another child, this time a boy. They had named him James, after their father. Isabella didn't know whether to be pleased or enraged. If only Hugh had shown such compassion when their father was alive.

As Isabella reread the letter she could feel tears of joy well in her eyes. Poor Frank had endured more than his share of mishaps and his nature caused him to magnify every one tenfold. It was about time for him to be happy. She could visualize the loamy soil on the banks of Turkey Creek and the tall green hills that rose not far beyond. She hoped Frank's land included some of the hills. Now that times were better in the west, she had every confidence that Frank would make a fine home for his Margaret. Isabella couldn't wait to meet her new sister.

William Torrance had begun his practice of medicine. He had completed his training and was beginning to gain the confidence of his neighbors. At first he was only summoned when Dr. Johnston or one of the other highly regarded men was unavailable. As his reputation grew, his summons were becoming more frequent. His father had willed him a specific portion of the plantation, and he was eager to be able to build his own house on it. But fate interfered. In the springtime, William took ill, possibly infected by one of his patients—the scourge of doctors everywhere. There was no remedy to the fact that great risk was involved in tending the ill. On the twenty-sixth of May 1852, he passed away. Margaret buried him at Hopewell near his father, leaving between them a plot for herself.

The day after the funeral Isabella and Rufus left for Salem to attend Nannie's graduation exercises. It was a bittersweet occasion, Nannie glowed in her accomplishments, but William was not yet cold in the ground. Bettie (who had not yet decided if she preferred "Bettie" or "Betsy") and Jane Camilla (who had decided since her aunt's death to give up "Jane" entirely and be called simply "Camilla") went with their parents. They were scheduled to enroll in the fall and took the opportunity to acquaint themselves with the school and the teaching Sisters. They walked up and down the streets, peeking into the shops and pondering where their pocket money would be spent. According to their mother, the pavement had been much improved over the years; perhaps they would not wear out their shoes as quickly as she had. Mr. Winkler's bakery was exactly where it had always been. They bought a sugar cake, pleased that some things never changed. Back at the hotel they shared it with Grandma Latta who had become a fixture at these events.

Over the summer Isabella amassed their wardrobe and the other things Bettie and Camilla would need for school. They were both sixteen, only a few months apart in age, and were closer than most natural sisters. By September, they were more than ready for Salem. Rufus was a loving father who believed in guiding his children gently into adulthood. His children were little flowers to be coaxed into blooming and indulged whenever necessary. On the fifth of October 1852, he wrote:

Dear Children
   Betsy & Camilla
      Rec^d Betsys letter in proper time & Camillas was rec^d very promptly. We are pleased to find that you feel like being content and happy   this is a great matter in learning. one discontented cannot learn well. With you there will be nothing to make you displeasured as you are on the stage road so direct that three times each week we can hear from you visit you if sick & send to you if you need.
      We are taking out the cotton very fast this good weather. If you were at home I would be tempted to put you in the cotton fields. our boy Ken picked 125 lb today by twelve oclock   Many of the hands picked 90 lbs & upward. W.Harris is here with three workmen at our mill wheel. I hope that we will be able to send you [pone] from our mill within three or 4 months. The girls & Margaret Niel were at church   Met Mrs Blackwelder on Sunday last & saw most of the world between this & Statesville   our country is healthy except for chills   Our family are well   Mr Simmond was here last night & is very busy at Caddle Creek Hopewell & other places singing
      We have not rec^d our full goods on acct. of the Rail Road Bridge

being off. Now here is a long letter for me & you must not expect [this] about letters with me. Write when you have time & feel like it.

Be courteous & kind to your teachers & all others without being so you will not expect to receive proper feelings from those with whom you associate

Our respects to Doc^{tr} D. Schumittes your teachers & all friends Say to Miss Isabella Sloan that her family were with ours Thursday last.

Yours affectionately
Rufus Reid
P.S. Enclosed is a dollar bill with it buy post office stamps of three cents each & place on your letters to home & your friends to me — as others   Divide the stamps between you.

The girls laughed at his spidery hand; it took both of them to decipher his letters, and even then some parts were not quite clear. He would not last a minute in this place with such penmanship. In November, he wrote again, this time with sad news:

Dear Betsy
I recv^d your letter & Camillas late not unattended. Some of the girls rec^d a letter from Camilla a few days since. We are pleased to have a favorable report from you as to health and general welfare

I have to report to you the early death of your brother James L Davidson of fever after about 14 days illness. Robert lossed a child about the same time   James died on the 2^d Inst & was buried in Charlotte on the 3^d.

I wish you and Camilla to write me as often as it is convenient and pleasant to you. With my business you will not look to me for much about letters. The Sisters will give you the news of our county
Love to Camilla
Yrs
Rufus Reid

James and Robert were two of the six boys of Betsy and Wilson Davidson who had moved to Oaklawn, then out again when their brother John brought a wife to the place. They were a good deal older that Bettie and Camilla but Bettie's brothers nevertheless. James had been thirty-two years old and left behind a childless widow.

There had been another death among their relations earlier that year. William Latta had written that his father had died of consumption at his home in Columbia on the twenty-fifth of July. He had suffered from the disease for many years. Isabella and Grandma Latta grieved together. To the older woman Robert was a son. Although she had not borne him, she had raised him and loved him as her own. Now all of her children were with God, a hard thing for a mother to bear. To Isabella, he was her sister Camilla's father-in-law, and their own father's dear friend. She could imagine them together in heaven sipping brandy and doing business with the angels. Perhaps Robert was telling her father of the progress with the railroad: there was only a tiny section of track yet to be laid. Late in October, she was sure they looked down from heaven beaming with pride as the first train huffed into Charlotte.

On the thirtieth of June 1853, William Latta married Miss Sarah Dews. His youngsters needed a mother, and he wished to put the loss of Camilla and his father behind him. Unfortunately his happiness was brief; Sarah died on the third of April 1854.

In January 1854, Isabella was blessed with another son. She named him Franklin, after all of the Franklins in her life: her brother, of course, Uncle Frank who had begun to take her father's place as advisor when Rufus was away, and her dear first husband buried in Coffeeville. She wrote of the birth to her brother who had married his Margaret the previous winter. His reply was a happy one, and he was flattered to be an Uncle Frank to her little Franklin. Married life had quieted his demons.

It was that same spring that Rufus suffered a slight attack of apoplexy. He had always been a robust man, suffering only occasionally from fevers and rheumatism which were expected at his age. He quickly recovered. Then there was another attack and another. Each time there was more paralysis. Isabella begged to send for the doctor as she watched him shuffling about the house trying to hide the fact that one hand was nearly useless. He told her in no uncertain slurred words, that he would have none of it. On the first of July, when she found him slumped in his chair, she disobeyed and sent for Dr. Houston. The doctor stayed most of the night, then returned the next day with medicine. He instructed Isabella on the care of her husband and asked her to send for him if Rufus was further attacked.

At first he seemed to improve or at least not decline, but it was not to last. On the eighth of July, the doctor was summoned again. During the next week he spent part of most days and several nights at Rufus's bedside, dispensing first one medicine then another. Isabella was frantic. Over two weeks time she watched her strong and able husband dissolve into an ashen sack of useless bones. Isabella was grateful for the doctor's attention. There was an epidemic of dysentery in the neighborhood, and he too seemed diminished in vitality. His only rests were brief naps in a chair at a patient's bedside. Finally, on the fifteenth of July, with no sap left in his body, Rufus Reid died in his sleep. Isabella thanked God for ending his agony but could not suppress her anger at Him for allowing it to occur in the first place. Grandma Latta, who was intimate with God, would help her find solace.

The older girls prepared his obituary:

> Died of Apoplexy at his residence, Mt. Mourne, in Iredell County, on the 15th inst. Maj. Rufus Reid, aged 57.
>
> The health of Mr. Reid had been rapidly declining for 4 or 5 months prior to his death, having been during that time constantly threatened, and several times attacked with the disease which finally terminated his existence. For nearly 4 days immediately preceding his death, he lay in a state of profound stupor, and neither spoke nor opened his eyes, nor moved a muscle of his body but passed away almost imperceptibly and without a struggle. Although he did not conform, or attach himself to any church organization of the world, his intimate friends are nevertheless satisfied, that he died with the elements of purely religious sentiments predominant in his heart. His life had been one of constant action and exertion, by which he has been enabled to leave his bereaved family surrounded with ample means to secure their comfort. He had the confidence and commanded the respect of all who knew him, and the citizens of his county had twice honored him with a seat in the legislative council of the State, having represented them in the House of Commons in 1844 & 1846. — His death to a large and interesting family, consisting mostly of females, is a loss which no imagination can compass, and no pen can describe; whilst no other object can ever fill the vacuum produced by it in a large circle of neighbors, friends and acquaintances. But let us hope that he approached his grave
> "Like one who draws the drapery of his couch
> About him, and lies down to pleasant dreams." [72]

Widowhood was different this time. At thirty-six Isabella was older and wiser. She had shared twelve years with Rufus, the most blissful years of her life. This time she was at home, financially secure, and surrounded by a large and loving family. All of these things made her grief deeper and comfort sweeter. Isabella called on Uncle Frank to help her manage her household and plantation. Since Grandpa Davidson's death twelve years ago, Frank traveled less often to his holdings in Alabama and elsewhere and was spending more of his time at his Mount Mourne plantation. He was close at hand and wise in the ways of business, an excellent person to come to her assistance.

Uncle Frank dove right into the business of collecting money owed Rufus, settling debts, distributing assets to the children, and managing daily finances. Frank was a meticulous man and kept exacting records for the Reid household. Isabella had selected a spot at the Centre Church graveyard to bury her husband, as close as could be found to her Davidson grandparents. Although he had not committed his soul to Christ, Isabella felt confident that this loving man was welcome in heaven. She knew he would not object to lying forever in hallowed ground, for it pleased her. Rufus had been intent on pleasing her. She arranged for a number of plots to be reserved for her family. She expected her daughters to marry and go to rest with their husbands' people and that she and Rufus would be surrounded by their sons and daughters-in-law. She laid him to rest near the center of the handful of plots.

With Rufus peacefully buried and Frank in charge of business, Isabella went back to work on the plans she and Rufus were devising when he took ill. Sallie's eyesight had always been a worry to them, and they had heard of new procedures being performed in Boston that sometimes helped the sightless. Perkins Institute, a school for the blind, had been established in that city many years before. Its fine reputation drew doctors and others whose interest was in restoring sight. Rufus and Isabella had made inquiries of a doctor who offered hope; now Isabella was following through by arranging transportation, boarding, and other particulars. This time Nannie would be her sister's eyes.

Outfitting the girls was the kind of activity that cheered Isabella the most. Early fall found them shopping most days for the expedition. Twenty-eight yards of alpaca would make sumptuous cozy cloaks for the Boston winter. They also bought velvet, flannel, linen, several shawls, shoes, bonnets, kid gloves, two parasols, needles and pins, hooks and eyes, and a bottle of cologne. When the finery was boxed up, they selected ordinary household goods such as coffee, sugar, spices, whiskey, and tobacco. Nearly every week a dozen or so chickens were bought. Isabella had about given up raising them since they could be had for ten cents apiece, and she had no interest in chasing minks and hogs. She was careful not to ignore the younger children in the excitement of planning for the Boston trip. She bought toys including marbles for the boys; and silk threads, linen, and sewing birds for Emma and Addie.[73]

Preparations complete, the young ladies were dispatched on their journey. Nannie at twenty-one felt quite grown up to have the responsibility of guiding Sallie on her quest for sight. On the twenty-fourth of November, Nannie wrote to Bud Rufus. Of course she knew everyone would read the letter, but his letter to her invited a reply:

My Dear Little Brother

You dont know how agreeably surprised I was this morning when I opened a nice long letter from our kind sister Flax and found one to me from you, which did very well considering it had not been corrected by any one but yourself. I didnt know that you could write so well, and such a good letter, it deserves answering right away and shall be. but I hope that you will not let this be your last. Sister wrote you last week We were so glad to find sister Flax's letter when we got home from the Dr's for we had been looking for one from someone at home three or four days, you know we must be glad to get letters for we are so far from home, which is very dear to us.

Sister and I went out to Lynn yesterday morning; and spent the night with a nice little lady who is a friend of Sisters and mine, we became acquainted with her at Dr G's room. I have her likeness, which I will let you see when we go home. Lynn is a city about nine miles from Boston we took the cars at twelve oclock and got out there about a quarter of one. Mr Breed, the husband of the little lady who invited us out to see them met us at the Depot, and took us to his house where we found Mrs Breed waiting for us to come. First she gave us dinner, which was very nice, then Mr Breed got a carriage and took us to ride out to Nahant which is a very fashionable watering place, that is where a great many persons go in the summer season for pleasure, many go from Boston. There is a very large Hotel there, where we were told that a gentleman with a small family boarded there a week last summer, and had to pay three hundred dollars, and another with a small family, payed either six or seven hundred, I forget which, we were told this, therefore we cant say whether it is true or not, but if it is, it is pretty dear living don't you think so? There are some very wealthy persons in Boston, but they might put their money to a better use, especially where so many poor persons are to be found, we see a great many who would be so glad to get it. We ought never to throw any thing away that will be of any use to someone or something else, for I think it is a great sin.

I didn't finish telling you about out ride. We came home, or I mean we rode about a mile and a half or three quarters on the beach or shore of the ocean, which is beautiful, just as smooth as it can be, and is more pleasant to ride on in the summer season, but nice even now, the sand is so hard that the horses feet, and the carriage wheels, don't sink more than half an inch into it when we are riding over it, and the waves are so pretty. I wish that you could see them, but you may perhaps when you are grown. It was just about dark when we got back. Mrs Breed has no little children, but she took us to see a neighbor of hers who lived just across the street after tea and there we found two very nice little ones, a boy by the name of Charles, who is about Johnies size, and a sweet little girl just Lucys size named Emma. We got back to Boston this morning between eleven and twelve. The first place we landed was at the foot of a street which took us right up to the Drs operating room, where we staid until about two, when we came to Mrs Reed's which you know is our boarding house. Sister and I received a letter from cousin Rufus Reid this evening. he and Helen were in Charleston where they expected to remain until last Tuesday when they would leave for Alabama. Sister got a very nice letter from Mr Frontis, which I expect she will answer soon, for we do love to get his letters. I have to read them to Sister, so you see we get the good of them together. I was sorry to hear that my bird and all the little Canarys were dead. I got Sister to ~~write~~ compose some lines of poetry for me on the death of my dear little bird. What has become of the dog? I hope that he is not dead too, we have not heard a word from him since we left home, tho he must still be in the land of the living, or we would have heard something of his departure.

Tell Mrs Brawley and Mrs Lemley for me that their bets on the new church are gone now. . . . Mr Frontis seems to regret that they can't get it done to preach in this winter and I am sorry that it cant be finished, but hope that he will find some place to preach in.

You must tell me when you write how many children you have in school and who they are. you must study hard, and try to improve in your writing, but I think you are trying to do that. Be a good boy, and do every thing that mother, Miss Cassie or sister Flax tells you in that way you will set a good example for your younger brothers and sisters. Sister will write to sister Flax soon as I will. I dont know which yet, but her letter shall be answered. Sister joins me in love to Grandma, mother, sister Flax, Miss Cassie, all the children with yourself and all friends. A kiss to little brother Frank.

I remain your very affectionate sister

Nannie [74]

Isabella read the letter with great interest. She hoped Sallie's treatment was going well. She would have to wait for a letter addressed to one of the adults for more on that subject. She was intrigued by Nannie's tale of the trip to Nahant; it sounded nothing like the Reid's watering place at Catawba Springs. The ocean must be lovely, but could it be finer than the mineral waters that bubbled up from the rocks nestled between green hills and the river? She pulled the atlas from the shelf and turned to the page containing Boston and its environs. Nahant was nearly an island in the Massachusetts Bay joined to Lynn by a long slip of land which looked hardly wide enough to bear a road. She tried to imagine the opulent hotel surrounded by beaches and ocean waves. She was glad the girls were finding amusement to supplement their serious mission.

Christmas was somber with Rufus gone, but the children would expect a celebration nevertheless. Molasses, apples, and spices were bought to prepare for the feast, and extra whiskey to reward the Negroes. In addition she gave them $257.90. She gave shiny coins to the little ones, a dollar or two to the field hands, and even more to the house servants. Rufus had left her over ninety people to provide for.

Although she missed Rufus dreadfully, by 1855 the most painful stage of grief had ebbed. In the relative calm of winter she could reflect on his wishes devised in his gentle manner to bring pleasure to his family. She determined to adopt his ways as if consulting with him daily.

In February, she received a letter from Frank relating the sad news that his beloved Margaret had died on the twenty-seventh of January at the tender age of twenty-five. They had been married barely two years and had not yet been blessed with children. He had buried her in nearby Grenada since her people were there. He had ordered from a stone mason a nine-foot-tall obelisk decorated with an engraved wreath. An elaborate scrolled shield was carved in relief to record her name and the dates of her birth and death. It would be the grandest monument in the cemetery. [75] Frank had lost interest in Mississippi and planned to visit Carolina in the summer; he hoped it would be a long visit. It was obvious to Isabella that Frank had been devastated by the loss of Margaret, and his melancholy had returned. She wept for her poor forlorn brother, and sadness for him revived her own grief. At least she had Rufus's children to bring her comfort.

As the spring unfolded she set aside sad thoughts; there was much to do to prepare for events ahead. Nannie and Sallie would be home from Boston soon; Nannie had reported that Sallie's vision was somewhat improved, but no miracle had been worked. Camilla and Bettie were completing their studies at Salem and would have their examinations on the first of June. Isabella scurried about to get them properly outfitted and was met with frustration at every turn. The railroad was a mixed blessing— goods could be delivered much quicker and in far greater quantities than by stage, but washed out bridges and broken rails made the system tauntingly unreliable.

Dick was slated to graduate from Chapel Hill; Isabella expected to see a lot of him at Mount Mourne that summer. He and Bettie had been exchanging letters and had become fast friends. Bettie had inquired again about the nature of their kinship and had been reassured that they were not blood relatives. Dick had grown to be a fine young man. Of all of Isabella's siblings, Dick shared her spirited nature most of all. Camilla's letters did not mention young men. She had taken notice of her sisters as they traveled to the great cities. Camilla's eyes were on the road and whatever lay at the end of it.

What a merry summer it was going to be with everyone at home, thought Isabella. Flax, Sallie, and Nannie were all in their early twenties, and Camilla and Bettie were both eighteen. She could hardly wait for the companionship of young women. Emma was twelve, little Frank was two, and Bud Rufus, Addie, John, and Lucy were like stair steps in between. Having them all under one roof would be quite the novelty and a delightful mad scramble. As she contemplated her family, she knew her father would be proud of her accomplishments. He was proud at the end of his days, but she wished he could see this fine crop of grandchildren. If he and Rufus could look down from heaven, they would approve of the way she was raising her assortment of children and caring for Grandma Latta. Isabella had become a fine woman, even if she thought so herself.

Enough reflection. There was work to be done. She must write to her girls in Salem and tell them of her lack of progress in finding suitable clothes for them. Cassie was preparing a box of their spring clothes and a few other things they needed, but commencement dresses still eluded her. She hoped Grandma Latta would be able to attend the examination in June, but Isabella would make no promise; at eighty, Grandma might not be up to the trip as much as she loved to go. No, thought Isabella, I will not mention that; I shall write a newsy letter and decide about Grandma when the time comes. On the first of April 1855, she wrote to Camilla:

My Dear Child

I send you a letter which came only yesterday from your cousin Mary   it had been missent, and I had concluded not to send it but as Cassie is sending a box I will just drop it in. I will also send some postage stamps half are for Bettie. Flax and I went to the college on yesterday to get you some dry goods but did not succeed very well the goods have not all come in yet   we got each of you a lawn dress and will try and get the other things which you need and send next week. We had a letter from Sallie this week in which she spoke of leaving about the middle of this month but I think it somewhat doubtful, she said her eyes were then better, the Misses Andrews were expected there this month so Sallie wrote and I think it likely our girls will remain and all leave together. This is Saturday and the children are all playing about. Addie & Johnny have very bad colds Johnny has been quite unwell all week. Cousins Robert & Eliza Davidson and children came here on last Saturday he went on to court on Monday and she and the little folks remained with us they left on Wednesday, we had quite a pleasant time of it. I suppose Flax wrote you that William D had been to see us after so long a time. Our garden is much more backward than usual this season. Almost every thing I had was killed during the severe weather but unless the fruit was killed this morning we will have plenty of peaches still. I suppose you are both very busy preparing for the examination, it certainly is no criteria by which to judge of a young ladies abilities but at the same time it would please both your teachers and myself for you to acquit yourselves well. Uncle Frank expects to go to Mississippi the week after next he has sent some 25 hands out there lately. I must close as Cassie wishes to close her box. We will try and get your box next week. I hope you get dresses in Salem instead of waiting. Give Bettie a kiss with my love, also love to all whom I should remember and accept a large portion for yourself from your

ever affectionate mother

I M Reid [76]

Epilogue

At Mount Mourne

Isabella's home remained vibrant for many more years. The keenest sculptor of her life and the entire country during the next decade was the Civil War, the infamous scourge that left no one untouched. Nevertheless, life went on.

Rufus Reid's daughters by his Latta wives all found husbands. Sallie Reid married her cousin, Rufus J. Reid, in 1855. Although he had business interests in Alabama, they appear to have spent the early years of their marriage in North Carolina. In 1869, they moved to Alabama and some years later to Saint Paul, Minnesota, where they are presumed to have died and been buried. They had no children.

In October of 1858, Flax Reid married Benjamin Franklin Little [Frank]. Frank was a graduate of Davidson College and the son of a planter from Richmond County, North Carolina. Frank and Flax established a plantation in that county on Homer Creek about three miles from the Pee Dee River. Flax must have honored the old tradition of bearing her first child at her mother's home. Their daughter, only a few weeks old when she died on August 22, 1859, is buried at Centre Church. Frank Little was in his thirties when war came and he followed his patriotic calling. He was wounded and captured at Gettysburg in 1863 and lost an arm for the effort. He further served his state in the North Carolina Legislature in 1864–65. Flax and Frank had seven more children; two of them died in early childhood during a diphtheria epidemic in 1865. Flax died in 1905; she and her husband are both buried in the family burial ground at Carlisle, their Richmond County plantation.

Nannie Reid stayed closer to home and on her twenty-third birthday, October 15, 1856, married Dr. George Johnston Houston who was probably a cousin of some degree to the Dr. J. H. Houston who attended her father's final illness. She and George lived on a plantation, carved from his father's land, which was also called Mount Mourne. The two Mount Mournes and Uncle Frank Davidson's place formed a triangle about three miles on a side which surrounded Centre Church. Nannie gave birth to nine children, the last two twin girls. Only one of this large brood ever married. Nannie died in 1874; she and her husband are buried at Centre Church along with their throng of single children.

After Bettie Reid completed her studies at Salem, she returned to Mount Mourne and waited impatiently for Dick Torrance to graduate from Chapel Hill, which he did in 1856. Their wedding that November followed Nannie's by less than six weeks. The next August Bettie gave birth to a daughter, Minna, and soon after the family was bound for the west. They settled in Richmond, Texas, which has been swallowed up by present-day Houston, where they encountered great difficulty in establishing a farm on the Brazos River. Maggie was born there in September of 1859, and Bettie died of coast fever on September 20, 1861. She is buried in Texas.

Only three of Isabella's children married. Addie Reid married a Mr. Brown, and a subsequent letter mentions John Reid's "wife" but not by name. What became of them remains a mystery. Lucy Reid married Robert Hall Morrison, Jr. He was the son of the first president of Davidson College who had long since left the stress of academic life and taken up farming near Morganton, North Carolina. Lucy kept up a lively correspondence with her famous sister-in-law, Anna Morrison Jackson, Stonewall Jackson's widow who became Charlotte's most revered citizen after the Civil War. Lucy died in 1925 and is buried in Morganton.

By July 1860, Bud Rufus was in military school in Hillsboro, North Carolina. He was only fifteen but war was in the air. His patriotic fervor was short lived. He died at Manassas, Virginia, on November 1, 1861. His monument at Centre Church states that he was sixteen years and eleven months old.

A year and a month later, Isabella's youngest child, Franklin Samuel, died at the age of eight and was buried next to his brother.

Mount Mourne became an enclave of women: Isabella, Jane Camilla, Emma, and Jane Latta lived there the rest of their days. Mrs. Latta died in 1864 at the age of eighty-eight. She is buried at Hopewell between her husband and her son, Ezekiel. The spinsterhood of Jane Camilla and Emma was a common fate of women of their time, widows of war rather than warriors. Jane Camilla died in 1901 at the age of sixty-six, and Emma in 1908 at sixty-five. They are both buried at Centre Church. Isabella never remarried and died on December 22, 1893, at the age of seventy-five. She is buried in the Centre graveyard next to her beloved Rufus.

From the West and Elsewhere

The war must have completely undermined Hugh's and Frank's ability to farm successfully in Mississippi. As usual Frank was first to notice the impending doom, although in fairness, the loss of his wife undoubtedly had its influence. He visited North Carolina several times over the next decade, then in 1863 sold all his land in Mississippi and returned permanently to his native state. He made his home at Mount Mourne with Isabella, and died there in May of 1869 at the age of fifty-three. He is buried at Centre Church among the Reids.

Hugh and Jane had four children, although their oldest died in childhood. Amazingly Hugh did visit his North Carolina kin at least once, in 1858. It is not known if he brought money. Sometime after the war he also gave up on Mississippi. By 1868, he had moved his family to Memphis, Tennessee, and sold his Mississippi farmland. He died in September of 1878 during a yellow fever epidemic in Memphis. He is remembered by a small stone in Elmwood Cemetery in Charlotte, but his remains are probably in Tennessee.

Franklin Davidson never married and lived out his life in his father's Mount Mourne home. He continued to help Isabella manage her affairs and preceded her in death by just six months. He died in 1893 at the age of eighty-eight and is buried at Centre Church next to his parents.

William S. M. Davidson married twice more but had no more children. He died in 1873, and his bachelor son, Jimmy Torrance Davidson followed him the next year at the age of thirty. An obelisk marking the graves of William and his second wife sits between those of his first wife, Jane, and their son Jimmy. One or both of William's subsequent wives may have been nieces of Rufus Reid.

William Latta also had two more wives after Camilla died. There were no children from his brief second marriage and one son with Anna Clark whom he married in 1856. William died in 1865.

At Cedar Grove

Margaret continued to manage the plantation with the help of her brother and sons. Her sister Jane had married and moved to Mississippi, and eventually her bachelor brother, John Allison, decided to go west and make his home with her. By this time Margaret's youngest, John Torrance, was a man and became the farmer of Cedar Grove.

The war was a watershed event for the Bratton clan who seemed unable to accept peace with their Negroes or the Yankees. Many scattered to the winds, some retreating to Canada to avoid their woes. Lettitia and Dr. Samuel Bratton's home in York County turned out to be temporary. They lived for a while in Mississippi before moving to Charlotte. Then in the late 1880s, in a state of great financial difficulty, they moved to Atlanta. The widowed Mary Torrance Bratton, who had married Dr. Witherspoon in 1851, moved with him to Mississippi where they had at least two children. By the late 1880s, Mary had been widowed again and was living with Lettitia and Samuel in Atlanta. As close as these sisters were knit, they are probably buried together in or near that city.

In 1856, Delia Torrance married John Johnston, a nephew of Rufus Reid, and settled with him on a plantation in nearby Gaston County where she died in 1861 at the age of twenty-nine. In 1857, Sarah Jane Torrance married Dr. John Brown Gaston of Montgomery, Alabama. She had at least one child and probably many more; she died in Alabama in 1914 at the age of seventy-eight.

Dick continued to farm his Brazos River plantation in Texas after he buried his beloved Bettie but curtailed his efforts when war broke out. He joined Terry's Texas Rangers and headed for Shiloh, Tennessee. On the way he left his daughters with his Aunt Jane in Columbus, Mississippi. He was wounded twice; the second time cost him his leg. While recovering at Cedar Grove he met Eliza Gaston of Chester, South Carolina. He married her in 1865 and took her to Texas where he tried once more to tame his land, but it was not to be. In 1869, they moved to Eliza's mother's farm and two years later back to Cedar Grove. In 1892, Dick gave up farming, and he and Eliza moved to Charlotte. She died there in 1916, he in 1927 at the age of ninety-four. They are both buried at Hopewell along with several of their nine children.

John Torrance was also called into military service and was present at several bloody battles. After the war he returned to Cedar Grove and worked his mother's farm for the rest of his days. The war that claimed Dick's leg stole John's spirit. He never married and was advised on more than one occasion to seek a cure for his love of strong drink. A remedy tucked in his papers suggests sucking on slices of raw potato which have been soaked in ice water until the desire to drink has passed. John died in 1904 and is buried at Hopewell.

Margaret lived out her life at Cedar Grove. Farming activity and visits to and from her scattered family were also interrupted by the war. In 1862, with her boys on battlefields, she hired James Brown as an overseer. Yet she worried that he would be conscripted before the crops were in. It was during those war-shattered years she wrote an anguished letter to Dick: "I have been distressed much. I do not know what your situation is. I can't help feeling like it was uncertain whether I am writing to the living or the dead." John did return at the war's end and Dick and his growing family a few years later, but the southern plantation lifestyle was gone forever. Margaret died in 1880 at the age of eighty-two and is buried in the Hopewell churchyard. Cedar Grove was inherited by Dick who divided the land among his eleven children. The portion of the farm containing Cedar Grove passed to Dick's daughter Delia who left it to her son, Richard Torrance Banks, the guardian and gatherer of the Torrance legacy.

Genealogy

Torrance Family

FIRST GENERATION:
Hugh Torrance b. 1743, d. 2/14/1816. On 5/29/1783 he married:
Isabella Kerr Falls b. 1740, d. 2/1/1816.
She had two sons and six daughters by her first marriage to Galbraith Falls.

SECOND GENERATION:
The only child of Hugh and Isabella Falls Torrance was: James Galbraith
Torrance b. 11/19/1784, d. 12/12/1847.
James's three wives were:
Nancy A. Davidson b. 10/28/1792, d. 11/11/1818; m. 2/9/1809
Mary Latta [Polly] b. 12/29/1799, d. 11/26/1824; m. 4/14/1821
Margaret Allison b. 1/16/1798, d. 1/19/1880; m. 1827

THIRD AND FOURTH GENERATIONS:
The five children of James and Nancy Davidson Torrance:
1. Hugh b. 1/5/1810, d. 9/10/1878; m. 10/?/1843 Jane Powell, b.1822.
Their four children were: Isabella b. 1845; Mary b. 6/23/1847; James b. 1852;
Martha b. 1853.
2. Jane Adeline b. 1811, d. 1820, at the age of nine.
3. Camilla Catherine b. 11/19/1813, d. 11/29/1851; m. 6/24/1834 William
Albert Latta, b. 1809, d. 1865. Their eight children were: William [Willie] b.
1835, d. 1841 at the age of six; Margaret b. 1837; Ada b. 1839; Annie b. 1841;
Adeline b. 1842; Jane Elizabeth b. 1845; Robert b. 1850; Florence b. 1851.
4. James Franklin [Frank] b. 1816, d. 5/17/1869; m. 1852? Margaret A., b.
1830, d. 1855. No children.
5. Isabella Malvina b. 1818, d. 12/22/1893; m. 9/9/1835 Franklin Smith b.
1807, d. 1837. Their only child was Jane Camilla Smith b. 1835 or 1836, d.
5/16/1901, never married.
Isabella next married on 4/19/1842 Rufus Reid b. 1797, d. 1854. Their six
children were Emma Catherine b. 2/11/1843; James Rufus [Bud Rufus] b.
12/12/1845; Addie Isabella b. 3/5/1847; John Hugh b. 4/21/1849; Lucy
Andrews b. 6/23/1851; and Franklin Samuel b. 1/24/1854.

The two children of James and Polly Latta Torrance:
1. William Latta b. 1/20/1822, d. 5/26/1852. Never married.
2. Jane Elizabeth b. 8/15/1823, d. 12/3/1844; m. 12/8/1842 Dr. William S.
M. Davidson. b. circa 1818, d. 1873. They had one child: James Torrance
Davidson [Jimmy] b. 10/21/1843, d. 3/4/1874.

The six children of James and Margaret Allison Torrence:
1. Lettitia b. 11?/1828, d. after 1888; m. 9/7/1847 Dr. Samuel Bratton. They had several children.
2. Mary b. 2/22?/1829, d. after 1888; m. 4/23/1849 Dr. Robert Bratton. Mary next married Dr. Sidney Witherspoon in 1851. They had several children.
3. Delia b. 1831, d. 1/3/1861; m. 6/17/1856 John Johnston [a nephew of Rufus Reid], children unknown.
4. Richard Allison [Dick] b. 12/7/1833, d. 5/22/1927; m. 11/26/1856 Bettie Reid. Their children were: Minna b. 1857, and Margaret b. 1859. Dick next married Patience Eliza Gaston [Eliza] on 10/3/1865. They had nine children.
5. Sarah Jane b. 1/12/1836, d. 1914; m. 1857 Dr. John Gaston, children unknown.
6. John Andrew b.1/28/1839, d. 12/21/1904; never married.

Latta Family

FIRST GENERATION:
James Latta b. 8/25/1755, d. 10/30/1837. In 1780 he married Elizabeth Houston b. ?, d. 1792.
James next married Jane Knox b. 1775, d. 7/1/1864.

SECOND AND THIRD GENERATIONS:
The two children of James and Elizabeth Houston Latta:
1. William b. 10/8/1781, d. 9/26/1829; m. 1811 Mary Pamela Woods. They had nine children including Mary b. circa. 1813, and Ann b. circa 1814.
2. Robert b. 8/21/1783, d. 7/25/1852; m. 11/4/1806 Jane Allison b. ?, d. 1819. They had four children including William Albert b. 11/15/1809, d. 1865 [see Torrance Family].
Robert next married Eliza Dilworth, b. 1795, d. 1869. They had four children.

The four children of James and Jane Knox Latta:
1. Elizabeth [Betsy] b. 2/9/1797, d. 5/4/1838; m. 1818 Benjamin Wilson Davidson [Wilson], b. 1787, d. 1829. They had six sons.
Betsy next married Rufus Reid on 1/24/1835; this was also his second marriage. They had one child, Elizabeth Eugenia [Bettie] b. 4/29/1836, d. 9/20/1861, and a stillborn infant b. 5/4/1838. Bettie Reid married Dick Torrance [see Torrance family].
2. Mary [Polly] b. 12/29/1799, d. 11/26/1824; m. 4/14/1821 James G. Torrance. They had two children [see Torrance Family].
3. Nancy b. 2/15/1804, d. 11/6/1833; m. 12/11/1828 Rufus Reid [his first

marriage]. They had three daughters: Sarah Latta [Sallie] b. 5/2/1830, d. ?; Mary Jane [Flax] b. 12/28/1831, d. 1905; and Nancy Elizabeth [Nannie] b. 10/15/1833, d. 1874.

4. Ezekiel b. 1810, d. 1820.

Reid Family

Captain John Reid b. 1752, d. 1821, m. Sarah Sharp. They had two daughters and four sons. The youngest was Rufus Reid b. 1797, d. 7/15/1854, see Torrance and Latta families.

Ephraim Davidson Family

General Ephraim Davidson b. 1762, d. 2/25/1842, m. Jane Brevard b. 1765, d. 9/28/1833. Their children were Nancy (see Torrance family), George Franklin [Frank] b. 1805, d. 6/16/1893, and at least three other daughters. Ephraim's father was a cousin of General William Lee Davidson, namesake for Davidson College.

John Davidson Family

Major John Davidson b. 1735, d. 1832, m. Violet Wilson b. 1741, d. 1818. They were the parents of ten children. The youngest was Benjamin Wilson b. 5/20/1787, d. 9/25/1829 (see Latta Family). Among John Davidson's grandchildren by son Jacky, was William S. M. Davidson b. 1817, d. 1873 (see Torrance family).

Notes

Most of the documents used to develop this story are in the Torrance-Banks Family Papers in the Rare Books and Manuscript Collection of the Adkins Library at the University of North Carolina at Charlotte. All of the quoted letters and documents and the photographs of them that are not cited in the notes below are from that source; when the collection is cited it is abbreviated TBFP.

The next largest source of documentation is the archives at Latta Plantation, currently operated as a public historic site. Most of the Latta papers are photocopies of original documents owned by various libraries; Latta archives and the owner of the original are both attributed. Some of the Latta papers are secondary sources compiled by an assortment of researchers over a number of years. Their authors are often unknown, and their sources are sometimes not attributed.

Additional original documents were consulted from the George F. Davidson Family Papers at Duke University, Durham, North Carolina. Land records, census reports, and cemetery lists were consulted in Yalobusha County, Mississippi, and in Mecklenburg and Iredell Counties, North Carolina. Some notes contain the author's comments, interpretations, and consternations. They should be obvious from context.

1 Mecklenburg 1825

1 The *Raleigh Register* of December 4, 1818, reported that "D in Mecklenburg County, N C on Wednesday morning the 11th inst of the typhus fever, Mrs. Nancy Torrance, in the 26th year of her age . . . " They had no knowledge that this horrible disease was spread by body lice.

2 Salem 1825~1827

2 Scots-Irish is a modern term; during the early nineteenth century they were called Irishmen. It was not until after the huge influx from Ireland following the 1840s potato famine that "Scots-Irish" was applied to the earlier immigration. Happily the new term better describes their origin and culture and is used in this text for clarity.

3 The details of Moravian life were taken primarily from *The Road to Salem*, by Adelaide Fries. This information was supplemented by Old Salem site brochures and other brief descriptions of early Salem, many visits there, and conversations with interpreters. The Salem Female Boarding School was opened to outsiders (non-Moravians) in 1805. It has been in continuous operation since that time and is now known as Salem College.

4 The ledger of the girls' purchases are in their school records in the Torrance-Banks family papers. It documents their academic needs, medical bills, and personal items, including numerous pairs of shoes. TBFP

5 The girls probably would have referred to both their mother and step-mother as "Ma," and the appropriate person would have been obvious to them through context. "Mother Polly" is used in this narrative for clarity.

6 Mary and Ann Latta were the daughters of James Latta's oldest son William. Their education at Salem is documented by the Latta Plantation archives, as is the depth of William's poverty and the rift between him and his father. All of this is confirmed by a letter from William to his father written March 16, 1825, in the George F. Davidson Family Papers, Rare Book, Manuscript, & Special Collections Library, Duke University, Durham, North Carolina.

7 The Cherokee chief's daughter and several other details of school life are described in the "Diary of Juliana Margaret Conner from June 10th to Oct. 17th, 1827," in which she recounts several days spent at Salem. The transcribed, unpublished diary is in the Conner Papers, #174, Southern Historical Collection, Wilson Library, University of North Carolina Library, Chapel Hill, North Carolina.

8 The 1840 list of Torrance Negroes records Peggy's birth year as 1818, the same as Isabella's. Another document from April 1817 states that Flora had a babe at the breast. TBFP. By 1840, James might have forgotten exactly when Peggy was born, or there may have been two children. In any event, since most children were nursed about two years, it is logical to assume that Flora took over Isabella's care. It is also possible that Flora nursed Isabella and her own infant simultaneously.

3 The Beginning

9 The census of 1790 indicates that four of Isabella's daughters were living with them. The older two may have lived there during part of the 1787-1790 period.

10 A letter of March 25, 1799 states that James, then fourteen, was in Salisbury. In another undated letter from Albert's wife, she volunteered to make him some clothes as he had "grown a good deal." TBFP

11 The census of 1800 lists two white males over forty-five. One of them was Hugh; it is assumed the other was an overseer. It is not known how long he was retained, but there are no non-family members in the 1810 census. In 1820, when James was between wives, there is an extra adult male and a teenage boy in the census. The only other indication of an overseer on the property was after James's death. In 1862, his widow entered a contract with James Brown to superintend the farm. TBFP

12 William and Robert were two and four when their father left Ireland and nine and eleven in 1792 when their mother died. It is not known exactly when they came to this country, but they were almost certainly here before their father remarried in 1796. Latta Archives.

13 At that time South Carolina was divided into districts, rather than counties. Today the town of Yorkville has become York, and the Yorkville District is York County.

4 The Store 1805~1825

14 Of the five Negroes Hugh acquired through marriage, the only male other than Phill was listed as a boy. Phill, a mulatto and the most valuable of the group, was probably in his twenties in 1784. Binah gave birth to a daughter about 1784; she and Phill could have been man and wife. The other two females were probably small children. TBFP

15 A perpetual calendar found in a book of English samplers, written by Averil Colby, provided the days of the week for the dates of James's transactions in Philadelphia and many other events in this story. Various journals, diaries, and other records of the period confirm its accuracy. James made his first purchase in Philadelphia on Monday, May 27, 1805. It is not known if he arrived that day or the previous one.

16 On many of the receipts the price of the individual items is given in pounds, shillings, and pence. After the prices were totaled, a dollar figure was often written on the bottom of the page. TBFP

17 It is not known how James occupied the Sabbath, only that no business was conducted that day. It was certainly in his nature to attend a religious service. The description of the Friends' meeting and the meeting house is typical of Philadelphia Quakers of the period. David Hackett Fischer, *Albion's Seed*.

18 There is some evidence that Albert Torrance might have been in Philadelphia during the last days of James's visit. Albert may have gone to New York or elsewhere and met up with James for the journey home, or James may have carried Albert's notes to Philadelphia as his agent. TBFP

19 The date of the addition to the log house has been the subject of much dispute. Some believe it was built in the late 1790s. The only logical reason for the earlier date would be to house one of Isabella's married children. The census of 1800 does not reflect this, and the addition is much too elegant to have been constructed for an overseer. A receipt of June 3, 1805, shows Hugh bought over five thousand feet of lumber milled to four specific thicknesses. TBFP. This could have been for an outbuilding, but the detailed milling instructions and the quantity of lumber in each category fit the dimensions and structure of the log house addition.

20 James's relationship with Albert may have been entirely one of respect and commerce. There were numerous transactions between them, but there are no surviving letters or receipts between James and Albert's family after his death. TBFP

5 Home Again December 1827

21 Camilla's sampler is extant and is privately owned.

6 Changes 1828~1833

22 The quotes are from a letter written from Philadelphia by Mary Laura Springs to her parents on September 29, 1830, and transcribed by her son, Edward L. Baxter Davidson, many years later. The letter is in the Davidson Family Papers, #204, Southern Historical Collection, Wilson Library, The University of North Carolina at Chapel Hill.

23 Oral tradition suggests the earlier brick house was also called Cedar Grove, but no documentation has been found.

24 In Richard Torrance's memoirs, written in 1916 when he was eighty-three, he said he was born a few weeks after the stars fell. TBFP. There are many historical accounts of the spectacular meteor shower on November 13, 1833, including that of Dr. J. B. Alexander in *The History of Mecklenburg County*.

7 Rebellion 1834~1836

25 Isabella's first two sessions cost fifteen dollars each; the sessions beginning in March 1834 cost seventy-five dollars. TBFP. It is inferred that boarding was not included initially.

26 James was involved in two lawsuits in 1834 and 1835. The first involved his debt with the plasterer, and the other was probably an appeal of the first. In any event he lost and was required to pay his opponents. F. L. Smith's signature (precisely the same handwriting as on his one surviving letter) is on both documents, but in what capacity is unclear. TBFP. After Smith's death, his obituary appeared in the *Charlotte Journal*. It stated that he "settled himself in Coffeeville [Mississippi] with the intention of devoting himself to the practice of the law . . . which was withheld from him by his native state." D. A. Tompkins' *History of Mecklenburg County* names an F. L. Smith who was a Charlotte lawyer in the early nineteenth century. Isabella's suitor may have been this lawyer, a court clerk, or involved in some other way. Since James lost about four hundred dollars, it could not have been a pleasant association.

27 There are conflicting records concerning the birth date of Jane Camilla Smith. Her tombstone is engraved July 26, 1836, and her school records list her birth year as 1836. The family history, a secondary source, states she was born in 1835 but gives no further date. TBFP. No primary sources confirm this. Isabella and Franklin's wedding date is confirmed by two newspaper notices. The 1835 birth date was chosen for this narrative for several reasons: The earliest letters from the west seem more descriptive of a one-year-old child than a six-month-old infant. Isabella's sister wrote a letter from Salem on July 7, 1836, and did not inquire about Isabella. And some momentous, unspeakable event must have caused the deep rift between Isabella and her father. It is certainly credible that her birth date could have been "altered" at some later time for the sake of propriety. The origins of Franklin Smith are obscure. There are no Smiths of the period in the Hopewell or Centre graveyards and no prominent Mecklenburg planters of that name. His gravestone states that he was from Charlotte. Jane Camilla's school records indicate that she was born in Iredell County, which may have been where his people lived and may be an indication that Isabella was unwelcome at Cedar Grove. Many years later, Franklin's mother wrote to Isabella from Charleston. A photocopy of this letter is in the Latta Archives.

28 In a document dated February 18, 1836, the court declared that James Latta was *non compos mentis* (mentally incompetent) and appointed Robert Latta and Rufus Reid as his guardians. A copy of this document is in the Latta Plantation archives; the original is in the Mecklenburg County court records.

29 The daily activity of the Negroes is described in some detail in a contract between Margaret Torrance and an overseer in 1862. Plantation life was probably not significantly different in 1836. It is not known which Negroes did which tasks. James's 1840 list of the names and ages of the Negroes indicates family groups and shows the demographics of the population. This suggests who would be suitable for which jobs. TBFP

30 The land records in the Office of the Chancery Clerk of Yalobusha County, Mississippi, confirm that Hugh, Frank, and Isabella made final payment and acquired title to three tracts of land totaling 204 acres "more or less," on November 29 and December 1, 1837. November 29th was the one-year anniversary of the loan from John Campbell. The seller of one of the tracts was John Campbell of Yalobusha who was in that county when the deed was recorded. He could not have been the same John Campbell who wrote to Rufus Reid from Mount Vernon, North Carolina, on November 11, 1837. They were probably father and son, and the younger Campbell was more likely the Mississippi pioneer.

The three tracts were close together but not adjacent. They paid fifteen dollars per acre for two tracts of eighty acres each, and about four dollars per acre for another tract of forty-four acres. They eventually bought up the intervening land.

8 The Journey 1836~1837

31 It is obvious from the letters and James's will that he gave his children Negroes who went with them to Mississippi. Their names and numbers are not known. According to census records James owned ninety-four Negroes in 1830 and ninety-two in 1840. His 1840 document "Ages of Negroes" lists thirty children under the age of ten. TBFP. Assuming similar demographics during the previous decade (the medical records give no indication of widespread death) and including James Latta's gift of six people in 1833 (TBFP and Latta Archives), James's Negro population should have increased by thirty-five or forty people, not decreased by two. His will states that he had also given Negroes to Camilla (TBFP); they were probably given as dowry in 1834. If the Negroes were divided evenly among Camilla, Hugh, Frank, and Isabella, about thirty would have gone to Mississippi.

32 A map in *The American Heritage Pictorial Atlas of United States History* describes the route reported by the letters as a major migration and trade route of the period.

9 The West 1837~1838

33 It is not known if John Smith is a relative of Franklin Smith. He is mentioned several times but only casually, and Franklin's sole surviving letter does not mention him at all.

34 The land records in Yalobusha County do not show that the sale of the lot in town to Smith or the Torrances was ever completed. The property may have reverted to the seller, or Isabella might have sold her half interest to a third party.

35 There was obviously an earlier letter announcing Smith's death which was received by James. It is not in the collection. A number of other letters referred to by those that survive are also missing. The irregularity of the mails was a constant lament. Many letters never may have reached their destination, some are probably lost, and some may be owned by descendants or other institutions.

36 The situation at Mount Mourne is derived from two transcribed letters in the Latta Plantation archives; one was written by Betsy to her mother on April 14, 1837, the other from Betsy to her son Robert on June 23, 1837. The owner of the originals is unknown.

37 Hugh may have been trying to settle the affairs of Franklin Smith. There were several Springs families in the Mecklenburg area; one of them may have owed money on notes held by Smith.

38 Franklin's gravestone now lies flat on the ground. Next to it is another small slab which may have been a foot stone or the larger stone's base. The slab is engraved "D. Bolles & Son. Cincinnati, Ohio."

39 Records of Frank Davidson's business and travel are in the George F. Davidson Papers, Rare Book, Manuscript, & Special Collections Library, Duke University, Durham, North Carolina.

40 Jane Allison did eventually marry Mr. Carson and move west. A letter she wrote in the 1860s survives. It is filled with good-natured teasing and reveals a sunny personality. TBFP

41 Betsy's acid stomach was mentioned in a letter she wrote to her mother on April 14, 1837 (transcribed copy in the Latta Plantation archives, owner unknown). A Latta family history (secondary source, author unknown, Latta Archives) states that she died of an abscess in her throat which ruptured while giving birth to a stillborn child.

42 Margaret's name is on the grocery receipt, so she may have been in Charleston or simply sent the order by way of James. She gave birth on January 28, 1839. The bill for meals and lodging was for only two nights. TBFP. It seems unlikely that a woman in her condition would have traveled so far and rested so briefly.

10 Troubles Deepen 1839~1840

43 No year is written on Frank's letters of July 19, and September 24, or Hugh's letter of July 29. Comparable information in other dated letters and documents place all three letters in 1839. TBFP

44 The 170.000 pounds refers to cotton not yet ginned, which can weigh three times as much as ginned bales. This fits with calculations from the letters that indicate their crop was generally between 50,000 and 70,000 pounds. TBFP, and *Our Fathers' Fields* by James Everett Kibler.

45 James paid his sons' debt in a series of installments. He did eventually pay the entire amount. TBFP

11 A Relative Peace 1840~1842

46 There is no record of James having sent stage fare to Isabella, but there is no other way she could have gotten to North Carolina so quickly. At the end of May she was in Mississippi with no prospect of going home, and by the third of September she had been at Cedar Grove long enough that her letter to Hugh had been received, probably at least a month. Her brothers had no money to spare, so James must have financed the trip. Isabella and Jane may have traveled alone, but it is more logical for them to have taken a few personal servants, leaving the majority of the Negroes on the Mississippi plantation.

47 William Smith is not mentioned in any other document. He may have been Franklin's father or brother.

48 The Latta Plantation archives contain several references to Rufus and/or his father buying and selling Negroes for James Latta.

49 There is no receipt for payment to the tutoress, nor record of her name; the notice appeared in the *Charlotte Journal*, Feb. 10, 1842. The receipt for the books is in the TBFP. The school was probably in session for a year or more. On January 26, 1843, the guardian of Miss Dorcas Lee wrote to James and asked for a bill of her expenses "as she will leave your house soon." Lettitia and Mary entered Salem in January, 1844. TBFP

50 The will of Ephraim Davidson and medical records of his final illness are in the George F. Davidson Papers, Rare Book, Manuscript, & Special Collections Library, Duke University, Durham, North Carolina. It does not state which of his daughters had an insane child.

12 Plantation Life 1843~1844

51 It is unclear why William Latta referred to James's wife as Cousin Margaret. The Torrance-Banks Family Papers contain an extensive genealogy of Margaret's family, the Allisons of Statesville. She does not appear to be related to William's mother, Jane Allison Latta, unless very distantly. The word cousin was sometimes used as a synonym for kin.

52 This is the most fragile letter in the collection. It is riddled with many small holes obscuring words or parts of words. Many of the bracketed words are probably accurate as a few letters or parts of letters could be discerned; some are educated guesses.

53 According to James's will he had given Isabella a piano sometime during his life. This letter addressed to Rufus indicates that James had paid for the instrument and probably concerns his gift to Isabella. The piano was shipped to the port of Charleston, then carted overland to Cheraw, S.C., by way of Georgetown. TBFP

54 The 150058 lbs. refers to cotton that has not been ginned. See note #44.

55 All of the information concerning Peter Stuart Ney comes from Dick's school records in the family collection, Dick's memoirs written in 1916 at the age of 83 (TBFP), a pamphlet titled *Ney - Was Peter Stuart Ney the Carolina School-master, Marshal Michel Ney The Great French Soldier?* by C. W. Allison, 1946, and excerpts from two books on Ney: *Marshal Ney: A Dual Life* by Legette Blythe, 1937, and *Marshal Ney Before and After Execution* by J. Edward Smoot, 1929. The Smoot book contains an interview with Dick conducted days before his death in 1927.

56 The cause of Jane's death is not recorded, however she did die during the epidemic of 1844–45. Vast numbers became ill, mostly in the northern part of the county, and about one-fourth of them died. Dr. J. B. Alexander, *The History of Mecklenburg County.*

13 Full Circle 1845~1847

57 A secondary source lists James Rufus's birth date as December 12, 1845. However his tombstone clearly states he died at Manassas, Virginia, November 1, 1861, aged 16 years and 11 months, which would place his birth one year earlier. The birth dates of Isabella and Rufus Reid's children come from a photocopy of a secondary document in the Latta Plantation archives. The document is in the Wilson Library, University of North Carolina at Chapel Hill, Chapel Hill, North Carolina.

58 The name might also have honored William's sister, Jane Elizabeth, who had died in 1824 at the age of eleven at boarding school in Philadelphia (Latta Archives), long before he and Camilla were married. Camilla may have known this Jane Elizabeth as a child since they were about the same age and their fathers were friends. Mrs. Latta was grandmother to both Jane Elizabeths.

59 Dilcy's position in the household is suggested by two documents. She was the only Negro woman specifically willed to Margaret that had not been part of her dowry, and the only Negro mentioned by name in the medical records. According to the Negro records her children were Stephen, Nancy, Phebe, Echo, and Alexander (not born until 1847). Stephen and Alexander were listed in James's estate, the others were not. Anecdotal evidence suggests Echo later became the family coachman, and a brief note written to Echo Torrance in 1891 survives. The medical records state that Dr. Johnston treated Sarah Jane and Dick on March 17th and 19th, staying twenty-four hours, then returned on the 28th and blistered a "Negro child - Dilcy's." He repeated the treatment on March 30th and April 2nd, at which time the child died. It is not known if the child was Nancy or Phebe. TBFP

60 It is assumed Edgeworth Seminary (Latta Archives) was chosen because of Sallie's needs. Whether it was recommended by Salem is speculative. Salem had not fallen into disfavor; in fact it was hugely popular and had to turn many girls away for lack of space, which also could have been a reason for sending Sallie and Flax to Edgeworth. Nannie, Jane Camilla, and Bettie all went to Salem in subsequent years.

61 A copy of this portrait is owned by Historic Brattonsville in McConnells, S.C., the site of the Bratton plantation. Information on the Bratton family came from Historic Brattonsville and the TBFP.

62 The letters reflect that James was ill during his last months, but the medical records do not indicate any doctor visits. James often bought a variety of medicines and perhaps had opted to treat himself. Among his papers are cures for asthma, rheumatism, and scrofula (a skin disease). The numerous references to his cough suggests his asthma was chronic and contributed to his death. TBFP

14 Mount Mourne 1848~1855

63 These numbers are from the inventory of James's estate dated February 1, 1848. An undated list of Negroes, which appears to have been made at the time of James's death, records 115 names. TBFP. Lettitia probably received some Negroes as dowry; she may have taken possession of them between James's death and the settlement of his estate.

64 A handwritten copy of James's will (primary document) is in the TBFP. All phrases and sentences in quotation marks are exactly as they appear in the will; the rest is paraphrased. The lists of Margaret's widow's allotment and the Torrance estate sale are also in the TBFP.

65 These notices appeared in the December 30, 1847, edition of the *Charlotte Journal*.

66 William Davidson did marry again, twice, but he had no more offspring. Chalmers Davidson, *The Plantation World Around Davidson*.

67 This information is documented by a letter to Isabella from Mary Smith dated April 5, 1848. It is unclear if Mary's benefactor was her son or brother; he is simply referred to in the letter as Jane Camilla's uncle. A photocopy of the letter is in the Latta Plantation Archives, the original is in the Southern Historical Collection, University of North Carolina, Chapel Hill, North Carolina.

68 This letter is in the George F. Davidson Family Papers, Rare Book, Manuscript, & Special Collections Library, Duke University, Durham, North Carolina.

69 The incident concerning the minks, chickens, hogs, and turkeys actually occurred in 1860. It is recorded in a letter to Dick from his mother on May 15th of that year. TBFP

70 Land records of Yalobusha County, Mississippi, Office of the Chancery Clerk.

71 Ibid.

72 Details of Rufus Reid's final illness and death were obtained from his medical records and from the obituary written by his daughters. It is not known which of his daughters wrote the obituary; the handwriting most closely resembles Nannie's, but it cannot be conclusively attributed to her. All of the girls probably contributed to its composition. Reid's medical records are in the George F. Davidson Family Papers, Rare Book, Manuscript, & Special Collections Library, Duke University, Durham, North Carolina. A photocopy of the obituary is in the Latta archives; the original is in the Rufus Reid Papers #12, Southern Historical Collection, University of North Carolina, Chapel Hill, North Carolina.

73 This and other shopping sprees are recorded in Frank's detailed accounts of the Reid household made after Rufus's death. George F. Davidson Family Papers, Rare Book, Manuscript, & Special Collections Library, Duke University, Durham, North Carolina.

74 Ibid.

75 No marriage bond was found documenting the union of Frank and Margaret nor any record of her maiden name. It is assumed they were wed at the time Frank established his own plantation. The only record found of her existence is the beautiful obelisk in Grenada's oldest cemetery which is inscribed:

"Sacred to the Memory of Margaret A., Wife of J. F. Torrance, Born Mar. 10, 1830, died Jan. 27, 1855."

There was no one else by the name of J. F. Torrance in any of the Yalobusha County land or census records during that time period.

76 George F. Davidson Family Papers, Rare Book, Manuscript, & Special Collections Library, Duke University, Durham, North Carolina.

Sources

Unpublished Sources:

George F. Davidson Family Papers. Rare Book, Manuscript, & Special Collections Library, Duke University, Durham, North Carolina.

Historic Brattonsville Archives. Historic Brattonsville, McConnells, South Carolina.

Latta Plantation Archives. Historic Latta Plantation, Huntersville, North Carolina.

Office of the Chancery Clerk, Yalobusha County, Mississippi.

Southern Historical Collection. Wilson Library, University of North Carolina Library, Chapel Hill, North Carolina.

Torrance-Banks Family Papers. Rare Books and Manuscript Collection, Adkins Library, University of North Carolina at Charlotte, Charlotte, North Carolina.

Published Sources:

Alexander, J. B. *The History of Mecklenburg County from 1740 to 1900*. Charlotte: Observer Printing House, 1902.

Alexander, J. B. *Sketches of Early Hopewell*. Charlotte: Observer Printing and Publishing House, 1897.

Allison, C. W. *Ney - Was Peter Stewart Ney, The Carolinas Schoolmaster, Marshal Michel Ney, The Great French Soldier?* Charlotte: Self-published pamphlet, 1946.

American Heritage Editors. *The American Heritage Pictorial Atlas of United States History*. New York: McGraw Hill Book Company, 1966.

Betts, Edwin Morris, Editor. *Thomas Jefferson's Farm Book*. Charlottesville: University of Virginia Press, 1987.

Bishir, Catherine W. *North Carolina Architecture*. Chapel Hill: The University of North Carolina Press, 1990.

Blythe, Legette. *Marshal Ney: A Dual Life*. New York: Stackpole Sons, Publishers, 1937.

Charlotte Journal, Charlotte, North Carolina.

Colby, Averil. *Samplers*. London: B. T. Batsford, 1964 & 1987.

Davidson, Chalmers G. *Piedmont Partisan; The Life and Times of Major General William Lee Davidson*. Davidson, N. C.: Davidson College, 1951 & 1968.

Davidson, Chalmers G. *The Plantation World Around Davidson, second edition*. Davidson, N. C.: The Mecklenburg Historical Association, 1973.

Davidson, Chalmers G. "Two Daughters of Mount Mourne." In *Briarpatch Magazine*. Davidson N.C.: Davidson College, March 1980.

Fischer, David Hackett. *Albion's Seed, Four British Folkways in America*. New York and Oxford: Oxford University Press, 1989.

Fries, Adelaide L. *The Road to Salem*. Winston-Salem: John F. Blair, Publisher, 1993.

Kibler, James Everett. *Our Fathers' Fields: A Southern Story*. Columbia: University of South Carolina Press, 1998.

Raleigh Register, Raleigh, North Carolina.

Smoot, J. Edward, M.D. *Marshal Ney Before and After Execution*. Charlotte: Queen City Printing Company, 1929.

Sommerville, Charles William. *The History of Hopewell Presbyterian Church*. Huntersville, N. C.: Hopewell Presbyterian Church, 1939, reprinted 1987.

Tompkins, D. A. *History of Mecklenburg County and The City of Charlotte from 1740 to 1903*. Charlotte: Observer Printing House, 1903.

Webster, Noah. *A Compendious Dictionary of the English Language, A facsimile of the first (1806) edition*. New York: Bounty Books, a division of Crown Publishers, 1970.

Site Sources that Are Open to the Public:

Hugh Torance House and Store
Gilead Road, P.O. Box 2674, Huntersville, NC 28070
704-875-3271
From I-77 take exit #23 onto Gilead Road. Travel west (away from Huntersville) on Gilead Road for about 2 miles. Hugh Torance House and Store is on the right. The site is generally open on summer Sunday afternoons. Call for tour schedule.

Historic Latta Plantation
5225 Sample Road, Huntersville, NC 28070
704-875-2312
www.lattaplantation.org
From I-77 take exit #16-B onto Sunset Road West. Turn right on Beatties Ford Road and travel 4.8 miles. Turn left on Sample Road (across from Hopewell Presbyterian Church) which leads into Latta Plantation Park. Continue all the way through the park to the plantation house. Call for times of guided tours.

Historic Brattonsville
1444 Brattonsville Road, McConnells, SC 29726
803-684-2327
From I-77 take exit #82-B onto Cherry Road in Rock Hill, S. C. Follow Cherry Road to SC 322. Stay on SC 322 for about 10 miles to Brattonsville Road. Turn left; the site is about a half mile ahead. It is open year round except major holidays. Call for hours.

Old Salem
P.O. Box F, Salem Station, Winston-Salem, NC 27108
1-888-653-7253
www.oldsalem.org
Old Salem and the adjacent Salem Academy and College are located near the heart of downtown Winston-Salem. Take the Main Street exit from Business I-40 and follow the signs. Old Salem is open daily except Christmas.

Southern Exposure Photography

Ann Williams is a Florida native and a graduate of the University of Florida. She has lived in Charlotte, North Carolina, since 1969 and has been a volunteer interpreter at a number of regional historic sites for nearly twenty-five years. Her research interests began with textiles and costumes with a practical bent toward their reproduction and have broadened to include many aspects of early American life, concentrating on the Carolina piedmont and its people.

She and her husband have three grown children. They spend much of their free time traveling the countryside to participate in Revolutionary War era reinactments, interpreting life as it once was.